NAMING
Thy NAME

NAMING
Thy NAME

CROSS TALK *in*

SHAKESPEARE'S

SONNETS

ELAINE SCARRY

Farrar, Straus and Giroux
New York

Farrar, Straus and Giroux
18 West 18th Street, New York 10011

Grateful acknowledgment is made for permission to reprint the following material:
Image from *The wonderfull combate (for Gods glorie and mans saluation)
betweene Christ and Satan Opened in seuen most excellent, learned and zealous
sermons, vpon the temptations of Christ, in the wilderness, &c. Seene and
allowed*, 8° C 260 Th, sig 3v. The Bodleian Libraries, University of Oxford.
Marriage portrait of James VI of Scotland, by Adrian Vanson (fl. 1580–1601).
Private Collection. Photograph © Philip Mould Ltd, London/Bridgeman Images.
Frontispiece by Nicholas Rowe for *The Tempest*. © The British Library Board.
The Works of Mr. William Shakespear, C.175.m.1, title page.

Library of Congress Cataloging-in-Publication Data
Names: Scarry, Elaine, author.
Title: Naming thy name : cross talk in Shakespeare's sonnets / Elaine Scarry.
Description: New York : Farrar, Straus and Giroux, 2016. | Includes bibliographical
references.
Identifiers: LCCN 2016016700 | ISBN 9780374279936 (hardback) | ISBN 9780374713867
(e-book)
Subjects: LCSH: Shakespeare, William, 1564–1616. Sonnets. | Shakespeare, William,
1564–1616—Characters—Men. | Constable, Henry, 1562–1613. | Love poetry,
English—History and criticism. | Sonnets, English—History and criticism. |
BISAC: LITERARY CRITICISM / Shakespeare. | BIOGRAPHY &
AUTOBIOGRAPHY / Literary.
Classification: LCC PR2848 .S33 2016 | DDC 821/.3—dc23
LC record available at https://lccn.loc.gov/2016016700

Designed by Jo Anne Metsch

Our books may be purchased in bulk for promotional, educational, or business use.
Please contact your local bookseller or the Macmillan Corporate and Premium
Sales Department at 1-800-221-7945, extension 5442, or by e-mail at
MacmillanSpecialMarkets@macmillan.com.

www.fsgbooks.com
www.twitter.com/fsgbooks • www.facebook.com/fsgbooks

1   3   5   7   9   10   8   6   4   2

for
Philip Fisher

CONTENTS

NAMING
Thy NAME

INTRODUCTION

Unable to find a shadow of you,
                a shadow of me,
I wandered lost, without a guide.
Beneath a double night with double light,
                you pressed down on me,
wayward love seizing me from exile.
Struck by twin thunderbolts, our eyes hurl light,
they tremble and flash like a star-filled night,
they ignite a torch—like the Northern Star
that sailors seek when the storm is through—
so that I might find traces of me,
                traces of you.[1]

This is a youthful and ardent poem. The author does not seem to have thought it worth preserving: it does not appear in his published books, or in his manuscripts; it survives only because it was published in a foreign language in a foreign land by someone who saw and admired his young writings.

But there is a reason to stop and listen to it. What we hear in this passage is a voice we have not heard before. It is the voice of Shakespeare's beautiful young man. We have heard many descriptions *of* him: Shakespeare speaks to or about him in more than 126 sonnets. But we have not heard *from* him—or, hearing from him, did not recognize his intimate bond with the playwright. In this poem, as in many others, he tells not just what it is like to be loved by Shakespeare but what it is like to be made love to by him. The claim of being struck by lightning recurs in seven of his poems. While the jagged lines of lightning are in part a salute to the zigzagging javelin of Shakespeare's surname, there can be little doubt that the poet, painfully in love, was struck by this friendship as by a radiant blow: harrowing and miraculous.

Having so often heard Shakespeare's account of their love, we might wish to ignore his voice for a brief time and submerge ourselves instead in the voice of the beloved friend. Though he often speaks in great distress, he also defends himself brilliantly against Shakespeare's complaints. In his most intimate poems, he conceives of himself and his lover as twins, and speaks with the tender confidence we associate with Romeo and Juliet.

> I send, Light, this narcissus bloom of earliest spring
>   so that our songs will be yoked together inside the blossom.
> To restore the balance, sing back to me with moistened lips.
>   In return for my flower, send your flower to me.[2]

While it may be hard to turn away from this lyric voice, we must open this story by listening for a time to Shakespeare. By doing so we will come to see what, with the help of patience and suspension of disbelief, may eventually stand forth with simple clarity: the beautiful young man is the poet, international diplomat, and brave defender of religious tolerance Henry Constable—or, as he was often called by contemporaries, "sweet Henry Constable."

Sweet Henry Constable? Ben Jonson spoke of Henry Constable's "Ambrosiack Muse"; an anonymous poet called him "England's sweete nightingale"; the sixteenth-century fin de siècle play *Return from Parnassus* reported, "Sweete Constable doth take the wond'ring ear / And layes it up in willing prisonment."³ In all three instances, what motivates the salute—and sense of belovedness—are Constable's poems, which were circulating by the early 1590s and in print by 1592: *Diana* was one of the two or three earliest sonnet sequences in England; it was widely read, admired, and emulated, and was reprinted with additional poems in 1594. But the sense that his voice was like nectar to other people cannot be attributed to the poems alone, however laden they are with the golden gifts of ingenuity and friendship.

In his person, too, Henry Constable had unusual allure. We know this because of a remarkable fact: it was reported of three different monarchs—England's Queen Elizabeth, France's Henry IV, and Scotland's James VI—that Henry Constable was "a favorite" of the sovereign.⁴ That he should be held in high esteem by one is interesting; by two is startling; by three, astonishing. What, more precisely, is astonishing is not just that he was liked but that, in a world where scores of people must have been vying for royal attention, his being liked was so conspicuous to onlookers that three different letter-writers in three different countries and three different years were incited to include the observation in their correspondence. Shakespeare again and again tells us his friend is singular; but this does not mean anyone else in the world need arrive at the same judgment. For the record, however, it appears that many people did.

It might seem, from the little that has so far been said here, that Henry Constable—the darling of poets, playwrights, kings, and queens—lived in a buoyant world of privilege and wealth. If one had to hold a single picture in mind to represent the full arc of his life, however, a more representative picture might be of an austere religious pilgrim covering thousands of miles on foot and on horseback, living in isolation, dedicated to his faith, which, after 1591, was Catholicism. Or perhaps a picture of him in a prison cell: Tower or Fleet Prison, one may take one's pick since he spent months in the first and years in the second. His "Spiritual Sonnets" to the Trinity and to an array of female saints, written in the 1590s but unpublished in his lifetime, have struck some readers as the most powerful of his poems. In them one hears an intensity of aspiration, suffering, and devotion that is matched only by his poems to a male beloved, the poems that we will attend to here.

In the initial years of their relationship, the two men were not yet the accomplished and worldly people they would shortly become. They inhabited that blissfully misty country of youth that guarantees a few brief years of privacy, off-limits to contemporaries and to later historians as well. Biographers of Shakespeare refer to the 1580s as his "lost years."[5] Biographers of Constable likewise refer to the 1580s as a decade during which he disappears from view for three or four years at a time.[6] The years are "lost" simply because both men were in their early to mid twenties and, like most people in their twenties, were not yet, or not often, conducting their lives on a public plane. In 1587, for example, Shakespeare was twenty-three years old. And Constable? No birth or baptism record for him has yet been found. Preliminary evidence suggests that his birth year may be the same as Shakespeare's, 1564, or that he was born two years later, or two years earlier.[7] Constable and Shakespeare (who was his own wife's junior by eight years) were close enough in age that they perceived one another as twins and delighted in their shared youth. While Shakespeare says his friend's skin is delicate and his own weathered, only in one sonnet does he designate himself older, and there he questions the reality of that very designation: "How can I then be elder than thou art?"

This book is written in the belief that what it describes is true. But its author only *believes* it to be true; she does not *know* it to be true. That would require more evidence than has so far been assembled. (The reader may therefore wish to insert before more than one sentence the phrase "For the time being, let us imagine that . . ."). But one dimension of what follows is certainly true: Shakespeare did not live in a world where he was the only person speaking; the people in his world, above all those he loved, certainly had voices. At the very least, what follows provides the texture of conversation, of call and recall, of words sent out and words returning that would have constituted the fabric of his life.

If the evidence about Henry Constable's place in Shakespeare's heart is incomplete, it is nevertheless—as we will see—elaborate. Shakespeare's devotion to his friend is present in the micro texture of the sonnets, in their overarching architecture, and in their deep fabric. It is with the first that we will begin, because it is here and in Henry Constable's answering poems that the two lovers spell out in full one another's names.

1

SPELLBOUND

Who will read, must first learn spelling.

—PHILIP SIDNEY

The sonnets never promise the dark lady that she will be immortalized, that her name itself is beloved, that her name will survive in the breath and speech and eyes of generations not yet born. But it is exactly this set of promises that the sonnets make to the beautiful young man. Over and over. How can such promises be fulfilled if no name is actually given? They cannot.

The first poem in which Shakespeare speaks the name—or, as he will later write, the poem in which "first I hallowed thy fair name"—is Sonnet 18, "Shall I compare thee to a summer's day?" Prior to Sonnet 18, the avenue to immortality is not poetry but biology. The poems urge the beloved to marry and have a child in order to perpetuate his name and family. Henry Constable *was,* in fact, the only child of an aristocratic family: his father, Robert, had been knighted by Queen Elizabeth, who made him lieutenant of the ordnance (the precursor of the Department of War); his mother, Christiana Dabridgecourt, was descended from one of the original members of the Order of the Garter.

It is often supposed that in urging the beautiful young man to father a child, Shakespeare must have been acting on behalf of that young man's parents. But Shakespeare may have had his own strong reason for making such an argument. If two young men find themselves ardently in love and one of them is married and the father of a child, the married lover might feel strong pressure to repudiate, or apologize for, his marriage. Shakespeare, always adept at occupying the high ground, does no such thing. He argues the reverse, faulting the beloved for failing to be himself married. Are you jealous that each night I return to my marital bed? You need not be; I would not be; I would in fact rejoice were you to marry. This hypothetical union need not cause Shakespeare any jealousy, for it is only hypothetical: further, if actualized, it would help keep the young man immune from love affairs with other men in his diplomatic travels to Scotland and the Continent (missions he was already undertaking in his twenties). Since Shakespeare has himself scripted the marriage, he might legitimately picture himself, should such a marriage occur, as the partial author of any ensuing births: "Make thee another self for love of me," he writes in Sonnet 10.

Between Sonnet 17 and Sonnet 18 a sea change occurs (perhaps an act of physical intimacy). Now in Sonnet 18 Shakespeare promises that he, not the imaginary infant, will directly provide his beloved's immortality: "But thy eternal summer shall not fade, . . . Nor shall death brag thou wander'st in his shade, / When in eternal lines to time thou grow'st." Then comes the final couplet:

So long as men can breathe, or eyes can see,
So long lives this, and this gives life to thee.[1]

The first of these two lines records the name of Henry Constable.

The "this" in the final line—"So long lives this, and this gives life to thee"—refers to the whole sonnet, but more specifically to the antecedent line with its precious cargo. One might object that a ten-syllable line has many letters and may contain, by accident, many names. This is a reasonable objection and no doubt accidental names do reside in the line. But there are fewer names than one might suppose: Philip Sidney is not in the line, nor Edmund Spenser, nor Christopher Marlowe, nor John Donne; nor, alas, has Shakespeare accidentally recorded my own name in the line, nor the name of the first five friends who come to mind, and many of us have fewer letters in our names than Henry Constable. Furthermore, put forward here is not any line but one that announces that the beloved is, at that very moment, inside our eyes, inside our breath, and that we are, by lending the line our live percipience, keeping the beloved alive.

A second instance is Sonnet 65, which asks, "How with this rage shall beauty hold a plea, / Whose action is no stronger than a flower?" How can delicate beauty survive if all other monumental substances—brass, stone, earth, boundless sea, rocks impregnable, gates of steel—are themselves subject to mortality? What resource or strategy can prevent this disappearance? The couplet answers:

O none, unless this miracle have might,
That in black ink my love may still shine bright.

The final line urges that his love is shining forth out of the line, and a man's name is indeed shining forth:

That in **BLAC**k i**N**k m**Y** l**O**v**E** may **ST**ill s**HiNE** b**R**ight.
H e n r y   C o n s t a b l e

In the handwritten poem sent to the beloved, perhaps the key letters were written in uppercase or ornamented. As in Sonnet 18, two crucial features are present: all fourteen letters appear; the line itself announces that the name is there for all to see.

The opening quatrain of Sonnet 55 makes the same argument as Sonnet 65:

Not marble, nor the gilded monuments
Of princes, shall outlive this powerful rhyme;
But you shall shine more bright in these contents
Than unswept stone, besmeared with sluttish time.

It is the third line—again a line that claims the lover is present in its own interior—that contains the beloved's name:

But **Y**ou sh**AL**l **SHiNE** more **BR**ight in these **CONTE**nts
H e n r y   C o n s t a b l e

The poem ends by reminding us what line 3 has already told us:

So, till the judgement that yourself arise,
You live in this, and dwell in lovers' eyes.

Even as one reads or recites this poem to one's own beloved—as over the centuries must have occurred millions of times—Henry Constable is present in our eyes and carried in our breath. It would be devastating, as noted at the outset, if the sonnets did not contain the lover's name, given how often Shakespeare says the beloved will achieve immortal life there. Shakespeare says not only that his powerful feelings of love will be eternally visible but that his beloved will be visible; and this cannot happen without a name. Further, he has made his promise come true: at every second of day and night someone somewhere in the world recites the sonnets, unknowingly carrying Henry Constable in their eyes and mouths. Humanity acts collectively as a dedicated relay team of rhapsodes, one person beginning to animate the beloved when the previous person drops off to sleep or dies.

In Sonnet 106, Shakespeare says that the beautiful countenance of the beloved is present to the world's eyes not only in the sonnet he writes, but in the poetry of all earlier centuries whenever it struggled to describe the beauty of a woman or the loveliness of a man:

> When in the chronicle of wasted time
> I see descriptions of the fairest wights,
> And beauty making beautiful old rhyme,
> In praise of ladies dead and lovely knights,
> Then in the blazon of sweet beauty's best,
> Of hand, of foot, of lip, of eye, of brow,
> I see their antique pen would have expressed
> Even such a beauty as you master now.

Beautiful men and women are constituted not just by body parts (foot, lip, eye, brow) but by language acts (rhyme, blazon, description, pen). The beloved, then, must surely be "figured" since he has been so often "pre-figured" and "prophesied" in these early writings:

> So all their praises are but prophecies
> Of this our time, all you prefiguring,
> And for they looked but with divining eyes
> They had not skill enough your worth to sing;

Prefigured and prophesied, the couplet now carries out the act of present-time figuration—

> For we which now behold these present days,
> Have Eyes to woNdeR, but laCk tONgueS To prAisE.
> H e n r y   C o n s t a b l e

—an instance of spelling remarkable for its presentation of the letters in almost the correct sequence: all fourteen letters are present, and eleven of the fourteen fall from the final line in the very position they occupy in the beloved man's name. It is, in fact, not just the final line of the couplet but both lines that contain Henry Constable's name—

> For we wHiCh NOw BEhoLd these pReSENT dAYs,
> H e n r y   C o n s t a b l e

> Have Eyes to woNdeR, but laCk tONgueS To prAisE.
> H e n r y   C o n s t a b l e

—even if the pyrotechnic feat of presenting the letters in sequence occurs only in the second of the two.

The spelling out of Henry Constable's name in this particular poem might have brought a special rush of pleasure to its recipient, since Sonnet 106—as scholars have long noted—echoes Henry

Constable's own sonnet about the way poets praising beauty in the past foretold beauty in the present.[2]

But all those beauties were but figures of thy prayse	So all their praises are but prophecies
And all those poets did of thee but prophecye.[3]	Of this our time, all you prefiguring.
—CONSTABLE	—SHAKESPEARE

Constable in his opening quatrain speaks in general terms of "former poets" and former beauties, then in the second quatrain focuses on the solitary instance of the fourteenth-century Italian poet Petrarch and his adored Laura. Shakespeare stays with the general and includes men as well as women: "descriptions of the fairest wights . . . In praise of ladies dead and lovely knights." Constable's precedent goes back two centuries; Shakespeare's general language of wights and knights drops us back down an even longer corridor of lost centuries. Both credit past writers with the power of divination: "in parables thy coming he foretold" (Constable); "they looked but with divining eyes" (Shakespeare). Constable and Shakespeare, far from acknowledging that the present borrows from the past, claim instead that the past borrows from the present by presciently seeing, then absorbing into its poetry, wonders yet to come. These two sonnets are (as we will see in later chapters) one of many pairs of poems in which we hear the murmur of emulation and affection between the two friends.

Whereas the name "Henry Constable" was deeply embedded in Sonnets 18 and 65 and 106, in Sonnet 55 it flashed into view in the word "contents" (containing five letters of the surname and two of the first name), as it also does in Sonnet 53 in the word "constant" (containing six letters of the surname and one of the first name). The poet in Sonnet 53 tells the beloved that he has the beauty of Adonis, of Helen, of spring, and of the autumn harvest, and ends with the couplet:

In all external grace you have some part,
But You LikE none, none you, for **CONSTANt HEaRt.**
H　　e　　n　　r　　y　　　　C　　o　　n　　s　　t　　a　　b　　l　　e

While this line fulfills the requirement for all fourteen letters, does it meet the second requirement: that the line itself call attention to its own orthography? Perhaps not so completely as the earlier sonnets. Yet the poem is about outward form: the first line of the couplet announces that the beloved is "part" of the "external" form; the closing line makes Henry Constable part of its external form.

Given the constancy of "constancy" in Shakespeare's sonnets, one might suppose that the full name would be spelled out in any line containing that word. Other than Sonnet 53, however, this is not the case. Shakespeare, as we will see in a later chapter, thinks of the words "constant" and "constancy" as synonymous with "Constable," and therefore abstains from the redundancy of tracing the name a second time (an insult to his own virtuosity), as he also abstains from what might become dangerously transparent. He is able to inscribe Henry Constable's name with characteristic ingenuity and grace, whether it is highly embedded within a line (Sonnets 18, 65, and 106) or closer to the surface (Sonnets 53 and 55).

That outcome is not so easy to achieve, as Henry Constable's poems attest. Either one will fail to include all the letters (and without *all* the letters there is no name) or one will include all the letters and the line will shriek out the name. "Forgive mee Deere, for thundring on thy name," Constable writes in a sonnet that goes on to explain the cause of this gracelessness. The beloved resides in his heart like insuppressible lightning and thunder: "So, not my selfe, but thou in mee would'st speake."

Forgive mee Deere, for thundring on thy name,
   sith tis thy selfe that showes my love distrest,
   for fire exhald, in freezing clowdes possest,
   warring for way, makes all the heavens exclaime.
Thy beautie so, the brightest living flame,
   wrapt in my clowdie hart by winter prest,
   scorning to dwell within so base a nest,
   thunders in mee thine everlasting fame.[4]

A much later writer, Emily Dickinson, often registers the lack of proportion between a fragile poem and her out-of-scale feelings, likening those feelings to a panther in a glove, a flood in a drawer. Henry Constable here gives us an equivalent: his beloved resides inside him and leaps out of him in jagged, visible letters the way lightning disdains the bird's nest that would contain it.

This description of bristling letters accurately describes several of Constable's sonnets—so much so that it is easy to imagine Shakespeare reprimanding him for nearly betraying their secret bond, a reprimand to which the poem above seems a reply and an apology. The double *s*'s, the *k*'s, and the *p*'s leap out of the lines even in modern typography and would do so more in printing or handwriting where the *s* is as tall as an *f*. Like the sonnet "Forgive mee Deere, for thundring on thy name," these sonnets are about his inability to suppress the name of the person who possesses him.

If ever sorrow spoke from soule that loves,
   as speakes a spirit in a man possest,
   in mee her spirit speakes, my soule it moves,
   whose sigh-swolne words breed whirlwinds in my brest.[5]

In this opening quatrain, the first line spells out "Will Shake-spere," the third line "Shakespere," and the fourth line, with its *wol-wor-whirl-win* sounds swirling about, almost seems to be trying to pronounce the name "William":

> If ever SorroW SPoKE fRom souLE tHAt LovEs
> W   i l l   S h a k e s p e r e
> in mee Her SpiRit SPEAKEs, my soule it movEs
> S h a k e s p e r e
> whose sigh-swolne words breed whirlwinds in my brest.

Though less successful, because less complete than Shakespeare's naming (the length of "Will Shakespere" and "William Shakespere" makes the task harder than spelling the name "Henry Constable"), the presence of the name in these three lines seems almost to shout. Even in lines 2 and 4, where the surname does not occur, the key letters are so prominent one may incorrectly suppose it to be present. The letters pick up the reverberations of the lines where the names are fully there.

    Indeed the next quatrain comments on and enacts this reverberation:

> Or like the eccho of a passing bell,
>   which sounding on the water, seems to howle:
>   so rings my hart a fearful heavie knell,
>   and keepes all night in consort with the Owle.

The reverberating call and recall pass from bell to knell, from howl to owl. Perhaps Constable is thinking here of the tawny owls (their quivering tremolo well matched to his lover's name), residents of Arden Forest, where not only Shakespeare's family but Constable's mother's family resided and where Constable's father leased several meadows.[6] Constable has indeed created a visual cacophony, even if the full acoustical cacophony of call and response had to wait for William Wordsworth's lyrical ballad "There was a boy," a boy who

> Blew mimic hootings to the silent owls,
> That they might answer him.—And they would shout
> Across the watery vale, and shout again,
> Responsive to his call,—with quivering peals,
> And long halloos, and screams, and echoes loud
> Redoubled and redoubled; concourse wild
> Of jocund din![7]

Howling, knelling, sharp shouts, and the tremolo of owls fill Constable's lines, which he elsewhere describes as "bellowings of dispaire."

The poem containing the phrase "bellowings of dispaire" dedicates one quatrain to placing the two lovers' names side by side:

> I call the heavens, ayre, earth, & seas, to heare
> my love, my trueth, and black disdaind estate:
> beating the rocks with bellowings of dispaire,
> which stil with plaints my words reverbarate.[8]

"Black disdained estate"? Is Henry Constable romanticizing himself here when he claims to be indifferent to the worldly benefits of wealth, class, coat of arms (the coat of arms for which Shakespeare, on behalf of his own family, would work so assiduously)? Surrounded by beautiful and wealthy women (such as Penelope Rich, the Stella of Philip Sidney's poem *Astrophel and Stella*), this is someone who nevertheless chose never to marry, who actively refused to perpetuate his distinguished family line. When his father died in 1591 he sold the estate to a cousin, forfeiting his patrimony and choosing instead his Catholic religious faith, which required him to go into exile in France, where he worked to support Henry of Navarre—the figure and the geography of Shakespeare's early play *Love's Labour's Lost*, whose central character is the King of Navarre. So much for his "black disdained estate."

But what about his "love" and his "trueth"? They are revealed in the names encrypted in words which, like resistant rocks, are themselves silent until conscripted into compassionate sound-making:

> My lOvE, mY tRuetH, aNd BLaCk disdaiNd ESTAte:
> H   e   n   r   y   C   o   n   s   t   a   b   l   e

> bEAting the rocKS witH bELLoWIngs of diSPAiRE,
> W   i   l   l   S   h   a   k   e   s   p   e   a   r   e

Shakespeare could not have complained that this last quoted line "thundered" out his name, since neither visually nor sonically does it hint at his name, even at the very moment it faults itself for "bellowing." (He could, however, complain that it is not a pretty line.)

In listening to Constable's poems, we have used a different standard, a different set of rules, than were in play in listening to Shakespeare. In the instance of Shakespeare, only the presence of the complete first and last name made the line eligible for our attention. The second requirement is that the line itself, or its immediate neighbor, announce that it contains the name. Sonnet 32 provides one more example. Shakespeare expresses the fear that he may die before having time to write the works that will make him a great poet, these sonnets being a record of his great love, not a record of his capacity for great poetry. The octave has several lines with eleven syllables, as though to enact and illustrate the rude quality of this, his early writing. Here are the lines that twice spell out Henry Constable, and an adjacent line telling us to look carefully at the lines, thus meeting the two criteria:

If thou survive my well-contented day,
WHEN that chuRl death mY BoNEs with duST shALl COver,
H e n r y   C o n s t a b l e
And sHALT BY foRtuNE ONCe morE re-Survey
H e n r y   C o n s t a b l e
These poor rude lines of thy deceased lover . . .

Without this second requirement, an instance can fairly be counted an accident, even if it occurs in a portentous location (each of Shakespeare's last two sonnets, 153 and 154, has a line with the full name in it), though location is one way of increasing the pressure of attention to individual lines. All lines—whether in Shakespeare or, say, Sidney's *Astrophel and Stella*—will have some letters of the name; many lines will have many letters of the name, but only a tiny number of lines—approximately two in one hundred[9]—have all the letters, and the odds against it occurring by accident are greatly increased by the second requirement: that it occur not just somewhere in an expanse of one hundred lines but in the very line (or an adjacent line) that announces it contains the name or invites close scrutiny of the line. In Shakespeare's sonnets, this happens nearly every time he instructs his beloved to scrutinize the line for evidence of his love, as Sonnet 32 does in its fourth line and again in its fourteenth. (In those few sonnets where a line calls attention to itself but does not spell Henry Constable's name, it instead calls out his intimate name or nickname, as we will see in chapter 4.)

Constable's two rules approximate, without matching, Shakespeare's. He often has the last name without the first, or the last name accompanied by the shortened name "Will" rather than

the full name "William." Of the seven ways in which Shakespeare signed his last name,[10] Constable takes the two most
inclusive spellings—"Shakespere" and "Shakespeare"—which
therefore also include all the shorter variants. Constable's second
rule again echoes without equaling Shakespeare's requirement for
announcement. Each of the poems cited above is about speaking
or suppressing words and names; but it is not the case that in any
of them a single crisp line explicitly crows (as in Shakespeare's)
that a name is herewith being delivered. The relaxation of the
rules makes it much harder to distinguish artful and intended
spelling of the name from accidental occurrences in the poems.[11]

We can see these two, perhaps overly supple, rules in play in
another of Constable's sonnets that is explicitly about the attempt
to carry out the double act of naming while suppressing the visibility of the name. Here are the first twelve lines. The beloved's
name occurs in the final line of the first quatrain, the second line
of the second quatrain, and the first and second lines of the third
quatrain.

You secrete vales, you solitarie fieldes,
    you shores forsaken, and you sounding rocks:
    if ever groning hart hath made you yeeld,
    or <u>wo</u>rds <u>ha</u>lfe <u>spo</u>ke that <u>sen</u>ce in <u>pri</u>son <u>lo</u>cks,
    W i l l   S h a k e s p e a r e
Then mongst night shadowes whisper out my death;
    th<u>at</u> <u>w</u>hen <u>my</u> <u>se</u>lfe <u>ha</u>th <u>se</u>ald my <u>li</u>ps <u>fro</u>m <u>spea</u>king,
    W i l l i a m   S h a k e s p e a r e
    each tell-tale eccho with a weeping breath,
    may both record my trueth, & true loves breaking.[12]
You <u>pre</u>ttie flow<u>er</u>s <u>th</u>at smile for <u>so</u>mmers <u>sa</u>ke,
    S h a k e s p e a r e
    pu<u>ll</u> in your he<u>a</u>ds before <u>my</u> <u>wa</u>tr<u>ie</u> eyes
    W i l l i a m

doe turne the Medowes to a standing lake:
by whose untimely floodes your glory dies.[13]

In the poem's final two lines, Henry's heart turns to moist air, which doubles the tears in his eyes.

While loneliness and pain inspire the dire imagery of the poem, the words "prison" and "death" may reflect the extreme legislation (initiated by King Henry VIII and reaffirmed by Queen Elizabeth) that arranged for homosexuals who acted on their love to be imprisoned or executed. Even amidst the isolation of the countryside—secret fields, solitary vales, forsaken riverbanks—to say aloud the beloved's name, to give half-spoken words sense, is to court prison. In turn, the threat of prison imprisons sense, requires it to be out of view. This being the case, he will dedicate nights in the countryside to whispering the name of the beloved, courting death so that when he suppresses his speech by daylight the echo of the whispered name will still reverberate among flowers, fields, vales, and riverbanks. But this solution lasts only a moment: the tears he sheds in response to his self-enforced daylight suppression submerge the compassionate landscape in a newly formed lake, erasing from the world what has already been erased in his own speech.

For Henry Constable, the stakes of both naming and failing to name were high. The question asked earlier returns: Was the poet overdramatizing himself? The answer seems to be no: he shows every sign of being someone who almost certainly would have risked imprisonment or death for the sake of love, just as he risked great hazards for his ardently held religious and political beliefs, going into exile in France in 1591, into the Tower of London in 1604, and again into prison in 1607, dying in double exile in 1613 while on a religious mission from Paris to Liège.

When Henry Constable left England in 1591, a poem by an anonymous hand surfaced and circulated throughout the city.

While the diction of the poem is intimate and tender, it portrays Constable's departure not as a personal loss but as a national loss, the loss of the country's beautiful singer, its sweet nightingale. The designation of the loss as countrywide—effortlessly accomplished in the salutation and sustained throughout—seems accurate. Constable was revered throughout the poetic community: four of his poems prefaced Sidney's *Defence of Poesy* when it was published in 1595;[14] his sonnet sequence *Diana*, which circulated in manuscript before it was published, is often credited with having instigated, or at least accelerated, the 1590s "craze" for sonnet sequences. Visual artists, too, found in him a fellow traveler: the brilliant miniaturist Nicholas Hilliard befriended him and entrusted him to deliver several paintings to their aristocratic and royal recipients. Henry Constable's poem about Hilliard is quoted in most studies of the painter.[15] For those literary historians who think Hilliard's exquisite miniatures include a painting of Shakespeare, Henry Constable would have provided the most direct avenue of access possible between painter and poet. Constable's welcome in political circles matched the welcome given him by artists: the "sister Swallow" in the anonymous poem who stirs the nightingale into flight may be his associate Robert Devereux, Earl of Essex, who in 1591 left England for a military campaign in France. Like the swallow, Essex was better known for his aerial displays than for his songs.

While the swallow in the poem may be a person or even the ship on which Constable traveled (ships named *Swallow* appear in the sixteenth century), it is first and foremost the actual bird. The swallow leaves England in late summer or early autumn and, like Constable, travels to France. Swallows, we know today, stop only briefly in France before crossing the Pyrenees and traveling to South Africa in their six-thousand-mile migration, a four-month-long trip (during which many of them perish).[16] By placing the nightingale in the company of the swallow, the anonymous poet is able to pivot attention from departure to return, for swallows arrive back on British shores so early—those in the vanguard arrive in February, many others in March, with waves still coming in April, May, and June[17]—that the bird is greeted throughout England as the harbinger of spring. By the opening of the second quatrain, the poem has already rotated effortlessly away from the certain sorrow of exit to a playfully indignant puzzle about why the migrant's return is not equally certain. Come. Return.

The poem is an odd, but not unfamiliar, conflation of adoration and chiding, tribute and reprimand. Don't be disloyal. Don't sing your songs to our enemies. The writer argues that Henry Constable probably does not need to leave England and should in any event return in the early spring. The anonymous poet's final reckless surmise that "ten to one" the sovereign will pardon the returning exile seems high-handed; its flippant diction is incommensurate with the gravity of Constable's situation, as though delivered by one who jests at scars that never felt the wound. Yet the jest pays tribute to Constable's poems, whose beauty not only will secure him a pardon, but will—like a theatrical romance—dissolve gravity into merriment, as though all the struggle and strain were much ado about nothing, a late summer night's dream.

TO HENRY CONSTABLE UPON
OCCASION OF LEAVING HIS COUNTRYE,
AND SWEETNESSE OF HIS VERSE

England's sweete nightingale!—what frights thee so,
As over sea to make thee take thy flight?

And there to live with native countryes foe,
And there him with thy heavenly songs delight?

What!—did thy sister Swallow thee excite
With her, for winter's dread, to flye away?
Whoe is it then has wrought this other spite,
That when as she returneth, thou should'st stay?

As soone as Spring begins she cometh aye;
Returne with her, and thou like tidings bring;
When once men see thee come, what will they say?
Loe, now of English poesie comes the spring!
    Come, feare thou not the cage, but loyall be,
    And ten to one thy Soveraigne pardons thee.[18]

The poem may not be by Shakespeare. Constable was so widely beloved that there are many candidates for its composition. But few would have so strong a motive for abstaining from signing the poem or, when writing the title, so strong a joy in saying aloud the name of the person addressed.

The entry of a new poem into Shakespeare's canon is not an event that can happen overnight, and there will no doubt be strong scholarly arguments for and against his authorship of "England's Sweete Nightingale" before a conclusion is reached. It is introduced here, for the time being, only as a possibility. Even at this early moment, however, it is useful to recognize that the stanza form is Shakespearean (three quatrains followed by a couplet) and that the language is consistent with that of Shakespeare's other writings. Shakespeare's possible authorship cannot be dismissed on the grounds that "he could not have said line 3," or "he never would have said line 5," since we hear him using these very words, phrases, or constructions throughout the early plays and poems.

(Other poets may well use these same constructions: the consistency does not prove that Shakespeare wrote the poem; it only shows that there is no reason he could not have written the poem.)

"England's Sweete Nightingale" is written in or near the year 1591, since that is when the young man it describes left England. Its wager "ten to one"—

> Come, feare thou not the cage, but loyall be,
> And ten to one thy Soveraigne pardons thee.

—recurs in Shakespeare's plays written in the late 1580s up through the mid 1590s. In *The Taming of the Shrew*, usually thought to have been written between 1590 and 1592, Hortensio urges, "Confess, confess, hath he not hit you here?" to which Petruccio responds, "A has a little galled me, I confess, / And as the jest did glance away from me, / 'Tis ten to one it maimed you two outright" (V.ii.61–64).[19] The scene continues with a debate about who will win the wager. The same language recurs several times in the *Henry VI* cycle, whose three parts are believed to have been written in or near 1591. In *Part II*, act II, scene i, Queen Margaret says to the assembled lords that she has not seen such high-flying falconry in seven years and continues, "Yet, by your leave, the wind was very high, / And, ten to one, Old Joan had not gone out" (II.i.1–4). The construction again occurs in *Part III*: "You left poor Henry at the Bishop's palace, / And ten to one you'll meet him in the Tower" (V.i.45–46). While these three instances are the closest to the one residing in the poem—since each is a casual wager—the "ten to one" ratio also occurs elsewhere in the early plays and in the sonnets.[20]

A second piece of language consistent with Shakespeare's early writings (and much less present as his writing continues) is the exclamation "What!":

What!—did thy sister Swallow thee excite
With her, for winter's dread, to flye awaye?

In *The Two Gentlemen of Verona*, written between 1589 and 1592, Lucetta says, "What, shall these papers lie like telltales here?" (I.ii.133) and Speed says, "What, are they broken?" (II.v.17). Again in *The Taming of the Shrew*, written between 1590 and 1592, Grumio exclaims, "What, this gentleman shall out talk us all!" (I.ii.247), Baptista says, "What, will my daughter prove a good musician?" (II.i.142), Petruccio says, "What! with my tongue in your tail?" (II.i.213), and a moment later, "What, you mean my face?" (II.i.229); and Baptista and Katharina have a rapid exchange of "what!" constructions (II.i.30–31).

> BAPTISTA
> What, in my sight? Bianca, get thee in.
>
> *Exit BIANCA*
>
> KATHARINA
> What, will you not suffer me?

"What" or "What!" is less a word than a punctuation mark coming at the beginning, rather than the end, of a sentence; it announces disbelief or indignation at the perception to follow. It is a slap of negation before the arrival of the thing that (distressingly) manages to survive the slap. In "England's Sweete Nightingale" the poet is less astonished that the nightingale exits with the swallow than that he does not plan to return with her.

The sonnet so successfully imitates a speaking voice that we may miss the artfulness with which it moves across three "what" constructions in its three quatrains: it begins with a sincere, nearly tender puzzlement ("what frights thee so?"), then scoffs at the very idea that there could be an acceptable answer ("What!—did thy sister Swallow thee excite . . . ?"), then quietly bows before the imagined spectacle of how the country will one day welcome the exile home ("what will they say? Loe . . .").

The interjection "Lo!" means "Behold!" and refers to some striking visual event or epiphany in the immediate physical environment, as when in "Sweete Nightingale" the poet describes the joyful greeting all England will give the émigré when he returns:

> When once men see thee come, what will they say?
> Loe, now of English poesie comes the spring!

"Lo!" is lavishly present in—though not confined to—Shakespeare's early writings. It recurs at moments of great physical intimacy throughout *Venus and Adonis*, written in the 1592–93 period, a work that is often seen as closely connected with the sonnets (lines 194, 259, 320, 853, 1128, 1135, and 1185), as it also appears in the very early play *Titus Andronicus*, written between 1588 and 1593 (I.i.71; I.i.159; V.ii.45).

Not all the words in "England's Sweete Nightingale" occur with the same frequency in Shakespeare's other works. The word "frights" occurs often throughout the early writings—such as *Love's Labour's Lost*, *Titus*, and *The Rape of Lucrece*—and continues to appear in late plays, such as *Othello* and *Macbeth*. "Excites," in contrast, is used in *Twelfth Night* (1601), *Troilus and Cressida* (1602), and *Macbeth* (1606), but does not seem to appear elsewhere; "incites" (which some printings substitute for "excites") tends to occur only in 1598 and beyond. "Aye" is used throughout Shakespeare's writing, where (as in "England's Sweete Nightingale") it has the usual meaning of always or forever, with an overlay of "Ay," "yes!"—and occasionally even (as in the conflation of "eyes," "ayes," and "aves" in *Measure for Measure*) the specific meaning of a yes vote. The word "poesy" is used almost only in the early writings—Sonnet 78, *The Two Gentlemen of Verona* (III.ii),

Love's Labour's Lost (IV.ii), and *The Taming of the Shrew* (I.i)—though it also appears at the opening of *Timon of Athens*, whose date is uncertain and which may have been written by multiple hands.

The construction "native country's foe" illustrates a feature of Shakespeare's early style that is noticed by Goran Stanivukovic: the tendency "to heap," to use two or three words that nearly repeat each other.[21] Where the poet might have said "foe" he adds "country's foe" (even though "foe" already implies "country's"), then triples it with "native country's foe." Would Shakespeare have said "*thy* country's foe" or "*thy* native country's foe"? That is a reasonable question, since he usually does use an article or possessive pronoun in front of "country" throughout his writing. But in addition to the fact that it would have disrupted the meter of the line, it is his way to sometimes drop the article. Shakespeare's songs often have nouns decoupled from articles, as in his use of the words "home" and "pail" in *Love's Labour's Lost*'s "Winter Song," "And milk comes frozen home in pail" (V.ii.890), or again the word "home" (stripped of both preposition and article) in *Cymbeline*, "Thou thy worldly task hast done, / Home art gone, and ta'en thy wages" (IV.ii.261–62). In the last play, *The Tempest*, "hands" is decoupled from article or pronoun: "Come unto these yellow sands, / And then take hands: / Curtsied when you have, and kissed / The wild waves whist . . ." (I.ii.378–81). The article is omitted before "dish" in Caliban's song: "No more dams I'll make for fish / Nor fetch in firing / At requiring, / Nor scrape trenchering, nor wash dish / 'Ban, 'ban, Cacaliban . . ." (II.ii.171–75).

The word "native" (though often accompanied by an article in Shakespeare's writings) seems to be a place where he is especially willing to drop the article. Thus Hamlet describes himself not as "a native" but "native"—"But to my mind, though I am native here / And to the manner born" (I.iv.16–17)—just as in *As You Like It*, Orlando asks Rosalind (whom he mistakes for a boy) not if she is "a native of this place" but if she is "native of this place" (III.ii.307). Perhaps more relevant, when Shakespeare uses "native" as an adjective the pronoun or article is often omitted. In *Henry IV, Part II*, Lancaster says, "We bear our civil swords and native fire" (V.v.100)—the "our" before "swords" carries over to "fire," but so in "England's Sweete Nightingale" "thy" carries over from the line before. Henry V repeatedly speaks of "native colours," "native punishment," "native graves," in each case without article or pronoun: for example, he does not say "these men have defeated the law and outrun their native punishment" but "these men have defeated the law and outrun native punishment" (IV.i.155–56); he does not say "many of our bodies shall no doubt find their native graves" or "find themselves in native graves" but "many of our bodies shall no doubt / Find native graves" (IV.iii.96–97).

The diction of "England's Sweete Nightingale" is, then (like the sonnet form itself), of a piece with the fabric of Shakespeare's writings, particularly his early works: the ten-to-one wager, the indignant "What!," the wonder-filled "Loe," the choice of "frights," "aye," "poesy," and a phrase—"native country's foe"—that manages to be at once redundant and shorn of any article or possessive pronoun. This consistency does not confirm his authorship of the poem, but it should hold us back from dismissing the possibility too lightly.

The claim that Henry Constable is the birthplace of English poetry—line 12 of "England's Sweete Nightingale"—may be too extreme for Shakespeare. He merely claims, as we will see in the next chapter, that Henry Constable is the birthplace of his own poetry.

2

THE BIRTHPLACE OF
SHAKESPEARE'S SONNETS

S hakespeare so often identifies his beloved as the source, inspiration, occasion, subject matter, and argument of his sonnets that there is no need to prove this proposition: the beloved is, as Shakespeare writes in Sonnet 38, his Tenth Muse, surpassing the other nine. What alone needs to be shown is that Henry Constable is in fact that beloved and hence that poetic source—or conversely, as this small chapter will argue, that Henry Constable is that poetic source and hence is that beloved.

This chapter, then, is not about the beloved's face, eyes, or heart, his constancy or inconstancy, his relation with the rival poet or with the dark lady—all subjects we will encounter later—but about one attribute only, his poems. In the overarching architecture of Shakespeare's sonnet sequence, Henry Constable's poetic influence is most overtly registered in three stations along the way: Sonnet 99 (the only sonnet with fifteen lines), Sonnet 126 (the final sonnet addressed to the beautiful young man and the only sonnet with twelve lines), and the two tonally anomalous poems that bring the whole sequence to a close, Sonnets 153 and 154.

Literary scholars have long recognized a link between the poets in a number of sonnets:[1] most often singled out is Shakespeare's Sonnet 99 and Constable's earlier written version of the same poem, which Shakespeare has borrowed. So far, nothing sounds remarkable: we know that Shakespeare's writings had many sources, Plutarch, Ovid, Chaucer, Holinshed, and many others. But two attributes make this borrowing in Sonnet 99 remarkable. First, the two poems are so close that Shakespeare's is not just derived from Constable's or influenced by it but is nearly a transcript or arch rewriting of it. Second and far more important, the poem itself is about theft. Shakespeare addresses himself in the sonnet to the sweet beloved who is being robbed; but he does this at the very moment he himself is robbing Henry Constable of his poetic lines! It is hard to escape the conclusion that Henry Constable and the beloved are the same person.

Love poems often say that the beloved has the beautiful attributes of some exquisite blossom. Shakespeare's Sonnet 99 reverses the claim. All the flowers have derived their attributes of freshness, color, and scent from the beloved boy. It asserts that the beauty of all the flowers has been borrowed—no, stolen—from the beloved. But at the very moment that Shakespeare-the-lover is telling his beloved that the flowers have made off with his attributes, Shakespeare-the-poet is filling his lines with flowers stolen from Henry Constable.

Constable's sonnet—entitled "Of his Mistrisse upon Occasion of Her Walking in a Garden"[2]—specifies four flowers: roses, lilies, marigold, and violet. Shakespeare's poem specifies four flowers: roses, lilies, marjoram, and violet. The lilies in both poems derive their whiteness from the hands of the person addressed. Constable's roses derive their red and Shakespeare's roses their red, white, and pink from the coloring of the person addressed. Most striking, the violet in each poem derives its purple by having been dipped in human veins. Constable's modern editor Joan Grundy says that she has searched all British and Continental poems and can find no other instance of a violet acquiring its color by being soaked in blood.[3] This fragile flower is the location where the two poems converge in a way that must have delighted the two writers: in Constable's poem, the other flowers derive their attributes from the lady addressed, while the violet's color comes from the speaker's own blood (which the lady has made his heart shed); in Shakespeare's poem the violet performs its theft from the same victim robbed by the other flowers. Hence in both cases it is Henry Constable (speaker in one poem, addressee in the other) whose veins are trespassed.

The violet is the final flower in Constable's poem, and the first flower in Shakespeare's. His poem opens,

> The forward violet thus did I chide:
> "Sweet thief, whence didst thou steal thy sweet that smells,
> If not from my love's breath? The purple pride
> Which on thy soft cheek for complexion dwells,
> In my love's veins thou hast too grossly dyed."

Appearing in spring even earlier than daffodils and swallows, the violet is indeed "forward." But the attribution may refer not only to its bloom time but to the fact that Shakespeare has repositioned the flower, moving it forward from the end of the second quatrain (its location in Constable's sonnet) to the poem's opening line. Shakespeare's beautiful formulation also emphasizes the tininess of the blossom, so tiny it can be dipped in veins (Constable's violet is dipped in blood that has been shed, and so may be on the surface of the body or pooled on the ground). The twice-repeated "sweet" in line 2 (an attribute of the violet but derived from the beloved) is an adjective often attached to Constable's name, as we earlier heard in Ben Jonson's reference to Constable's "Ambrosiack Muse," again in the anonymous poem "England's Sweete Nightingale," and a third time in contemporary lines from *Return from Parnassus*, "Sweete Constable doth take the wondring ear / And layes it up in willing prisonment."[4]

In a daring departure from Constable's poem—an act of "pseudo-originality" the lovers must have found hilarious—Shakespeare changes Constable's fourth flower from the trisyllable blossom beginning with *m*, marigold, to the trisyllable blossom beginning with *m*, marjoram. The kinky or wiry or curly locks of the beloved are appropriated by the marjoram with its tiny knotted buds running the length of its multiple stems.[5] What, in a nice Shakespearean somersault, is actually original is his emphasis on robbery. Shakespeare makes the poem uniquely his by confessing that none of its merits are his own.[6]

Far from suppressing the record of his theft, Shakespeare foregrounds it: it is, in fact, the heart of the poem. Constable's flowers acquire their attributes by the comparatively gentle routes of emulation (the roses "blush for shame" to see the lady's red lips) or envy (the lilies' whiteness is bred from envy of the lady's hands) or mistake (the marigold opens its petals in the lady's presence, believing her to be the sun). Shakespeare's flowers are outright thieves, miscreants that deserve chiding and punishment, condemnation (line 6) and curse (line 13). Even the delicate violet is not just a thief, but a greedy thief, annexing so much purple that it is "grossly" dyed. The vocabulary is relentless: "sweet thief," "had stol'n," "had stol'n," "his robb'ry," "had annexed," "his theft." The sonnet ends: "More flowers I noted, yet I none could see, / But sweet or colour it had stol'n from thee." Shakespeare foregrounds his own act of theft in a sonnet whose portentous number (99) already calls attention to itself, and whose number of lines (15) similarly guarantees scrutiny. The sentence it so clearly speaks— "My beloved is the man from whom my flowers in this poem are swiped," or, more simply, "I am in love with Henry Constable"— is not just the accidental revelation of the sonnet but its point and substance.

Far, then, from his having resorted to an act of plagiarism out of want of invention, Shakespeare's whole invention resides in the naked act of transcription. He has made himself legible. We can appreciate the ingenuity all the more by remembering that this poem follows one of the most powerful and painful sonnets in the whole sequence, "From you have I been absent in the spring," whose lily and rose are, like those in Sonnet 99, derived from the beloved, and whose final couplet contains the excruciating and exquisite lines "Yet seemed it winter still, and you away, / As with your shadow I with these did play." If the figure in Sonnet 98 is borrowed from Constable, it is in a poem so transfigured, so magnificent, that its origins have been left far behind. By comparison, 99 is a charming jest—a piece of mischief, but mischief with a mission and with spectacular revelatory force.

Constable had an inventive mind: one contemporary praised him, saying that no one in the country had "a more pure, quick, or higher Delivery of Conceit."[7] Other poets often borrowed, and elaborated, individual metaphors, lines, or even entire poems. Poets who emulated him include Alexander Montgomerie (the royal poet of Scotland who signed his own name to one of Constable's poems after rephrasing it in a Scottish dialect), Richard Barnfield, Barnabe Barnes, George Chapman, and Michael Drayton.[8] No wonder Shakespeare complained in Sonnet 78 that he himself was just one imitator in a sea of followers:

> So oft have I invoked thee for my Muse,
> And found such fair assistance in my verse,

> As every alien pen hath got my use,
> And under thee their poesy disperse.

Shakespeare ends this sonnet by claiming the distinction of being far more indebted than the others, since the beloved not only
"mend[s] the style" of his poems (true of all the other poets) but
provides his exclusive subject matter: "thou art all my art."

Because Sonnet 78 is about Shakespeare's poetic indebtedness
to his beloved, it should come as no surprise that the poem en-
codes a beautiful salute not just to the beloved's person but to
his poetry. Constable's own most complete manuscript of poems
opens with a poem whose first four words—"Grace full of
grace"—deserve to be firmly attached to his name, a hope expressed in the choice to place the poem at the threshold. Shakespeare ends the second quatrain of Sonnet 78 with an echo of
these words:

> Thine eyes, that taught the dumb on high to sing,
> And heavy ignorance aloft to fly,
> Have added feathers to the learned's wing,
> And given grace a double majesty.

As Constable's "grace full of grace" is a doubling of grace, so
Shakespeare here has doubled grace, as he will again at the end of
the third quatrain:

> Yet be most proud of that which I compile,
> Whose influence is thine, and born of thee:
> In others' works thou dost but mend the style,
> And arts with thy sweet graces graced be.

The doubling of grace, accomplished in the eighth and twelfth
lines, has itself been doubled by occurring in both places.

> And given grace a double majesty.
> And arts with thy sweet graces graced be.

Shakespeare's sonnet seems openly addressed to Constable. Is Constable's addressed to Shakespeare? Shakespeare's allusion to the poem is wholly independent of this question: to echo "grace full of grace" is to write a signature only slightly less explicit than spelling out the letters "H-e-n-r-y-C-o-n-s-t-a-b-l-e." Nonetheless it is a haunting question to ask.

In Constable's beautiful sonnet—nominally addressed "To his Mistrisse"—the speaker tells his beloved that the ostensible addressees in the poems (which are sometimes untitled, sometimes addressed to an unspecified lady, sometimes addressed to named persons, such as the King of Scotland, Lady Clinton, Lady Rich's infant daughter, the miniaturist Mr. Hilliard) are not the recipients of his deepest and truest love; his feelings have been directed to these others by mistake or lack of self-knowledge:

> Grace full of grace, though in these verses heere
> My love complaynes of others then of thee
> Yet thee alone I lov'd and they by mee
> (Thow yet unknowne) only mistaken were[9]

His love for the beloved is so strong that he is here willing to repudiate (or at least call into question the sincerity of) lines written to others with such apparent affection and admiration. (If any of the poems were intended to flatter, that goal has certainly been subverted here.) Formerly distributed among many, his love now has a single and unified recipient:

> The fire indeed from whence they caused bee
> Which fire I now doe knowe is yow my deare

> Thus diverse loves dispersed in my verse
> In thee alone for ever I unite.

The eleventh line is an extreme instance of the "volte," or "turn," associated with the Petrarchan form of the sonnet (but usually coming in line 9). In a single line, the speaker lets it be known that this solitary great love is hopeless for reasons already so well-known to the beloved that it is pointless to rehearse them again. Having turned away from the beloved in line 11, in the last three lines he turns toward God, who will either give him the love he yearns for or free him forever from love. Here the promise of grace in the opening four words is secured:

> But follie unto thee more to rehearse
> To him I flye for grace that rules above
> That by my Grace I may live in delight
> Or by his grace I never more may love.

The recipient of the poem may have read this ending in a different way than that proposed above. In line 11, the speaker turns away from the fiction of addressing a feminine person and openly identifies the beloved as male by whom he hopes to be loved and with whom he hopes to love with heavenly grace. While it may seem that "grace that rules above" can only refer to God and not to a human lover, we will see that both poets repeatedly allude to the act of love as one in which one of the two lovers (Shakespeare) is above. It is also the case that Constable often puts his human beloved and God in the same skyward location, as in the line "for live I doe, on heaven and thee to call" from a poem we will next come to.

To whom is this sonnet, "Grace full of grace," spoken? The title tells us it is spoken "To his Mistrisse."[10] But the poem tells us that the poems in the rest of the collection are not actually, or ultimately, destined for the persons named in their titles. Further, there is no biographical record of a woman to whom Henry Constable was devoted other than in friendship and courtly admiration. Either answer—the poem was spoken to a lady unknown to us; or the poem was spoken to a man whose name and gender Constable had good reason to withhold—could be true, and there is probably no way to decide between them.

It is worth stating the obvious here, however, that calling a male beloved "mistress" would not be foreign to either of the poets. Both Shakespeare and Constable often imagined themselves as feminine. Shakespeare is widely said to have portrayed himself as Venus in *Venus and Adonis*; he entered into the minds and hearts of countless women in his plays; and he loved writing scenes in which a woman was addressed as a boy or a boy as a woman. Sonnet 20 tells us he first perceived his beloved young man as a woman: "A woman's face, with nature's own hand painted, / Hast thou, the master mistress of my passion." In the 1609 Quarto, "master mistress" is uppercase: "Master Mistris."

In Constable's poetry, too, gender is fluid. One of his love poems about the separation of the lovers ends with the distressed lines:

> one will look for but nowhere find
> the boy within the woman, the woman within the boy.[11]

At its very heart, according to this poem, the loss of the beloved is the loss of gender fluidity. One of his poems to Queen Elizabeth addresses her as "prince": it opens "Most sacred prince why should I thee thus prayse."[12] (Elizabeth often used this same appellation in speaking of herself.)[13] This capacious view of gender extends to those who are spiritually exalted. He slides effortlessly from one gender to another when he describes God as a mistress, writing from exile to the Countess of Shrewsbury that he will "serv[e] no other Mistress than God Almighty, whom I know will love me if I love him, and in whose company I can be when I will."[14] In his divine sonnets, Constable cherishes the feminine soul as his own. In a sonnet addressed "To St Mary Magdalen," he writes, "So shall my sowle, no foolysh vyrgyn bee / with empty lampe: but lyke a Magdalen . . .";[15] in another sonnet with the same title, he writes, "For lyke a woman spowse my sowle shalbee";[16] and his sonnet "To St Margarett" ends:

> Teache me (o virgyn) how thou dydd'st prevayle:
> *Virginity* thou saiest was all thy Ayde:
> gyve me then purity in steade of power,
> and let my soule mayd chaste, passe for a Mayde.[17]

The yearning to pass for a Maid was well-known to both poets.

While we can never be certain whether "Grace full of grace" was written to a woman or to a man, another "grace" poem—omitted from the 1592 edition of Constable's poems but included in the 1594 edition—is clearly addressed to the male beloved, a male beloved whom Constable regards as a great poet. To be without him is to dwell outside all love, outside all poetry.

> Fayre Grace of Graces, Muse of Muses all,
>   thou Paradise, thou onely heaven I know,
>   what influence hath bred my hateful woe,
>   That I from thee and them am forst [forced] to fall?
> Thou falne from mee, from thee I never shall,
>   although my fortunes thou hast brought so loe,
>   yet shall my faith and service with thee goe,
>   for live I doe, on heaven and thee to call.
> Banisht all grace, no Graces with mee dwell,
>   compeld to muse, why Muses from mee flye,

excluded heaven, what can remaine but hell?
exil'd from Paradise, in hate I lye.
Cursing my starres, albe I find it true,
I lost all these when I lost love and you.[18]

To be with the beloved is to reside in the realm of poetic transubstantiation: "Fair Grace of Graces, Muse of Muses all." To be rejected by the beloved is to be in exile from that same realm: "Banisht
all grace, no Graces with mee dwell." If doubly graced, then
doubly disgraced.

When for the sake of his religion, Henry Constable was eventually forced to leave England and go into exile in France, his
heartache was great: we have the record of his efforts over many
years to return to England, his insistence that England was the
country he loved. That longed-for return had an almost impossible premise: he could return only if he could first convert the
country to religious tolerance or, more extreme, convert the country to Catholicism—both projects to which he arduously and
unsuccessfully dedicated himself.[19] But he knew how to live in a
foreign country. He was, after all, a world traveler, having often
moved across the European continent or up the English coast to
Scotland. The Catholic God to whom he now turned could even
be more easily adored in these other lands. As in earlier years he
had been well received by the Scottish king and the British queen,
so he was now on good terms with the French king, whose sister
provided him with a stipend.

To live outside England he knew how to do, having begun
his ambassadorial travels at a very young age. To live outside the
sphere of his beloved he did not know how to do. The reason for
the separation of the lovers is already well-known to us—at least
as the story has been told to us by Shakespeare: the beloved slept
with a woman Shakespeare regarded as exclusively his own. The
account given by the other lover awaits us in a later chapter. For

the time being, it is Constable's poetic presence in the architecture of Shakespeare's sonnets that is our subject, and to which we return. Perhaps Shakespeare learned of Constable's departure only when he was already aboard a ship, and thus needed to communicate with him by a poem that would circulate publicly and so eventually reach France. Perhaps his cheerful wager—"And ten to one thy Soveraigne pardons thee"—reckless as a prediction of royal actions, was a way of predicting the likelihood that he himself would forgive the beloved. Shakespeare's sometimes arch statements about the separation (as well as this whistling wager in "England's Sweete Nightingale," if indeed he is its author) might make us underestimate the pain Shakespeare suffered at the separation. But that pain is visible in many other poems, among them Sonnet 126.

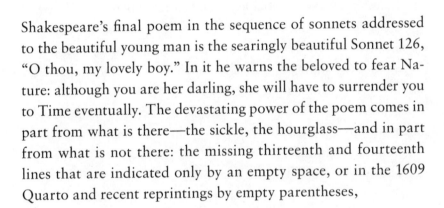

Shakespeare's final poem in the sequence of sonnets addressed to the beautiful young man is the searingly beautiful Sonnet 126, "O thou, my lovely boy." In it he warns the beloved to fear Nature: although you are her darling, she will have to surrender you to Time eventually. The devastating power of the poem comes in part from what is there—the sickle, the hourglass—and in part from what is not there: the missing thirteenth and fourteenth lines that are indicated only by an empty space, or in the 1609 Quarto and recent reprintings by empty parentheses,

(   )

(   )

which themselves form an hourglass signature.[20] There is perhaps no silence anywhere in literature, not even in *Hamlet*, more crushing than the cessation of this last poem at its twelfth line.

What makes the poem so painful is its combination of great distance and great intimacy. Distance is required for factual truth telling: you will be slain. The intimacy comes from the image of the lovers in an hourglass position, one on top of the other, the beloved below gaining the sands that are emptied out from the one lying above:

> O thou, my lovely boy, who in thy power
> Dost hold time's fickle glass, his sickle hour,
> Who hast by waning grown, and therein show'st
> Thy lovers withering, as thy sweet self grow'st.

This coupling is sonically magnified by the six pairs of rhyme words in the six couplets where sound is laid on top of sound—power/hour, show'st/grow'st, wrack/back, skill/kill, pleasure/treasure, be/thee—like lovers in the act of love, pressed forward by the internal rhymes (fickle/sickle)[21] and near rhymes (grown/grow'st/goest; mistress/minute/minion). It is not clear whether it is more true to say that the sonnet is missing its final couplet, or to say that the sonnet is only a set of relentless final couplets. By picturing the lovers in hourglass form, Shakespeare makes of himself and the beloved a couplet. He also converts the couplet form into an iconographic register of their lovemaking, a record of a long-ago embrace.

The downward fall of the first quatrain gives way to a rocking motion in the next quatrain, as the tide carries the beloved—a "wrack," a hybrid of seaweed and debris[22]—now forward, now back. Pairs of words sustain the rocking: waning/grown; withering/grow'st; goest onwards /pluck thee back; detain/not keep. Again the lines merge perfect distance (the brutal announcement that the beloved is a plaything of Nature) and perfect intimacy (the tidal rocking, coming after the hourglass position, seems a love act). It is as though while making love to one's beloved, one were to press the beloved into an admission that he must die; or as though while coaxing one's beloved to recognize his coming death, one were to make love to him.

In a deservedly famous article on numerology in the sonnets, René Graziani observes that the number 126 is a doubling of the number 63, the age believed by Elizabethans to be the "climacteric" year in a person's life—a year fraught with spiritual change and the risk of death.[23] In supporting this hypothesis about contemporary perceptions, Graziani cites a quotation from the first known reference to the climacteric sixty-third year in English. The cited speaker is, yes, Henry Constable. Constable attaches a note to the sixty-third poem: "When I had ended this last sonet and found that such vayne poems as I had by idle houres writ did amounte iust to the climatericall number 63, me thought it was high tyme for my follie to die and to employe the remnant of [my] wit to other calmer thoughts lesse sweete and lesse bitter."[24] If Constable conceived of this note at the moment he collected his poems, he would be at most twenty-nine or thirty; if at the time he wrote the sonnet, younger.

This link between Shakespeare's Sonnet 126 and Constable's note attached to his sixty-third sonnet is not nearly so portentous as that between Sonnet 99 and its precursor poem. Graziani mentions Constable's note not to indicate lines of influence but only to illustrate a belief of the era that at least two poets shared. But when Constable's sonnet sequence went from manuscript to book publication in 1592, it acquired another feature that bears far more directly on the poem.

On the title page of the book appears a seal used by the printer, Richard Smith. It has the motto "Occulta veritas tempore patet"— hidden truth is revealed in time—with a picture of an hourglass (bottom right) and a sickle (top center) carried by a satyr-legged Time leading a female figure of Truth up out of a cave (see figure 1). The shared images in the seal and the sonnet are striking: a sickle,

FIGURE I
Image on the title page of the 1592 and 1594 editions
of Henry Constable's *Diana*[25]

an hourglass, Time demanding a final reckoning, a passive figure who must be led to face this Truth. Neither the motto nor the combined elements in the emblem were widespread conventions. Partial sources certainly existed (in which some, but not all, of the elements were present), but they appear to be scattered.[26]

Richard Smith's printing of Henry Constable's poems, in contrast, would surely have been in the hands of every London poet in 1592. Would the appearance of the book have been painful for Shakespeare? Constable, though still himself in exile, would suddenly seem back inside the city gates, read and talked about wherever the still-aspiring playwright went.[27] (Shakespeare would have also found many of the poems directly addressed to a male beloved excluded from this first printing; they did not appear until the 1594 edition.)

If Sonnet 126 was written at the moment Constable's published poems appeared, it would also explain why Shakespeare here acknowledges that the beloved seems to be flourishing, seems to be augmented rather than diminished by time—in contrast to other sonnets, where the trajectory for lover and beloved alike is perceived as straightforward decline. In Sonnet 126, it is the very fact that the beloved appears exempt that instigates the insistent reminder: you are not exempt.

We have so far seen that Henry Constable's poetry, like an underwater garden of coral, breaks above the waterline and surfaces into clear visibility at two important stations in Shakespeare's sonnet sequence: Sonnet 99 and Sonnet 126. We have also had occasion to contemplate the tidal currents beneath the surface that flow from Constable's "Grace full of grace" to Shakespeare's Sonnet 78 back to Constable's "Fayre Grace of Graces, Muse of Muses all," creating a chamber of underwater echoes that we will soon hear much more fully in other poems, but that are not part of the architectural skybridge that goes from 99 to 126 and is then completed at 153 and 154. It is to the two final sonnets that we now turn.

The oddity of these two final poems has been noticed by many readers and literary scholars. As Helen Vendler writes, the poems seem willfully minor.[28] It is not just that they lack the searing finality of many of the other poems; they abstain even from the aspiration for such finality. If there is a sense of finality, it is achieved by formal means only, by the fact that Shakespeare has essentially repeated his own sonnet with slight variations, so that together 153 and 154 seem a decisive chord, or—in effect—a final couplet where the unit of the pairing is not now a line but an entire sonnet.

The beautiful Sonnet 116—"Let me not to the marriage of true minds / Admit impediments"—argues that true love is unalterable and unswerving. The final sonnets—153 and 154—make a counterclaim about erotic desire.[29] It is not quite the case that eros is unalterable. It is instead that it can only be altered in one direction: increase. Try to intervene to erase it from one geography and it will not only continue to reside in that first geography but spread to a second. Try to intervene to lower its temperature and it will not only maintain its heat but convert the would-be agent of cooling to its own fever. Eros, unlike sonnet sequences, never runs out.

In arguing this thesis, Shakespeare had many metaphors, idioms, and mythological tales to choose from. The view being argued is close to the view held by the fairies in *A Midsummer Night's Dream*, who are the champions of promiscuity. They disapprove of monogamy as bourgeois ill will, think it delightful and sweet that lovers should be randomly matched in the middle of the night. Peaseblossom and Mustardseed do not raise their eyebrows, if they even have eyebrows, when Titania and Bottom fall in love, nor do they disapprove when Oberon enters the body of a male shepherd so he can make love with the maiden that shepherd loves. (Titania complains, but only out of jealousy, not moral disapproval.) As for the erotic misadventures of the human lovers, the only sorrow is their return to chaste living.

Of the hundreds of possibilities Shakespeare had when writing Sonnets 153 and 154, he chose as the vehicle of his argument a mythological story, and of the scores of mythological stories, he chose Diana (Titania's Ovidean namesake). Henry Constable's sonnet sequence was by no means the only contemporary invocation of this chaste goddess, but it was certainly a celebrated one. The 1592 volume was republished with additional poems in 1594 and may have had a third printing in 1598.[30] Here in these final moments, Shakespeare has raised Henry Constable's flag over the sonnet sequence as a whole.

The erotic triangle comprised of Shakespeare, his young man, and his mistress is, in the other sonnets, a source of acute distress, even when Shakespeare is being forgiving. Here in Sonnets 153 and 154 the story is retold with cosmic acceptance, almost a celestial shrug. The lady—Diana, or one of her water nymphs—tries to rid the world of Cupid's charismatic sexuality by stealing his brand while he lies sleeping and by then submerging it in Diana's pool. The pool, far from cooling the brand, itself becomes a hot spring. When Shakespeare now comes to this chaste retreat and submerges himself in its waters to preserve himself from eros, he instead catches fire from his lady where (to close the triangle) Cupid himself originally caught fire.

This triangle—as presented in the earlier sonnets—will be described in the next chapter, where we will see that the terrible pain it caused Shakespeare was matched, and possibly exceeded, by the pain it caused Constable. But three features of Sonnets 153 and 154 should be noted. First, the lovers are here all without blame: the female goddess's intentions are wholly honorable (her acts of enclosing the brand "in her maiden hand" and then submerging it in her pool are undertaken in the service of chastity), and the god himself is asleep when the trespass takes place.

Perhaps more important, the "I" of the poem—Will Shakespeare—is a latecomer to the scene, the third to arrive. This may seem like a small point, but his self-righteousness in all the other sonnets seems to have no basis other than priority: the mistress is his, the man is his, so for them to have relations with one another entails a two-directional trespass on his intimate territory. If his temporal priority is not the basis of Shakespeare's objection, it is hard to see what the claim is, since the two miscreants are not doing anything that Shakespeare himself is not doing (sleeping with two people to each of whom he regards himself as true). It is therefore a graceful and large-spirited step to retell the story giving Diana and Cupid the primary relation and to describe himself as the third to arrive.

As in Sonnet 126, Shakespeare combines the distant with the intimate, though here the merging is much more extreme and probably less successful. While he invokes the mythological or allegorical figures of Diana and Cupid, the sexual imagery is almost embarrassingly explicit. The love god's brand, Diana's pool, and Shakespeare's act of submerging himself in the pool all have such explicit bodily locations in three concrete, nonfictional persons that the poems become graphic beyond what the delicate framework of a sonnet can bear. The poet confesses that his female beloved has become more intensely and permanently erotic to him once he experiences her interior as a place where the male beloved had been (an outcome Shakespeare acknowledges in several other sonnets addressed to his mistress).[31]

Is Shakespeare's portrayal of the young man as Cupid—"the little love god," "the general of hot desire"—diminutive or condescending? Not to sixteenth-century ears. Constable's own poems contain two sonnets describing his beloved as Cupid. The first begins with the description of a sculptor who makes a statue of the son of Venus in cold marble in an attempt to contain and control his heat. He includes in the sculpture a fountain so that rain will fall on him to further cool his ardor; the water instead augments the temperature of the boy.

> A Carver, having lov'd too-long in vaine,
>   hewed out the portrature of *Venus* sonne
>   in Marble rocke, upon the which did raine
>   small drizling drops, that from a fount did runne,
> Imagining, the drops would eyther weare
>   his furie out, or quench his living flame.

> But when hee saw it bootlesse did appeare,
> hee swore the water did augment the same.

In the final six lines, the poet describes his own parallel efforts to carve a portrait of the beloved in his poems to contain him and thereby diminish his charismatic power. Instead, the presence of the beloved in the poems only magnifies his erotic power.

> So, I that seeke in verse to carve thee out,
>   hoping thy beauty will my flame alay,
>   viewing my verse and Poems all throughout,
>   find my will, rather to my love obey.
> That, with the Carver, I my worke doe blame,
> Finding it still th'augmentor of my flame.[32]

It is not clear who Cupid is in these final lines: the beloved, since he is the one who, like the statue, is carved out; or the speaker, because he is the one whose fever, like Cupid's, requires diminution but instead undergoes augmentation. Shakespeare's 153 and 154 may be in part a response to this poem, as again to the next.

More intimate and concussive is Constable's second sonnet. Once the poet has pained his beloved ("thine eyes, eyes that my soule hath paind"), he fears that the beloved's erotic commitment to him will disappear and so searches to see if the beautiful love god is still in his bower. He believes Cupid has vanished until a mere glance from his lover's eyes hits him with a powerful flash of erotic confirmation.

> Wearie of love, my thoughts of love complaind,
>   till Reason told them there was no such power,
>   and bad mee view faire beauties richest flower,
>   to see if there a naked boy remaind.

Deere to thine eyes, eyes that my soule hath paind,
> thoughts turn'd them back in that unhappy hower
> to see if Love keepe there his royall bower,
> for if not there, then no place him contain.
There was hee not, nor boy, nor golden bow,
> yet as thou turnd thy chast faire eye aside,
> a flame of fire did from thine eye lyds goe,
> which burnt my hart through my sore-wounded side.
Then with a sigh, reason made thoughts to cry,
There is no God of love, save that thine eye.[33]

The image in the third quatrain is connected to the array of poems Constable wrote in which his beloved acts on him like a bolt of lightning. Though almost certainly written in the 1580s, these two poems, like Constable's others that thunder out Shakespeare's name, are omitted from the 1592 edition, then included in the 1594 edition. They are part of the haunting music of conversation between the two poets that lies beneath the surface of the poems. It is not this music, however, but the act of raising the flag of Diana over the sonnet sequence as a whole that makes the two final sonnets part of the overarching architecture of acknowledgment.

That each of the two friends associates the other with the winged boy reminds us that both poets are young. If one hears only one person's voice in a love duet, one may mistakenly believe that each time the singer says his beloved has quality "x," the singer himself must have quality "not-x." If Shakespeare praises the youth of his beloved, he himself must be old; if he praises the beauty of his beloved, he must be plain. Shakespeare praises the freshness, aliveness, and youth of the beloved (as did other people in describing Henry Constable[34]). But Shakespeare also describes himself as a small child (Sonnet 143), as a beginner who wields a "pupil pen" (Sonnets 16 and 32); when his mistress flatters him by saying he is young, she believes she can get away with the lie because she thinks she is speaking to an "untutored youth"—in other words, she really *does* think him young (Sonnet 138). Conversely, Shakespeare moans about his own tanned and weathered skin (Sonnet 62), but even more often he expresses terror and fury that his beloved resides on a precipice a half-step away from the gouging and scarring soon to be inflicted by heartless Time (Sonnets 3, 5, 6, 7, 11, 12, 15, and 19). The Cupids of Sonnets 153 and 154 when placed side by side with Constable's two Cupids remind us that lovers the world over echo one another's praises, often each marveling at the very feature that has, in turn, transfixed the beloved.

One final detail of Sonnets 153 and 154 entails a digression, but one that will eventually carry us back to the main path. Shakespeare in both sonnets alludes to but does not name Diana's water nymphs. Ovid, however, does name them. They are Crocale, Nephele, Rhanis, Hyale, Phiale, and Psecas[35]—in English, Sea-Shore, Cloud, Rain-Drop, Crystal, Water-Bowl, and Rain-Shower. Hyale, or Crystal, is a name with some interest for us. As we will see in a later chapter, the two poets had intimate names for one another: Shakespeare sometimes called his beloved Hal; Constable sometimes called his beloved Hyella. The call and response of their beautiful intimacies must be postponed until the story of their erotic distress is contemplated, especially as it is retold from Henry Constable's perspective.

In designating Henry Constable the birthplace of Shakespeare's poetry, there is no suggestion that he is an equal or a nearly equal poet. "I grant thou wert not married to my Muse," says Shakespeare, who *was* married to his Muse. Shakespeare lived by his poetry, wrote under duress and obligation and abiding commitment. He must have spent almost every waking and sleeping moment in acts of composition. By an early age, he had probably carried out what is today considered the prerequisite for the highest skill in any craft: ten thousand hours of practice.[36] Henry Constable, in contrast, was an ardent but only very occasional practitioner; he had incurred no obligations to the craft. If Shakespeare was sometimes incited to write in response to something Constable had written, what began as breath or vapor lying close to the ground in Constable's song was, once taken up and sung back by Shakespeare, given residence in the sky. This, in any event, is the way Henry Constable perceived it.

> As drawes the golden Meteor of the day,
>> Exhaled matter from the ground, to heaven,
>> and by his secret nature, there doth stay
>> the thing fast held, and yet of hold bereaven,
> So by th'attractive excellence, and might,
>> borne to the power of thy transparant eyes,
>> drawne from my selfe, ravisht with thy delight,
>> whose dumbe conceits divinely syranyze.[37]

Under Shakespeare's sway, ravished with feeling, Constable initiates dumb conceits, which the beloved draws forth and lifts into heavenly siren songs that need no support to keep their celestial position.

Would Shakespeare have begun writing poetry if he had not met and fallen in love with someone steeped in British, Continental, and classical poetry? Someone able to spark and speak metaphors in an instant? Someone able to talk and talk back? Someone able to hoot to the owls in Arden Forest, then slip off to the court of the Scottish king, where he was regarded as a favorite of James VI, then to the British court, where he was, as a foreign observer noted, a favorite of Queen Elizabeth ("favorito de la Regina"[38]), then to France to befriend Henry of Navarre, the future king of

France (who also regarded him "a favorite")? Probably Shakespeare would have written no matter what life put in his path. But this is the person life *did* put in his path; this is the person he wrote to and for; this is the Juliet he met after having thought the world contained only Rosalines. Accidental or instrumental or incidental, this is the person who merits the reverence Shakespeare asks us to give him.

3

A DAY TO REGRET

Shakespeare's sonnets speak of a beloved man and of an act of infidelity that man carried out one day. Constable's sonnets speak of a beloved man and an act of infidelity he himself carried out one day. This parallel alone would not suffice to connect the two poets, since acts of infidelity are fairly widespread. But Shakespeare describes a far more specific and unusual form of faithlessness, an instance of infidelity in which the beloved, rather than straying away from him to some other neighborhood, trespassed onto his own most intimate ground and had sexual relations with his mistress. Constable describes this same trespass, excoriating himself for having betrayed his beloved friend by sleeping with that friend's mistress.

Whether the mistress described is Shakespeare's wife or another woman seems unanswerable. Many features of the sonnets indicate that the dark lady is his wife, Anne Hathaway: several sonnets give a scene of sunny domesticity; in one of them, Sonnet 135, he addresses her in a state of pregnancy (asking whether, with so much of himself already inside her, he can sexually enter her); and the name "Hathaway" is universally acknowledged to be prominent in Sonnet 145.[1] But the conviction that the dark lady is someone else has been held by generations of readers and will no doubt endure across time. The term "mistress" can mean either wife or unmarried beloved. But for clarity, the term "mistress-wife" might be most accurate; for if the woman addressed is his wife, she is also the object of immense sexual desire traditionally (albeit wrongly) reserved for an extramarital mistress; conversely, if she is an extramarital mistress, the term "mistress-wife" best describes the sense of ongoing commitment and personal possession that Shakespeare feels toward her.

Whoever she is, Shakespeare regards her as decisively "his," we might even say "his property," since the pain-filled sonnets about the infidelity repeatedly accuse the male beloved of an act of theft. In Sonnet 35 he addresses his male friend as "that sweet thief which sourly robs from me." In Sonnet 40 he says, "I do forgive thy robb'ry, gentle thief." In Sonnet 41, he is aghast that the errors of "straying youth," which might lead "in their riot" almost anywhere and still be comprehensible, have instead carried him to the place of all places that ought to have been exempt, "my seat"—his private residence, his home, his center.

But the specific language of robbery—"sweet thief," "gentle thief"—is the mildest of Shakespeare's reproaches, usually spoken at the moment when he is in the midst of forgiving, or is about to forgive, the infidelity. In some instances, the act of forgiveness comes only after having described the male friend's act in a brutal idiom of moral disgust, a blight on what had been beautiful, the "mud" on a silver fountain, the "rotten smoke" obscuring the sky, the "stain" of an eclipse taking away the moon, a "loathsome canker" living secretly inside the "sweetest bud." Even to make such comparisons (by acknowledging that the wrongdoer has something in common with the once-beautiful bud, fountain, or sky), says Shakespeare, "corrupts" the speaker, making him complicit in the apparently unspeakable wrong the beloved has carried out. The effect of this poisonous vocabulary is to make it clear that the beloved who committed this trespass is worthless and contemptible; and though he can be forgiven (by the large-spirited mercy of the speaker), he probably cannot be actively desired, any more than one longs to moisten one's lips with water from a muddy fountain or caress with one's hand a disease-covered rose.

Centuries of readers must have noticed something wrong with Shakespeare's thinking here. It is not that the marriage bed (or the bed of an enduring female partner, if unmarried) should not be trespassed. Marriage in both religious and secular law entails a reciprocal transfer of rights over the body to the spouse. (We know that for the political philosopher Thomas Hobbes, taking someone's spouse was only slightly less injurious and unjust than taking the person's life or cutting off a limb.)[2] But if this is a precious bond deserving of protection, why is Shakespeare himself already violating the bond by his relation with a male beloved? If it is so precious to him, why has he been addressing the young man as the true love of his life? If, on the other hand, having a female mistress and having a male beloved are compatible acts (presumably the position Shakespeare has taken up to this point), then the lovemaking of the mistress and beloved should seem (or almost seem) harmonious as well. This is how the situation strikes Henry Constable, who absorbs the horrifying vocabulary of moral error, but then questions the coherence of the charge. Noticeably, and mercifully, he accomplishes this final pivot, hurling the charge of moral incoherence back onto Shakespeare, without subjecting Shakespeare to the same idiom of contamination and moral degradation.

We see Constable's acceptance of moral blame, followed by a sudden protest in the sonnet "Mine eye with all the deadlie sinnes is fraught," most starkly in a version of this sonnet in the Marsh manuscript that is believed to be an earlier draft than the published version.[3] The act of trespass takes place when Constable's beloved male friend is away from home and—worse—has explicitly entrusted him to act as guardian of this home front while he is away (the Stratford cottage for those who believe the mistress is Shakespeare's wife, a London residence for those who believe the mistress is distinct from Shakespeare's family). Constable describes himself as succumbing to each of the deadly sins in turn in order to arrive at the act of sleeping with the mistress-wife. More accurately and more virtuosically, he describes his "eyes" as subject to each of the deadly sins in turn while his own heart and mind are the victims of his eyes' wrongdoing. The published version actually numbers each of the sins—pride, sloth (here, idleness), envy, wrath (here, murder), avarice (or covetousness), gluttony, and lust. Constable follows the traditional sequence from most sinful, pride, to least sinful, lust, changing only the position of sloth: fourth in the usual hierarchy, here it is promoted to second place.

The published sonnet opens with a quatrain acknowledging pride and idleness:

> Myne eye with all the deadlie sinnes is fraught
> 1. First proud sith it presum'd to looke so hye
>   A watchman being made stood gazing by
> 2. And idle tooke no heed till I was caught.[4]

Pride prevented him from comprehending that anyone was off-limits to him. The specific formulation—"proud sith it presum'd to looke so hye"—cannot be an allusion to social status, since Constable was descended from the nobility on both his maternal and paternal sides, from a young age wrote poems to queens and kings, and flattered and flirted with high-born ladies. It is his status in relation to his own male lover (we will see in later quatrains) that ought to have placed her off-limits.

When the opening quatrain is compared with the draft in the Marsh manuscript, we see that the draft has less clarity and rhythmic strength than the published version.

> Myne eye with all ye deadly sins is fraught
> first Prowde, because it is cause that so highe
> my love presume: & Slothfull is for why
> save only gaze about it, it doth naught.[5]   .

Because "Sloth" has an ungainly sound, it is a hard word for poetry (even while being onomatopoetic); "idle" in the alternative version acknowledges the sin while avoiding the tone. The poet in both versions acknowledges that if he was going to sleep with someone, he might have looked around; instead, out of laziness he took no effort to look around and simply carried out the act with someone already at hand in the immediate environment. The published version explains how he came to occupy the woman's environment: "a watchman being made," he was entrusted to protect her. Counted on to be a guardian, he was too lazy even to act as watchman over himself, failing to notice his own desire and protect against it until it overtook ("caught") him.[6]

The second quatrain acknowledges the sins of envy and wrath. Constable often has poems, as does Shakespeare, in which there takes place an internal competition among eyes, heart, and thoughts. While the friend is away, the speaker's thoughts get to be near the woman. His eyes are envious that his thoughts get to be nearer to her than does the rest of him; and so he trespasses into her physical vicinity; in so doing his eyes carry out the "murder" of his heart, the site of his true love.

3. And enviouse beares envie that my thought
   Should in his absence be to her so nye
4. To kill my heart myne eye let in her eye
   And so was accessarie to a murder wrought.

The Marsh manuscript version is close to the published version:

And Enviouse which envith that my thoughte
should in his absence be to hir so nighe
to kill my hart: it hath let in hir eye
& so consent gave to a murder wrought.

In both versions of the second quatrain, the poet acknowledges that he has passively allowed the fatal event to occur, acting as an accessory, consenting to an act not initiated with premeditated design.

The third quatrain quickly paces off the sins of covetousness (or greed), gluttony, and lust, with the crushing identification of his eyes (and by implication, the woman he beholds with those eyes) as "a baude" between the speaker and his true love:

5. And covetouse it never would remove
   From her fayre hayre, gold so doth please his sight
6. A glutton eye with teares drunke every night
7. Unchast, a baude between my hearte and love.

Is the description of the "fayre hayre, gold" at odds with the "dark" hair of the dark lady? Perhaps. The color does not occur in the Marsh manuscript and may have been placed in the published version explicitly to deflect attention from the real person who is at the center of the scandal the poem describes. But brown or honey-colored hair is often called dark by some and gold by others (as contemporary portraits confirm, a sitter depicted with light blond locks in one painting turning up with dark brown or black locks in a second painting).[7] Further, it is clearly placed here primarily to reinforce the sin of greed, since gold is associated with wealth. The image it replaces in the Marsh version is more complicated: the miscreant is covetous of the "ritche treasure" belonging to his true love residing in his heart; thus he covets what his own heart already owns.

His eyes are a "glutton" in their masochistic thirst for perpetual tears. His gluttony therefore anticipates and assists the damnation and exile that will come in the final couplet:

> These sins procured have a goddesse ire
> Wherefore my heart is damn'd in loves sweet fire.

It is the goddess of love whom he has trespassed against and whose scorn he must endure. With the final image—"damn'd in loves sweet fire"—the poem ignites into crisscrossing flames of meaning: he suffers in painful fire which, because it belongs to the love goddess, is a sweet fire; he suffers the fire of his friend's anger, sweet because it belongs to that friend (a friend who will in his own poem on *Venus and Adonis* identify himself with the love goddess); and he is damned in the sweet fire of the erotic desire that caused the trespass.

But this ending should be put aside. The last six lines of the original poem in the Marsh manuscript are far more powerful. Here is the third quatrain (lines 9 through 12):

> And covetous whose only god is this
> beawtyes ritche treasure hourded in my hart
> a Glutton eye with teares which drunken is
> And all these sins shew how Unchast thou art.

Suddenly in the last four words of the quatrain—the last four words of the body of the entire poem—the center of gravity shifts, effortlessly and profoundly. The person spoken to, rather than the speaker, is charged with lack of chastity, with sexual trespass, and hence—since this was the sin that was buoyed up by the other six—of all the other sins retroactively. Poetically and psychologically, this is a powerful moment. The sudden shift is sustained in the final couplet of the Marsh version, which now has the beloved (rather than the speaker) as the object of the goddess's displeasure:

> And therefore thou deservst a Goddesse ire
> & therefore I am dampnd in Love his fire.

The conflation of damned and dampened suggests the flames at once engulf the suffering speaker and extinguish the hopeless love.

The sudden pivot at the end occurs because the person addressed has all along been guilty of the very acts for which the speaker is now condemned. Generations of readers have surely wondered as they read Shakespeare's sonnets why Shakespeare's beautiful young man and mistress-wife should be perceived as guilty of inconstancy if Shakespeare himself, up to the moment of their trespass, has without guilt loved, and probably made love to, them both. If having two loves is compatible—if they somehow exist on different, nonconflicting planes—there should be no grievance when the lovely friend and the mistress-wife sleep together. If instead Shakespeare is so alarmed by their sleeping together, that very alarm exposes the fact that his own love for them, which may formerly have seemed compatible, was compatible only in his own eyes. Was his mistress-wife really not supposed to feel forsaken by the ardent love Shakespeare had for his male friend? Was his male friend really not supposed to feel heartsick when they parted, knowing he would be going to the bed of his mistress-wife?

In a beautiful poem entitled "Of the thoughtes he nourished by night when he was retired to bed," Henry Constable describes the felt experience of losing his beloved each night.

> The sun his journey ending in the west
> Taking his lodging up in Thetis bed
> Though from oure sightes his beames be banished
> Yet with his light the *Antipodes* be blest.
>
> Now when the same tyme brings my sun to rest
> Which me so oft of rest hath hindered
> And whiter skin with white sheete covered
> And softer cheeke doth on softe pillow rest.
>
> Then I Oh sun of suns and light of lights
> Wish me with those *Antipodes* to be
> Which see and feele thy beames and heate by night
> Well though the night both cold and darksome is
>   Yet halfe the dayes delight the night grants me
>   I feele my suns heate though his light I misse.[8]

The poem has the metaphysical inventiveness found in John Donne. The disappearance of the earth's sun into the west and the disappearance of the speaker's lover at night are parallel events, since the lover is the speaker's personal sun. Without him, the world is dark and cold. Constable gives a graphic description of his lover in bed, the visual and tactile beauty of his body: "And whiter skin with white sheete covered / And softer cheeke doth on softe pillow rest." He does not need to say that lying beside the beloved is a woman, since in the parallel universe the earth's sun lies beside Thetis at that very moment. There would be no need to introduce Thetis's bed into the architecture of the poem if the phantasy taking place involved thoughts of the male beloved only; it is the male beloved in the company of a woman that the poem bodies forth. So painful is the nightly separation from the beloved that he wishes he were on the other side of the earth. But that mental transit, rather than enabling him to escape, carries him into the arms of eros; for the wish to be on the other side of the earth is a wish to be Thetis, made love to by the sun, or to be the sun, making love to Thetis. Within his own world, it is the wish to be in the mistress's position made love to by the man, or to be the man making love to the woman: to "see and feele thy beames and heate by night." This phantasy leads to the couplet which confesses that distress has been replaced by arousal: by night he feels his sun's heat though he cannot see his light. The agitation of physical separation is each night followed by the agitation of phantasized lovemaking. (Perhaps the trespass he eventually carried out with Shakespeare's mistress had been mentally rehearsed many times, prompted by the ache of nightly separation.)

In response to Henry Constable's distress and restlessness, the beloved man gives the answer that a lover in that position might truthfully give: "When I am away from you at night, it is only you I think about." Shakespeare being Shakespeare, what results is not a simple sentence of reassurance, but an exquisite sonnet, Sonnet 27.

> Weary with toil, I haste me to my bed,
> The dear repose for limbs with travel tired;
> But then begins a journey in my head
> To work my mind, when body's work's expir'd.
> For then my thoughts (from far where I abide)
> Intend a zealous pilgrimage to thee,
> And keep my drooping eyelids open wide,
> Looking on darkness which the blind do see.

> Save that my soul's imaginary sight
> Presents thy shadow to my sightless view,
> Which, like a jewel hung in ghastly night,
> Makes black night beauteous, and her old face new.
>   Lo, thus, by day my limbs, by night my mind,
>   For thee, and for myself, no quiet find.

The face of the beloved appears as a luminous mental image suspended in an otherwise black field. Romeo will say of Juliet, "she hangs upon the cheek of night / Like a rich jewel in an Ethiop's ear." Juliet on the balcony is actually present to Romeo, who reports a perceptual act, not an act of the imagination. But Shakespeare in Sonnet 27 describes the ability of the imagination to place on the mental retina the face of the beloved.[9]

Shakespeare's Sonnet 27 and Constable's "Of the thoughtes he nourished by night when he was retired to bed" are about the disquiet of nightly separation after being together in the day. Shakespeare's beloved, the couplet concludes, incites him to exhaust his limbs by day and his mind by night. Are his limbs exhausted during the day because of the arduous travel to reach him or because of ardent lovemaking when they are together? The idiom of travel in lines 2, 3, and 6 weights the answer toward the first, though Katherine Duncan-Jones points out that "journey" in line 3 is a pun on "*journée*," the French word for day (or day-long task), thereby shifting the weight toward the second. The association of motion with erotic performance is more extreme in Sonnet 51, where Shakespeare describes the unwilling forward motion of the creature between his thighs (his horse) when facing away from his beloved and the fiery speed and adrenalized momentum when facing him; the creature he rides seems less a horse than his own body, in one direction immobilized, in the other direction thrust relentlessly forward.

The possibility that the ambiguity is intentional is heightened by the fact that Constable's poem contains an almost identical ambiguity. Is the antecedent of "which" in line 6 "tyme" or "my sun"? Is it time "[w]hich me so oft of rest hath hindered"? If so, it means nightfall allows his beloved to rest but makes it impossible for the speaker to rest. It may instead, however, be "my sun" "[w]hich me so oft of rest hath hindered." If so, it means that during the day his lover makes love to him relentlessly. Both poems, if only glancingly and ambiguously, while describing the torment of separation and abstinence, not only credit the capacity of the imagination to make the beloved present in nightly phantasy but salute their exhaustive acts of lovemaking during the day.

But we have permitted ourselves to slip back into a relatively happy period where the only torment was nightly separation. And it is the crisis in their relation that we must return to. We have seen in the draft of the Marsh manuscript Henry Constable's call for symmetry: if what he did was wrong, then surely his lover can now see that his own actions were wrong; conversely, if the lover's former actions were without fault, then surely the same blamelessness adheres to the newly erring beloved.

But this response on the part of Henry Constable is only one genre of response. Just as Shakespeare lurches among an array of attitudes to the betrayal, so, too, does Constable, as together the troubled pair search for ways to diminish one another's pain and recover their serene confidence in one another. We may call the first genre of response—the one audible in the Seven Sins poem— "not guilty by reason of symmetry" or "guilty, but only if you are equally so." In the next two forms of response, Constable accepts his own action as wrong but assigns partial responsibility first to the woman herself, then to the beloved man. In one sonnet he suggests the woman initiated the flirtation: posterity will see "I did not force her hart, / and tyme shall make it knowne to other men."[10] Her responsibility was present even in the Seven Sins poem where the dangerous reciprocal gaze the two shared originated with the woman: his error was to let his eyes meet her already-looking eyes (line 7). His designation of his eye (and by implication, the woman his eye looks upon) as a "baude" also assigns responsibility to her, whether he uses the word to convey only her carefree merriment or her promiscuity. In describing the woman, there is no right alternative, no way of diminishing the male beloved's pain: if she is Thetis, that suggests she resides in the same neighborhood of his heart where his male beloved resides; if alternatively, she is a baude who means nothing to him, that is equally crushing. To betray your true love because you deeply admire someone else, or instead to betray your true love for a meaningless sexual encounter—which of these could possibly assuage the pain that the true love will feel (even as the mirror flashes around and shows that man his own alternating exaltation and repudiation of the mistress-wife to be equally painful to his male friend)?

In another poem, Constable assigns responsibility to the beloved man. Already this possibility was latent in the Seven Sins poem where the speaker describes himself as having been made a watchman, hence placed by someone else's hand in harm's way. (Was he placed in the position of watchman as a love test?) But that poem emphasized the greater weight of obligation the speaker had to abstain from desire, since he had been entrusted with the post of watchman. More direct blame of the male beloved is given in the opening poem of a seven-sonnet sequence entitled "The last 7 of the end and death of his love." I am in torment, says the speaker, a torment made worse by knowing my own folly brought this about; the one explanation that would make me gladly accept my pain would be to know you so take pleasure in my torment that you scripted the entire event; if my pain gives you pleasure, I can accept my pain. Here are the final six lines:

> So when this thought my sorrowes shall augment
> That myne owne follie did procure my payne

Then shall I say to give my selfe content
Obedience only made me love in vayne
   It was youre will and not my want of wit
   I have the payne, beare yow the blame of it.[11]

Inventive wit is a hallmark of Constable's poetry, so perhaps this dispersal of blame to the beloved is only poetic ingenuity. But it is worth remembering that Shakespeare begins his theater career with a play—*The Two Gentlemen of Verona*—in which, inexplicably and outrageously, one man shows his love for his closest friend by offering him his own female beloved.[12] More important, Constable's intuition that he acts on his beloved's will is mirrored in Shakespeare's identical intuition: throughout the sonnets, Shakespeare describes himself as acting on the will of the beloved, gladly arguing against himself if the beloved does, repudiating himself if the beloved does, hating himself if the beloved does. These two are surely in a nightmare of reciprocal adoration and loyal bondage, despite the ostensible subject of disloyalty.

Eventually, of course, the lovers do recover the ground of their love. But before turning to that happy outcome, we should pause to appreciate Shakespeare's moral high-handedness. In many of Shakespeare's sonnets, the sting of moral condemnation burns into the poem despite nominal forgiveness in the couplet. Infidelity, as G. Wilson Knight says in *The Crown of Life*, was death-like for Shakespeare.[13] The many moments in the plays where a suspicion of infidelity leads to a hate-filled denunciation of a wholly innocent person[14] was perhaps Shakespeare's penance for the brutality of his treatment of his own beloved: the curses hurled against Hero or Desdemona or Cordelia are far more lethal than the charges Shakespeare levels in the sonnets; and so, too, Hero and Desdemona and Cordelia are far more innocent than Shakespeare's beloved. By intensifying both the denunciation and the innocence—by driving the two further and further apart—he perhaps acknowledged a profound moral error on his part in his own many-years-long love affair.

The aura of moral rightness almost always belongs not to the most morally good person but to the most articulate; and because no one could ever be as articulate as Shakespeare, no one could ever be as morally right. What Henry Constable suffered at his hands can be appreciated by *reading aloud* Constable's brilliant poem in which he describes the many ways in which his lover has brutalized him. The final and worst is this: his moral self-esteem has been so thoroughly damaged that he has lost the right to complain about all other losses.

> I Doe not now complaine of my disgrace,
>   ô cruell fayre one, fayre with cruell crost:
>   nor of the hower, season, time nor place,
>   nor of my foyle for any freedom lost;
> Nor of my courage my mis-fortune daunted,
>   nor of my wit, by over-weening strooke,
>   nor of my sence, by any sounde inchaunted,
>   nor of the force of fierie poynted hooke.
> Nor of the steele that sticks within my wound,
>   nor of my thoughts, by worser thoughts defac'd,
>   nor of the life I labour to confound;
>   But I complaine, that beeing thus disgrac'd,
> Fyerd, feard, frantick, fetterd, shot through, slaine,
> My death is such as I may not complaine.[15]

Shakespeare had fallen in love with someone who, even when devastated, could talk back.

Shakespeare's tumultuous accusations against his friend begin with two sonnets about the weather. Sonnet 33 opens with the gold and green of radiant summer sunlight:

> Full many a glorious morning have I seen
> Flatter the mountain tops with sovereign eye,
> Kissing with golden face the meadows green,
> Gilding pale streams with heavenly alchemy.

The beautiful, trust-inspiring break of day soon gives way to "basest clouds," "ugly rack," and racing "disgrace." By the twelfth line, the golden sunlight that lasted just one hour seems forever gone. Even the couplet, which provides a sudden, about-face act of forgiveness, does so only on the basis that a lover, like the sky, may "stain." The word occurs twice in the final line and provides the final word: "Suns of the world may stain, when heaven's sun staineth." The line seems to insist on the friend's uncleanness at the very moment it pretends to wave his error away.

The couplet of Sonnet 34 is more convincing in its forgiveness:

> Ah, but those tears are pearl which thy love sheds,
> And they are rich, and ransom all ill deeds.

The "stain" of Sonnet 33 is now muted in the less graphic word "ill," which is mercifully relegated to obscurity by being merely the next-to-the-last word and uttered only once. Yet the body of Sonnet 34 is more relentless in its anger than is its predecessor. It opens with two lines of innocent puzzlement about why the lover gave no warning of the impending change of weather:

> Why didst thou promise such a beauteous day
> And make me travel forth without my cloak . . .

But by lines 3 and 4 the beloved is portrayed as actively taking advantage of the "rotten" sky to cloak his own dishonesty.

> To let base clouds o'ertake me in my way,
>   Hiding thy bravery in their rotten smoke?

How cruelly Shakespeare inserts the word "bravery." According to him, the beloved not only has sauntered forth in jaunty disregard of the impending injury, but has comported himself as though he were carrying out an act of courage. Under the false flag of bravery, he has aped this virtue only to desecrate it. Shakespeare carries out—rather than merely describing—an act of corrosion; before our eyes the most unassailable of virtues deteriorates, rots. Worst of all, the next eight lines insist there can be no remedy: the beloved has no power to "cure" the "disgrace"; his "shame," should he feel it, will not lessen the speaker's "grief"; his "repentance," should he offer it, will not diminish the speaker's "loss"; his "sorrow," should he suffer it, will afford only "weak relief." Shakespeare has cut his lover off at every pass, blocking four avenues of repair before any one of them can even be entertained. The couplet sounds magical in its sudden reprieve: these are the pearls that were his eyes. But the portrait of the beloved in tears reinforces the portrait of impotence and is not free of falsehood, since the young man is pictured as buying his way out. When read by third parties like ourselves, Sonnet 34 seems an elegant, forgiving poem. But when read by the person to whom it was addressed, how could it be anything other than excruciating?

Henry Constable also assesses the pair's moral disarray in images of changing weather. Far less intense than Shakespeare's two sonnets, Constable's poem aspires to reason with, rather than humiliate, the beloved. He begins by acknowledging that he has wronged his beloved and that his beloved has justly withdrawn his affection. But that admission is just prelude to the real import of the opening quatrain, which ends by counseling the beloved against luxuriating in his moral superiority:

> Deare, though from me youre gratiouse lookes depart
> And of that comfort doe my selfe bereave,
> Which both I did deserve and did receave,
> Triumph not overmuch in this my smarte.[16]

Constable's ability to accommodate the fresh speaking voice is here in evidence, and continues in the completion of the octave, where he directs the beloved to feel sorry not for him but instead for those now in the beloved's favor. The shift in focus from the rejected speaker to the anonymous persons held in esteem by the beloved may baffle us momentarily, but permits the location of blame to slide from the speaker to the beloved, who is guilty of inconstancy. Had he been constant, he would have continued to love the speaker even when the speaker committed a wrong:

> Nay, rather *they* which now enjoy thy heart
> For feare just cause of mourning should conceave,
> Lest thow inconstant shouldst theyre trust deceave,
> Which like unto the weather changing art.

Now the sestet takes that capricious weather, and amplifies it— turns it into a sonic atmosphere of braided song and silence— through the response of birds so subjugated to the weather's inconstancy that in foul weather they sing in hope of fair, and in fair weather stop singing out of alarm that it will cease:

> For in foule weather byrds sing often will
> In hope of fayre, and in fayre tyme will cease
> For feare fayre tyme should not continue still;

So they may mourne which have thy heart possest
For feare of change, and hope of change may ease
Theyre hearts whome griefe of change doth now molest.

The speaker's wrong (Constable's wrong) is now completely eclipsed by the wrong of the beloved (the wrong of Shakespeare), who has withdrawn love and, through that inconstancy, baffled the feathered world of small singers.

The distance between the diction used by the two poets is striking. Shakespeare's vocabulary of stains, rot, ugliness, and illness is morally condescending. Constable's aim in his sonnet is to puncture that smugness ("Triumph not overmuch in this my smarte"), but words like "smugness," or any of the hundred images he could enlist to provide a portrait of that unseemly state, are avoided altogether. His aim is only to reassert level ground, equality, not to rise above, look down upon, or humiliate his already badly wounded friend. How carefully Constable works to maintain equality can be seen in the shift from the octave to the sestet. While the diction of the octave is free of condescending language, the sheer force of argument in these eight lines risks creating the aura of superiority. Hence, the sestet replaces the confident momentum of argument with an image of sweet confusion, and makes it clear, in its closing lines, that this sonnet itself is like the song of a bird who sings to ease his heart in the hope that fair weather lies ahead.

And fair weather does lie ahead; or more accurately, stormy weather lies ahead but now it does not matter. The argument Henry Constable makes in "Deare, though from me youre gratiouse lookes depart" is the argument Shakespeare adopts in "Let me not to the marriage of true minds / Admit impediments" (Sonnet 116). Shakespeare's first outbreak of anger against the beloved—"Full many a glorious morning have I seen" (Sonnet 33)—seemed in its imagery a direct repudiation of what could be called his poem of betrothal, "Shall I compare thee to a summer's day?" (Sonnet 18), as though the exquisite world of that poem were now gone. So in turn Sonnet 116, which many readers see as the pair's marriage poem,[17] reclaims the ground of betrothal by its direct acceptance of changing weather. Even should the base clouds and ugly rack feared in Sonnet 34 swell into a raging storm, love will not swerve: "it is an ever-fixed mark / That looks on tempests and is never shaken" (Sonnet 116, lines 5 and 6). In this sonnet, the golden green world suffers more damage than ever it did in Sonnet 34, since here Time moves across that meadow with "bending sickle" slaying blades of grass and beautiful youths alike. Still, love does not flee:

> Love's not Time's fool, though rosy lips and cheeks
> Within his bending sickle's compass come;
> Love alters not with his brief hours and weeks,
> But bears it out even to the edge of doom.

The sonnet might have ended by swearing the truth of its assertions on a Bible. Instead, it swears on itself—the unswerving love is as true and real as the fact that this poem is in writing, as true and real as the love of a man for a man:

> If this be error and upon me proved,
> I never writ, nor no man ever loved.

The word "man" in the last phrase can be either the subject or the object of the verb "loved." The couplet may say: "This assertion of unswerving love can no more be an error than it can be shown that I never wrote a word, or shown that no man ever fell in love." Alternatively and more likely, it may say: "This assertion of unswerving love can no more be an error than it can be shown that I never wrote a word or that I never loved a man."

The fourteenth line is self-validating. It thus notarizes the poem—and the marriage it describes—as a whole. Since it is impossible to read the couplet's nominally disputable assertion without noticing that the speaker has written words, and since the speaker here and elsewhere is, by this very speech act, in the midst of loving a man, the line *enacts* the two forms of proof it at that same moment *designates* as the double seal of attestation.

Within the compass of the sonnet, this circularity and self-validation may seem merely ingenious—literary critics have sometimes faulted the couplet for what they mysteriously see as "pomp" and "swagger."[18] But when one takes a step back, or ten steps back, or ten thousand steps back, one sees the almost unthinkably heroic, deeply moral, act of validation that has occurred. Shakespeare is publishing these poems in 1609, probably more than twenty years after first falling in love. Why? Because, as is sometimes surmised, he believes his fame will come from these sonnets? Can we really believe that Shakespeare had the matchless poetic genius to write *Hamlet, Lear, Othello*, but not the poetic discernment to see that there in the plays, even more than in the sonnets, his greatness lay? (Sonnet 32 explicitly tells us that the sonnets record only his love, not his poetic genius; he worries he may not live long enough ever to demonstrate that genius.) No, his motive cannot be fame. By 1609, the sonnet sequence craze was over. The story the sequence tells had no peer and hence no predictable audience. In form, then, the sequence was stale, and in content a scandal. The act of publishing promised nothing except—profoundly—the act of fulfilling, enacting a marriage promise. He writes before the eyes of the world and, before those same eyes, proclaims his love for a man.

How many extended and explicit—undisguised, nonallegorical—love poems from a man to a man were written *before* the sixteenth century? *In* the sixteenth century? The seventeenth?

Eighteenth? Nineteenth? Twentieth? With no ground behind him and no ground in front of him, Shakespeare stood his ground, made naked his love, bore it out, even to the edge of doom.

Henry Constable's sonnets are often equally forthright and sometimes more explicit. But he—perhaps at his lover's request—cast them upon the world in only the most fragmented and dispersed way. He included them in the 1594 edition of his poems with an ambiguous signature attached to them: *Diana, or, The excellent conceitful Sonnets of H. C. Augmented with divers Quatorzains of honorable and Lerned Personages*. This attribution was technically accurate—some poems soon known to be by Philip Sidney were included—but willfully misleading, since it allowed the other poems, almost certainly by Constable, to reside in an unsigned limbo. Other early poems—poems we have already begun to encounter here and which we will come back to before long—were carried out of England into the Netherlands, translated into either Dutch or Latin and published there in 1591, where they have lain, largely unnoticed, for four hundred years. Three of these have duplicates which appeared in English in the 1592 or 1594 editions of Constable's poems, thereby confirming that the person called Henry Constable in the two countries is the same man. In the Netherlandish book, the three whose duplicates made it into the English edition reside side by side with twelve others that did not: all are grouped together under the single rubric "Adumbratum de Anglico Henrici Conestabilis,"[19] or "An Adumbration of the English Henry Constable." The word "adumbration"—whose root is "*umbra*," or "shadows"—was just at that time first coming into use. The title may simply mean "A Presentation . . ." or even "A Foreshadowing of the English Henry Constable." The Dutch poet Janus Dousa the Younger (who published the volume and who included some of his own poems under the rubrics "Epigrammata Juvenilia" and "Epigrammata

Puerilia") would be well aware that he was publishing the other poet's earliest compositions—a sample, a whisper, a prefiguration of work to come.[20]

One solution to the crisis, then, audible in the sonnets of both Shakespeare and Constable is the generous marriage oath, the promise—for better or for worse—that a true lover will be constant even when the beloved fails in any of the thousand ways that a beloved may fail. The second solution (again audible in both poets) is that the two men are twins, or even a single person, and that therefore it is incoherent to worry that one could "take" something from the other, since each already possesses what the other has, as we hear in Shakespeare's Sonnet 40:

> Take all my loves, my love, yea, take them all;
> What hast thou then more than thou hadst before?
> No love, my love, that thou mayst true love call;
> All mine was thine, before thou hadst this more.

In Sonnet 133, Shakespeare tells his mistress-wife that after seducing him, she seduced "my next self." The final couplet of Shakespeare's Sonnet 42 confidently asserts:

> But here's the joy, my friend and I are one;
> Sweet flattery! then she loves but me alone.

Twinship includes all that is bright and beautiful, but it also includes the symmetry of wrongdoing that Constable described and Shakespeare accepted.

Pairs of twins appear throughout the early plays; and inevitably one of the pair will have an erotic encounter with a person who was "originally"—or eventually—the beloved of the other twin. In *A Midsummer Night's Dream*, Helena and Hermia are "Like to a double cherry . . . Two lovely berries moulded on one stem" (III.ii.210–12). Given their inseparability, it is inevitable that once night falls over the forest, Helena's male paramour will be overcome with yearning for Hermia, and Hermia's male paramour will be overcome with yearning for Helena. In *Twelfth Night*, Cesario (Viola disguised as a boy) woos and wins the heart of Olivia, whom Cesario's twin, Sebastian, soon marries; Cesario (Viola still in disguise) suffers Olivia's dismay when he fails to remember he has married her just a few hours earlier.

If twinship excuses and erases sexual trespass in Shakespeare's sonnets and plays, in Constable's poems—as we earlier heard—twinship is simply the sweet fact of yoking itself, quite apart from the confusions it generates or apologies it affords.

I send, Light, this narcissus bloom of earliest spring
so that our songs will be yoked together inside the blossom—

yoked together like the beautiful boy and his reflection in the pool; or like the single flower Shakespeare's Helena and Hermia together embroider: "We . . . / Have with our needles created both one flower, . . . / As if our hands, our sides, voices, and minds, / Had been incorporate so we grew together." In the sonnets, Shakespeare—rather than phantasizing that the two lovers will merge into a single creature—instead takes their merged singularity as his starting point and contemplates the romantic benefit to be gained by pretending to divide themselves. How can I praise you when to do so is only to praise myself? he asks in Sonnet 39:

O how thy worth with manners may I sing,
When thou art all the better part of me?
What can mine own praise to mine own self bring?
And what is't but mine own, when I praise thee?

Let us pretend to split ourselves into two (the sonnet continues) so
that your absence will free me to sing of you:

> Even for this, let us divided live,
> And our dear love lose name of single one,
> That by this separation I may give
> That due to thee which thou deserv'st alone.

But this playful division, were it to be literalized, would be too
dreadful. Instead, the couplet tells us, an imaginary "absence"
(personified and addressed in the final lines) will enable Shakespeare to praise his beloved while still remaining securely merged
with him as a single bodied being:

> And that thou teachest how to make one twain,
> By praising him here who doth hence remain.

If the Ovidean hybrid of the yoked pair surfaces in and out of
view in any one of the sonnets, it is writ large in the overarching
design of the published sonnet sequence. The person to whom the
sonnet sequence is dedicated, "the only begetter of these ensuing
sonnets," Mr. W.H., may be the William-Henry hybrid whose
union did indeed beget the ensuing sonnets.

The ornament at the top of the 1609 title page has two Cupids
face-to-face (like Narcissus and his reflection), each riding the
curling stem of a central blossom. Scattered across the full design,
individual blossoms shoot forth stamens that at their tips become
yet another flower: blossom, stem, stamen, and root are indistin-
guishable; fish, fauna, mammals, and mermen are entwined and
envined in a composite creature that could begin at the periphery
or instead at the center or instead at the bilateral midpoints where
the floral spray that the Cupids ride may be their own genitals,
out of which the composition proceeds forward and back.

FIGURE 2
Ornament on the title page of the 1609 *Shakespeare's Sonnets*.[21]
The book opens and closes with two Cupids face-to-face.

As the sonnet sequence opens with the two Cupids face-to-face, so it ends by the placing edge-to-edge of two Cupids in the final two sonnets. They face each other. Equally important, they together face back across the sonnets to mirror the pair on the title page. Shakespeare may have written Sonnets 153 and 154 once he had selected the ornament that would be used for the title page—or, at the very least, once he had seen the ornament the printer had selected; for it is hard to believe that without foreknowledge the book (which up to the final sonnets contains only a few explicitly named mythological figures)[22] suddenly invokes at the end the very creatures who appear at the threshold. While many of the sonnets were probably first written in the 1580s, and a few, such as Sonnet 126, in the early 1590s, a small number were written, or at least revised, in the first decade of the 1600s, including perhaps the final pair at the time of the 1609 publication. It is equally possible that the final two Cupid poems—each of which contains, if only by accident, a line with the name "Henry Constable" in it—were written long before Shakespeare carried the poems to the printer. If so, it was not the threshold design that prompted the poems, but the poems that prompted Shakespeare to choose the threshold design we now find there.[23]

The youthful Cupids at the gateways into and out of the sonnets license us—for at least one chapter—to contemplate Shakespeare's capacity for unembarrassed tenderness. We will look for it in the place where it is most in evidence: the speaking of first names, private names, and nicknames. After this brief respite inside the nectared world of reciprocal caress, we will return to the realm of strife, specifically the distress caused by the rival poet.

4

BRIEF NAMES,
BELOVED NAMES:
HAL, HYELLA, HEN

Among all those who are beloved in Shakespeare—Romeo, Juliet, Antony, Cleopatra, Cordelia, Bottom, Beatrice, Benedict . . . the list is long—none seems more greatly loved than Prince Henry, in part because Falstaff takes every occasion to say his name aloud: "Now, Hal, what time of day is it, lad?"; "Indeed, you come near me now, Hal . . ."; "Well, Hal, well . . ."; "But, Hal, I prithee trouble me no more with vanity." Sometimes Falstaff even says Hal's name twice within a single sentence: "Why, Hal, 'tis my vocation, Hal"; or in two sentences in close proximity: "Thou has done much harm upon me, Hal. God forgive thee for it! Before I knew thee, Hal, I knew nothing." These sentences occur in the first hundred lines of the first scene in which we see Prince Hal (1 *Henry IV*, I.ii.1, 11, 60, 71–72, 81–82, 92), and the play as a whole is an extended meditation on the act

of name calling whose beauties and mysteries might well preoc-
cupy us here. But it is instead the act of naming in the sonnets
that is our subject, and we may find that we have not, after all,
strayed far from the woodland world of "Diana's foresters" in
Henry IV.

Shakespeare addresses Henry Constable through two intimate
names derived from "Henry." Intimate, even prayer-like, is the
name "Hal," uttered as softly and as regularly as though it were
breath itself. He directly tells us this in a poem which opens with
a quatrain asking if he has anything new to say to his beloved,
and continues:

> Nothing, sweet boy; but yet, like prayers divine,
> I must each day say o'er the very same;
> Counting no old thing old, thou mine, I thine.
> Even as when first I hallowed thy fair name.
>
> (Sonnet 108)

When the poet describes the act of having "hallowed thy fair
name," he means in part that he has consecrated the name, conferred on it the status of that which is holy. But he also seems to
mean—as we will eventually see—that he has converted the beloved's fair and formal name, "Henry," into the name "Hal"—
that he has "halified" or "hallowed" the beloved's name. Now
there is a third meaning: "hallowed" can also mean "helloed," as
in the sentence "When I first greeted you by name" or "when first
I spoke your name in greeting." In her commentary on Sonnet 108,
Katherine Duncan-Jones notices that the meanings of consecra-
tion and greeting are both present in the line "hallowed thy fair
name," and she notes that Falstaff conflates those two meanings
by saying, "For my voice, I have lost it with hallooing and singing
of anthems" (2 *Henry IV*, I.ii.172–73). But surely present in Falstaff's sentence is also the meaning "I am hoarse with having said

Hal over and over again"; and it is that verb—the act of saying the name "Hal"—that is key in Sonnet 108, where it is also merged with prayer and greeting.

Shakespeare's own intimate and abbreviated name is "Will," the same word as the verb and the noun, as he delights in telling us in Sonnets 135, 136, and 143. Here is Sonnet 135:

> Whoever hath her wish, thou hast thy Will,
> And Will to boot, and Will in over-plus;
> More than enough am I, that vex thee still,
> To thy sweet will making addition thus.
> Wilt thou, whose will is large and spacious
> Not once vouchsafe to hide my will in thine?
> Shall will in others seem right gracious,
> And in my will no fair acceptance shine?
> The sea, all water, yet receives rain still,
> And in abundance addeth to his store;
> So thou, being rich in Will, add to thy Will
> On will of mine, to make thy large Will more.
>   Let no unkind, no fair beseechers kill;
>   Think all but one, and me in that one Will.

As Katherine Duncan-Jones notes, in Sonnet 135 alone, Shakespeare uses the word "will" thirteen times and in the Quarto capitalizes *and italicizes* it seven times! In Sonnet 136 he uses "will" six times and concludes, "for my name is *Will*."

This acrobatic act of turning his own name into a hoop through which he somersaults into an uncharacteristically obvious pun—over and over as though performing a roll call where there is only a single name yet where the "rolling" motion must nonetheless be literalized—allows him to italicize and underscore a way of naming which he then need *not* do for Hal, whose name he embeds in another auxiliary verb—"shall"—without ever having to depart from the prayer-like tone into antics and acrobatics. How Shake-speare brings "WILL" and "sHALl" together will be described in a moment; but for now let us just listen to the way the sound "Hal" becomes the "phonetic jewel" at the center of Sonnet 55 (and many other sonnets addressed to the beautiful young man).[1]

I will underscore the name in these sonnets the way Shake-speare underscores his own name, so that the name "Hal" will be (as Shakespeare promises) unmistakable in our eyes. But this may be misleading, since sonically the word, far from being stressed, is the softest sound in the poem. No capitalization or italics are necessary if one speaks the poem aloud, for acoustically "Hal" and "shall" are nearly identical, so much so that the unac-cented name "Hal" runs through the sonnet like a soft brook of under-sound.

> Not marble, nor the gilded monuments
> Of princes, *shall* outlive this powerful rhyme;
> But you *shall* shine more bright in these contents
> Than unswept stone, besmeared with sluttish time.
> When wasteful war *shall* statues overturn,
> And broils root out the work of masonry,
> Nor Mars his sword nor war's quick fire *shall* burn
> The living record of your memory.
> 'Gainst death, and all-oblivious enmity,
> *Shall* you pace forth; your praise *shall* still find room
> Even in the eyes of all posterity
> That wear this world out to the ending doom.
>   So, till the judgment that yourself arise,
>   You live in this, and dwell in lovers' eyes.

Line 3 of the poem—"But you shall shine more bright in these contents"—spells out the name "Henry Constable," as we saw in chapter 1. But now, in addition, comes the persistent caress of intimate naming.

How can future time imperil the beloved when the beloved already is, in his very name, embodied and carried forward in the word that designates the future: "shall." "Shall" is defined by dictionaries as "something that will take place or exist in the future." The soft, almost always unstressed "shall" occurs six times, twice in a single line (like one of Falstaff's sentences): "shall outlive," "shall shine more bright," "shall . . . overturn," "shall burn," "Shall you pace forth," "shall still find room / Even in the eyes of all posterity." Beautifully understated, the unstressed auxiliary is more important than the verbs it sustains: it is less the shining, the overturning, the burning than the abiding fact of being—and still being, and being once more—in all futures that Shakespeare means to, and does, accomplish. In four of the phrases, the beloved is the subject of the verb ("outlive," "shine more bright," "pace forth," "find room"), and in two, a transmuted subject: it is war that will overturn statues and fail to burn the living record of his name, but by yoking the word "shall" to these verbs, it is as though the beloved is the agent of even these powerful acts, burning or burnishing the living record.

In Sonnet 55, then, the beloved is promised that he will live "in the eyes of all posterity"—even as, at this very moment, he *is* in our eyes. In Sonnet 81, in addition to our eyes, it is in the breath of posterity that his name (line 5) will live:

> Or I ***shall*** live your epitaph to make,
> Or you survive when I in earth am rotten,
> From hence your memory death cannot take,
> Although in me each part will be forgotten.
> Your name from hence immortal life ***shall*** have,
> Though I, once gone, to all the world must die:

> The earth can yield me but a common grave,
> When you entombed in men's eyes *shall* lie.
> Your monument *shall* be my gentle verse,
> Which eyes not yet created *shall* o'er-read,
> And tongues to be, your being *shall* rehearse,
> When all the breathers of this world are dead;
>> You still *shall* live, such virtue hath my pen,
>> Where breath most breathes,—even in the mouths
>> of men.

"Shall" occurs once in the first quatrain, twice in the second quatrain (opening and closing the unit), three times in the third quatrain, and once in the final couplet. The nearly soundless sound of "shall"—its unstressed assistance to or carrier of other words—makes it like breath itself under the voice.

The word "hal" is the word for breath in the Latin, "*hal-are*," "to breathe," as is visible in the English words "inhale" and "exhale." Subvocal and "over-read" (line 10), it is overlooked by our eyes at the very moment it passes over our tongues (line 11) and inhabits our mouths (line 14). We, like many generations before us, and many generations after us in the 2100s and 2200s—"eyes not yet created . . . / And tongues to be"—will be successively conscripted, whether knowingly or unknowingly, into animating the beloved's name. In this sonnet, as in others we will come to, it is less "fame" or "memorialization" that is promised than the astonishing fact of aliveness itself; and it is we—we breathers, we readers—who lend our aliveness to Shakespeare's beloved friend.

Like breath, the word "shall" is part of the deep iterative fabric of the poems. "Shall" occurs in many—in fact, thirty-two—of the beautiful young man sonnets; and because it often occurs multiple times (six "shalls" in Sonnet 55, seven "shalls" in Sonnet 81, four "shalls" in Sonnet 63, three in Sonnets 18, 51, and 65) it recurs fifty-four times in these poems. In the many beloved man sonnets where it appears only once, it often inhabits a threshold position, the poem's opening line (Sonnets 22, 70, and 101) or the poem's final line (Sonnets 19, 38, 54, and 77)—as it also sometimes occupies that threshold position in poems where it occurs multiple times.[2]

It is crucial to notice that the word nowhere occurs in the sonnets exclusively addressed to, or describing, the dark lady. After Sonnet 126—where the sustained sequence to the male friend ends—"shall" is almost absent from the poems. The word occurs in only three poems, one in which Shakespeare addresses his soul rather than a person (Sonnet 146, "Poor soul, the centre of my sinful earth"), one in which both the young man and the dark lady are present (Sonnet 144, "Two loves I have of comfort and despair"), and one which is addressed to the mistress-wife but where the single "shall" is lost in a sea of "wills" and where the isolated auxiliary might even legitimate a reading of the sonnet that includes the beloved man (Sonnet 135).[3] Literary critics have long cited the "shall" line in this sonnet as meaning that the woman has had lovers other than Shakespeare: the reading we propose differs only by observing that the woman has not had multiple unnamed lovers but one very specific, and named, lover. Because the meanings of "Will" are so yoked to Shakespeare's name in this poem, he perhaps had to use a different auxiliary at the single moment in the poem where no self-referring pun was wanted. Yet it is conceivable that this appearance of the word "shall"—the solitary instance in any of the many poems addressed to his female beloved—means that even here Hal is present.

In this sonnet, Shakespeare tells his lady: you already have me and my will so present inside you that there is no longer any room for me to enter. He then cajoles her into letting more of himself in. It is a poem that one might say to a woman who is carrying one's child and who is therefore already visibly swollen with one's own presence. But perhaps it is not a child here but the male beloved, who, because he is identical with Will, makes her already full of "Will," an interior space he would nevertheless, in his own body, like to enter.

We saw in chapter 1 that Sonnet 18 is the first poem in which the name "Henry Constable" is spelled out in lines that claim they carry a special cargo. It is also one of the "shall" poems: "Shall I compare thee to a summer's day?" As though to prepare for the transubstantiation of his friend into our own breathing, Shakespeare in this beautiful sonnet differentiates the beloved from the sometimes untender breathings of summer:

> Thou art more lovely and more temperate:
> Rough winds do shake the darling buds of May,
>
> . . . .
>
> But thy eternal summer *shall* not fade,
>
> . . . .
>
> Nor *shall* death brag thou wand'rest in his shade,
> When in eternal lines to time thou grow'st;
> > So long as men can breathe or eyes can see,
> > So long lives this, and this gives life to thee.

"Shall" is especially likely to occur in poems about breath and about aliveness, as it does here, and again in the final line of Sonnet 38, which begins: "How can my muse want subject to invent, / While thou dost breathe . . ."; or again in Sonnet 70, where the beloved is "heaven's sweetest air."

The sexual act is a stunning act in part because it entails entering into, and exiting from, the interior of another person's body. But this is what breath does as well; it is part of our own and every other person's deep interior. As breath resides inside a person, so Shakespeare accomplishes a second ingress into the interior—the interior of the interior—by registering the scent of breath:

The rose looks fair, but fairer we it deem
For that sweet odour which doth in it live.
(Sonnet 54, lines 3, 4)

The sonnet goes on to conclude that like "sweet roses" (line 11),

Of their sweet deaths are sweetest odours made:
And so of you, beauteous and lovely youth,
When that *shall* vade, by verse distils your truth.
(Sonnet 54, lines 12–14)

Shakespeare ensures that future generations—those responsible for keeping Hal alive and breathing—will not only repeatedly whisper his nickname but also deepen their breathing. Descriptions of scent invite, perhaps even require, a small rush of air into the nose so that the nostrils of readers flare ever so slightly when they come to such lines. Even when Shakespeare is abusing his beloved, as his anger adrenalizes our heartbeat, so his frequent recourse to aversive odors enlists the reader into deeper inhalations: "lilies that fester smell far worse than weeds" (Sonnet 94).

Again in Sonnet 65 Shakespeare distills person into breath, breath into scent:

How with this rage shall beauty hold a plea,
Whose action is no stronger than a flower?
O, how *shall* summer's honey breath hold out
Against the wreckful siege of batt'ring days . . . ?
. . . .
O fearful meditation! Where, alack,
Shall time's best jewel from time's chest lie hid?

The sonnet answers that question. Time's best jewel is Hal and he is hidden in the word "shall." Hal is the sweet summer morning scent in the rose whorls of "shall." Hal is "time's best jewel" hidden from Time in "time's chest."

By enclosing Hal in the future, he is made immune to the ravages of time. By the time any reader—whether living in the 2010s or the 1610s (or, alas, even the middle or late 1590s)—reads Sonnet 63, old Time will have injured the beautiful Henry Constable, will have "crushed and o'erworn" him, "drained his blood," and "filled his brow / With lines and wrinkles." But these verbs are all securely in the past tense (that form of past tense misleadingly called "present perfect" when Time has galloped ahead to swallow into its entrails what briefly seemed out in front). Safely enclosed in the simple future, Hal is always a hair's breadth ahead, always just beyond the reach of time's knife. Hal cannot be cut away from "shall":

> For such a time do I now fortify
> Against confounding age's cruel knife,
> That he *shall* never cut from memory
> My sweet love's beauty, though my lover's life.
>   His beauty *shall* in these black lines be seen,
>   And they *shall* live, and he in them still green.

Though some of the naming sonnets both spell out Henry Constable's name and lace the poem with "shalls," here the intimate name alone suffices. It fulfills the couplet's announcement that the beloved is right now right here: visible, alive. Twice present, he grows and greens, freshened with the breath of each new, ever more numerically generous, generation of readers.

There are places on the body of the human being that are difficult for the person to reach; usually they are places on the back of us. For Time, the opposite holds true. It can always reach and ravage its own back but cannot reach its own front, no matter how fast it runs. Hidden out front in the one pocket of time that even time itself cannot reach, Hal is made secure. The beloved lives in the safe space of shall-time.

> Yet do thy worst, old Time: despite thy wrong,
> My love *shall* in my verse ever live young.
>
> (Sonnet 19)

Shakespeare sometimes combines the "shall" and "will" auxiliaries at a moment when he is giving a promise, or requesting a promise, as though to fold his own name and Hal's into a speech act that resembles a marriage vow. In Sonnet 123 Shakespeare defies time—"Thy registers and thee I both defy"—and concludes:

> This I do vow, and this *shall* ever be,
> I *will* be true despite thy scythe and thee.

Venus in Shakespeare's *Venus and Adonis* sometimes addresses her beloved in words that echo the sonnets. Her repeated vocative "sweet boy," "sweet boy" (lines 155 and 583) is continuous with the "sweet boy" of Sonnet 108 and the "O thou, my lovely boy" of Sonnet 126. This poem, too, occasions a brief moment when the two men's names converge in the language of the marriage vow—Wilt thou take this man? Wilt thou take this woman?—

> Tell me, Love's master, *shall* we meet tomorrow?
> Say, *shall* we? *Shall* we? *Wilt* thou make the match?
>
> (*Venus and Adonis*, lines 583–86)

Both passages carry out a kind of word magic in which, for a split second, the two—Will and Hal—seem poised on the edge of being married.

Though their love for each other almost certainly began in the mid to late 1580s, it is not unreasonable to believe they remained true to one another over the next two decades: "For term of life thou art assurèd mine," Shakespeare avows in Sonnet 92. His 1609 publication of the poems (his open and risk-filled acknowledgment of his passionate love for a man) and Henry Constable's ardent avowals of chastity and dedication in his holy sonnets both, in different ways, affirm this possibility. If it is odd to believe in Shakespeare's capacity for keeping promises, it is more odd to doubt that capacity. Four centuries—not two decades—have substantiated his vow that his beloved will be kept alive by the breath of future readers. That he kept his love alive for one brief human lifetime should not be doubted.

HYELLA

Shakespeare called his beloved Hal. Constable called his beloved Hyella. The poems in which the beloved is called by that name are among the Latin poems published in the Netherlands in 1591. Despite the apparently feminine name, it seems likely that he is here addressing a male beloved.

Even more acute than Constable's pleasure in the sending and receiving of poems is the pleasure of being in the beloved's presence, watching the world transformed before his eyes. We find this in "Carmen xix," a four-line poem:

With you, Light, I see. I seem to see all
Even though our eyes see nothing different.

Turn your face to me at all times, Hyella, do not refuse;
Otherwise I gaze around at everything, and discern nothing.[4]

Earlier we saw that Constable compares the felt experience of being made love to with the felt experience of being struck by lightning. Given the power of Shakespeare in the poems and plays, is there any reason to suppose that this description of intimacy with him is an overstatement? Here in "Carmen xix" we might ask the same question about the gift of Shakespeare's perceptual acuity. With Shakespeare at one's side, would not the beauty of trees, faces, flowers, poems skate from surface to surface with such flashing brilliance that his disappearance from one's side would be, as Constable implies, like the sudden fall of night? "Turn your face to me at all times, Hyella."

For Constable, the beloved rearranges the universe, from the celestial canopy overhead to the flowers at the poet's feet.

You ask why the clouds disappear from the whole sky
And the Trojan urn does not pour out its customary waters.
Why the wandering sea rises up with no waves,
And why it is that the Pole star shines brighter than is its way;
Why a more beautiful forest springs up in fertile plough
    lands,
Beginning to spread its luxurious canopy;
Why the face of the beautiful earth laughs with every kind
    of flower,
And the river breaks into lustrous whirlpools?
The breeze of the western zephyr does not cause this,
Nor the clear dry air from the south,
Nor does the wrath of the north wind subside in such a way.
After Hyella has moved into the joyful fields,
Calming everything gazed upon,

The fair one exhilarates even heaven,
Deserving[5] as much of the gods as of mortal hearts.[6]

This delight-filled poem, "Carmen xiii," has an odd feature, a feature found in several of the Latin poems that does not seem to occur in the English poems. In the English poems, Constable is always full of admiration, even reverence, for women, whether it is in his elegant poems praising Lady Penelope Rich (the sister of Robert Devereux and the woman said to be Philip Sidney's adored Stella) or in the much more ardent poems to St. Mary Magdalen, St. Katharyne, and St. Margarett in the "Spiritual Sonnets." In the Latin poems, in contrast, the poet—while ascribing feminine attributes to both himself and his beloved—sometimes explicitly places himself apart from the female world, even speaking of it with disdain. (This goes along with the fact that the poems seem to be written by a poet slightly younger than the man writing the English poems.)

"Carmen xiii" above provides an instance. The poem consists of a list, a succession of small bursts of surprise, even though, with one exception, no item is surprising: in response to Hyella's presence, the sun shines, the stars gleam, the earth laughs, flowers bloom, streams flow. One item amidst this luminous sequence is, however, startling: the sudden rising up of a forest into the midst of plowed fields. A field that has been worked and yields a crop is a long-standing metaphor for marriage and childbearing, as when Shakespeare in Sonnet 3 writes, "For where is she so fair whose uneared womb / Disdains the tillage of thy husbandry?" Constable's line seems a fairly open repudiation of the world of heterosexual reproduction, and conceivably (along with other, similar statements) provides an answer to Shakespeare's first seventeen sonnets, in which he counsels the young man to get married and bear children. It is the only image in the list to which he dedicates two lines.[7] It is also the image most allied with Hyella, since his or her entry into the poem precisely reenacts the entry of the forest into the fields: the forest enters into and displaces the happy (that is, fertile) fields in line 5, as now Hyella enters into the joyful (that is, fertile) fields in line 12.

A second instance of this repudiation occurs in "Carmen xviii"—a difficult love poem to which we will return in chapter 6. Relevant here is the end of the poem. The final four lines contrast the unreliable world of women with the chaste (and presumably male) world of poetry:

> He who is swept along with Mercury
> Finds only the unreliable trust of a woman.
> In the end it is Diana who measures out Olympus,
> Joining radiance to ice.[8]

When Shakespeare moves from the first seventeen sonnets to Sonnet 18, he shifts from an immortality based on biological fatherhood to an immortality based on poetry. Constable here does the same. He describes the unreliable sphere of women and procreation: Mercury was in the ancient Arcadian religion "the fertilizing god of the earth," particularly responsible for overseeing the birthing of sheep.[9] Constable contrasts this realm with Olympus, the immortal realm of poetry achieved by walking in the path of chaste Diana. Enlisting a chiastic structure, the poem makes a male god the guide in the territory of female instability, while a female goddess, revered for her refusal to participate in heterosexual escapades, leads us to the world of Olympus. We will encounter a third instance in which the poet distances himself from heterosexual love at a later moment in contemplating the Hyella poems.

Is the name "Hyella" a transcription of the name "William"? Is it a name for Will and Hal united, as suggested by the fact that the first three letters reside in "Henry" and the next three letters in "William"? Shakespeare addresses his beloved as a beautiful youth. Constable in turn addresses his beloved as a youth, child-like, as we saw in his two Cupid poems, his skin whiter than white sheets, as we saw in his poem about missing him at mid-night. (Shakespeare describes his own countenance as weathered, but presumably he is speaking only of his face and hands.)

In his Hyella poems, Constable may be translating, or adapt-ing, or at least alluding to the poetry of the late fifteenth- and early sixteenth-century Italian poets—Andrea Navagero and Marcantonio Flaminio—who wrote Latin love poems and epi-taphs to a young girl named Hyella, who had "died of disap-pointed love."[10] She is beloved by Cupid, as this prose poem by Navagero tells us:

> Wandering by chance through flowering gardens my
> Hyella was weaving together white lilies with fragrant
> roses, when behold, among the roses she came upon Love
> hiding, and entwined him forthwith in her garland of
> flowers. He struggled at first; and fluttering his bright
> wings, the fierce boy tried to loosen his chains. Soon,
> when he saw her milk-white breasts, worthy of his mother,
> and a mouth fit to move the very gods, and as he became
> aware of the ambrosial perfume of her hair, of that per-
> fume which the wealthy Arab gathers in abundant har-
> vest, "Go, my mother," he said, "seek for yourself a new
> Love. This seat will be fit for my throne."[11]

As the pair thrive in a garden in daylight, so, too, they thrive by night. Here is Navagero's prose poem entitled "Prayer to Night That His Love Remain Hidden":

> Kindly Night, thou who embracing earth in silent dark-
> ness, concealest the sweet thefts of delightful Venus, while

I hurry to the embraces and soft kisses of my beloved
Hyella, be thou my only companion on my way. Lest
anyone find out about our love, condense the air more
compactly into coal-black clouds; he who confides his
secret joy to anyone else does not deserve any girl ever
willing to be called his own.[12]

The love god himself (we are told) wants the level of secrecy ordinarily reserved for Eleusian mysteries and rituals. Only the nurse
who leads him to Hyella's room knows of his love. The poem
brings to mind another very young person who wants only her
nurse and kindly night to witness her love acts: "Come, civil
night, / Thou sober-suited matron, all in black / . . . Come, night;
come, Romeo. Come, thou day in night; / For thou wilt lie upon
the wings of night / Whiter than new snow upon a raven's back. /
Come, gentle night, come, loving, black-brow'd night / . . . O,
here comes my nurse" (III.ii.10–11, 17–20, 31).

The Hyella poems, as noted earlier, are in the group collected
in the Netherlands and published by the Dutch poet Janus Dousa
the Younger. Dousa, like so many other national and international figures, must have admired Constable either in person or in
writing: he took care to translate five of Constable's poems into
Dutch and ten into Latin (though some of those ten may have
been originally composed in Latin). Dousa included them in the
1591 book containing his own poems. We know that Dousa and
his father were in England in 1585 and met Philip Sidney, a friend
of Constable's, though there is no record of his having met Constable himself.[13] One of Shakespeare's biographers thinks Shakespeare might have been in the Netherlands in 1586 in a theater
group serving with Leicester forces;[14] quite independently, one of
Constable's biographers surmises he might have been in the Netherlands in 1586–87 serving under Leicester.[15]

Did Henry Constable himself give the poems to Dousa? Did

someone else do so? Is it possible that it was Shakespeare who did so? Shakespeare's Sonnet 77 describes a blank journal ("vacant leaves," "waste blanks") he gives to the beloved friend with a specific request that he fill its pages with "thy mind's imprint." In the space between Sonnet 77 and Sonnet 122, the beloved has written out his poems and given the book to Shakespeare. But Shakespeare, astonishingly, has given the gift away to a third person! The beloved's dismay at this turn of events is addressed in Sonnet 122, where Shakespeare (as always residing on moral high ground even at a moment when he has performed an act acutely painful to his lover) explains that what might be construed as a careless disregard for his beloved's poems is instead a regard so high and permanent that no written record is needed. "Thy gift, thy tables, are within my brain" (line 1); and "Therefore to give them from me was I bold" (line 11).

Shakespeare's story dovetails with elements in Constable's own. If the poems were given to Dousa by Shakespeare, Shakespeare's words once more turn out to be validated; for he told the beloved when he gave him the blank journal that the poems once recorded would be as children who outlive him. Sonnet 77 contrasts the mirror and the sundial, which tell the beloved he must age and die, with the notebook that lets pieces of his mind leave home like children sent to a wet nurse, making new acquaintances in the world.

> Look what thy memory cannot contain,
> Commit to these waste blanks, and thou shalt find
> Those children nursed, delivered from thy brain,
> To take a new acquaintance of thy mind.

The etymology of "deliver" is "to set free." Only by being set free from the poet's brain can the poet's mind outlive that brain, reaching acquaintances he himself can never meet. Although in the Netherlands collection we find three poems that are published later in England, other poems—such as the Hyella poems—appear to survive in this place only. (It seems equally plausible that the blank pages that Shakespeare requested, then gave away, are what is now called the Todd manuscript, since there Constable organized his poems into a coherent order, and there, too, are found poems not elsewhere surviving.)

The intimate Hyella poems are usually tender, even reverential, in tone. But not always. One Hyella poem announces that the distress between the lovers has successfully killed their love, thereby freeing the pair from their bonds. There is—the poem proudly announces—no sorrow or mourning or elegy for the love that has died; there is instead celebration and self-congratulation. They have both been liberated! Entitled "Triumphus xxi," the poem might equally be called "Exultation!" or "A Coup!" Here is its opening:

TRIUMPHUS XXI

Hey! At last we have conquered. We have won.
We have put out the savage fires. We have won.
Love has exited from my now-hardened heart.

Be gone, frivolous games, jokes, blandishments,
And farewell to you, too, torturer of my mind!
From here on, I shall not marvel at your
eyes, Hyella, or at your flushed cheeks
or at your artful verses.[16]
I shall not endure your disdain,
nor will I supply the occasion for
your thousand reproaches.
I shall no longer place garlands of flowers
before your rigid doors.[17]

In the next section of the poem, his triumphant announcement of regained sovereignty looks a bit shaky, since he now moves to a generalized rant. So thoroughly have the pair destroyed their love that the speaker now magnifies and accelerates his boasts: he will not only cease to enter with the beloved into their play, their fights, their rituals; he will even cease to mention him to other people, as we see in a section of the poem that addresses him as the winged boy. The pivot to Cupid occasions a general denunciation of the mayhem eros routinely instigates.

> Nor shall I speak about you, Cupid,
> along with your foam-born mother.
> From you, hatreds and madness and slaughter and bloody
>   wars!
> From you are born all sorts of evils for the race of man.
> You wield weapons dripping with the slaughter of mortals.
> You hurl dire darts into tender hearts.
> You corrupt gullible hearts with your flattering poisons
> As the Sorceress Circe is accustomed to do with her
>   Aeaean Island practice,
> where there spring up cares and tears, and no cure
> of healthy Bacchus or Ceres comes to the rescue.[18]

For a moment it may seem his self-congratulation has exhausted itself.

But no. He now creates a victory garland and places it on his own head. He creates that garland in front of our very eyes: this section of the poem (as the classicist Richard Thomas points out) literally brings into being a circle by both beginning and ending with an optative speech act addressed to the garland:

> Therefore, gird my temples, laurels of victory!

he exclaims, and then, eighteen lines later:

> So I repeat, for a second time:
> Gird my temples, you victorious laurels.[19]

Lest we miss the act of encirclement, he prefaces the circling back with the announcement that he is doing so.

The garland is made up of strange blossoms. Between the two addresses to the garland comes a series of portraits of all the noble gods and humans who have endured abject humiliation once they have succumbed to the erotic: Apollo, forced by his own acts of trespass to become a laughable and laughed-at herdsman; Mars, sneaking off in what he and Venus believe is a private act of love-making only to be entangled, exposed, and ridiculed in the humiliating chain-link net of Hephaestus, where they are kept on display; Eurydice, still in love with Orpheus even when she can see that love has landed her in hell.

The garland of flowers he once placed in front of Hyella's door in an act of wooing and cherishing now instead resides on his own head. So, too, the victory once happily ceded to Cupid now belongs to the speaker. Hyella and Cupid have merged: the poet initially addresses Hyella, then without ceasing to speak to Hyella, turns effortlessly to address Cupid, attaching the adjective "savage" to each: "We have put out the savage fires"; "Savage Boy, let the triumph go from you to me."[20]

The end of the poem celebrates the strength of mind that can distance itself from such ravages. A king is "not the person who holds many thousands of men beneath him, harassed by fear or desire or the favor of the fickle people," but the person able to conquer the storms of his own mind. Having so disparaged the erotic tumult of his relation with the beloved, and having so celebrated his triumphant separation from that love ("shattering all your charms and allurements"), an odd note suddenly enters when, toward the end, he appears to disdain women for their distance from these very rages:

> May I be such a one,
> May Fate allow me to survive the springtime of my life,
> No woman may ever feel our ragings,
> Nor drag me bound by the neck beneath her laws.
> Therefore, O Sound Mind, I store myself away in your
>   sanctuary.
> Drive all these evils from my heart
> Which have not allowed me to spend restful nights,
> And restful days, while harsh Amor has tortured me.[21]

The Latin poems—both the Hyella group and those containing no name—introduce gender puzzles: usually no pronoun is used, but when one occurs it is sometimes male and other times female. Here is the opening of one Latin poem:

> O beautiful Narcissus, O dazzling white lilies,
>   gifts of my Hyella, presents worthy of a mistress,

Narcissus and Hyella are closely associated, just as Cupid and Hyella merged in "Triumphus xxi." Yet one phrase later the poem describes the gifts as "worthy of a mistress." Did Constable himself introduce this gender instability? Did he compose the poem in Latin? Or did the instability enter only at the moment the poem was translated from English into Latin? Since we do not have an original English version, we do not know the answer.

We saw in chapter 2 both Constable's and Shakespeare's commitment to gender fluidity.[22] It may be useful to return briefly to the gender question. Shakespeare's first 126 sonnets are clearly addressed to a man; yet even here the history of publication has sometimes confused the issue. A 1640 printing of the sonnets changed some of the pronouns from male to female, replaced the word "boy" with the word "love," and introduced at least one sonnet title specifying a female beloved. A 1711 collection of the poems restored the male pronouns but used the subtitle "154 Sonnets all of them in Praise of A Mistress."[23]

It should not be surprising to discover some of the same mystification occurring with Constable's poems, mystification that continues today. The male addressee in Constable's poetry is obscured in two ways in the otherwise superb edition by Joan Grundy (the main edition used today and one with countless merits, though a new edition with modern English is needed). She places the most openly erotic poems addressed to a man in an appendix and calls them "Doubtful Sonnets" because she believes they are not by Constable. As mentioned earlier, the ambiguity originates with the 1594 edition of Constable's *Diana* that prints the poems without stating the poems are by Constable. The two reasons Joan Grundy gives, far from persuading us to reject their association with Constable, provide strong evidence that they are by Constable. The first reason for rejecting them is that they are homoerotic. Grundy writes that she has tried unsuccessfully to prove they are not his. She wishes she could prove they are not his, she tells us, because they have caused him to be "censured . . . for vices not his own."[24] The second reason draws on her fellow biographer George Wickes, who observes that Constable—in the poems universally accepted as his—always uses the Italian or Petrarchan form of the octave, with variation in the closing six lines. In contrast: "Of the forty-one unidentified sonnets, twenty-five are Shakespearian in form, five more employ adaptations of the Shakespearian form."[25] Constable's adaptation of the poetic form his beloved habitually used strengthens, rather than sabotages, our conviction that they are his.

So one problem a reader of the English poems encounters is

the downgrading of an important group—a homoerotic group written in Shakespearean form—to the appendix. Even when indexing the poems by first lines Joan Grundy sets this group in a space separate from the others (with the rubric "Doubtful Sonnets") so that their opening lines do not mingle with the others. But there is a second problem with the English edition, this time affecting poems not in the appendix but in the main body of the work. With the exception of poems written to specific, named persons (such as Lady Rich and the painter Nicholas Hilliard),[26] many of Constable's poems did not have titles in the 1592 edition of *Diana*, in the 1594 *Diana*, or in most surviving manuscripts. In a single manuscript—called the Todd or Dyce manuscript—elaborate descriptive titles have been added to the poems. These makeshift titles are included in the Grundy edition without a clear-enough warning to the reader that they have only a single source and contradict all other sources; they are placed in a large font at the top of each page. Despite the fact that the pronouns in many of the poems are neutral—an unusual feature of the sonnets that almost no poet other than Shakespeare shares[27]—the cumbersome titles inevitably introduce a "Mistrisse" or a "Ladie" as the subject of the poem.

Here are three examples (each of which might have been richly useful to the present book, but none of which have been used because of their mystifying titles). One gender-neutral sonnet that complains that the poet sees his beloved only by day, not by night, has the title "Of his Ladies goeing over earlye to bed, so depriving him to soone of her sight."[28] Unlabeled, as it stood in the printed editions and most manuscripts, it enabled one to picture either a male or a female beloved while reading the poem; but with this lengthy rubric as a gateway, one is conscripted into picturing a female all the way through the poem without even recognizing that the source of the picture is the title, not the poem. Another gender-neutral poem—in fact, the one translated into Dousa's

Latin—has in Grundy's English edition the title "An excuse to his Mistrisse for resolving to love so worthye a creature."[29] Once again this gender assignment at the threshold preempts our ability to read the poem openly. A third instance is a lovely sonnet in which the poet defends his tongue, his pen, and his heart against the accusation that they have each flattered the beloved; our capacity to feel the heat of the song that is sung is diminished by the title, "Of the slander enuye gives him for so highlye praysing his Mistrisse."[30]

The titles, as Grundy herself acknowledges, may have been added by a hand other than Constable's.[31] Or they may have been added by Constable himself, but added as a form of protection—in case his love relations were ever questioned, the heavily titled manuscript could be brought out to document the fact that, despite the absence of "shes" in the content of many of the poems, they were each written to a "she." (As Grundy notes, the provenance of the manuscript before 1800 is unknown.)[32] The Grundy edition includes the cumbersome and potentially misleading titles. The nineteenth-century Hazlitt edition also includes them, though places them in square brackets to signal more clearly their ephemeral character; a prominent note on the first page of the Hazlitt edition explains the source of titles or "prefixes": "This and following prefixes between brackets are added from Todd's MS."[33]

The Hyella poems in the Dousa collection—usually delicate, lyric, and loving, but sometimes, as in "Triumphus xxi," distraught—present us with gender mysteries, while making us sensitive to similar mysteries (and potential obfuscations) even in the English poems.

HEN

Amidst the whispered "Hals" and "Hyellas," Shakespeare had a second shortened name for his friend, the name "Hen." This is unsurprising: there has probably never been a Henry alive on earth who was not called Hen by intimates, if only at moments of contracted speech, as at dawn ("Awake, Hen?") or in a rush ("Over here, Hen!"). In Henry Constable's case, the name was probably used more widely: manuscript records show the way Henry Constable consistently signed his name. Here is one, from a letter he wrote in October 1596:[34]

Two other letters—one written in January 1596 from France and the other in May 1604 written from the Tower of London—show the same abbreviation.[35] He signs his name not just "Hen" but "Hen:"—full stop.[36] Thus the original circumstances imagined above, where the intimate name is followed by a highly inflected piece of punctuation—"Awake, Hen?" "Over here, Hen!"—is warranted not just by the special circumstance imagined there but by the ordinary currents of everyday conversation. As "Hal" is a name full of quiet reverence, "Hen!" is a name full of playful animation and delight.

In the sonnets, "Hen!" is embedded in the word "hence," a word that by the addition of the crisp final consonant carries its own punctuation. Rhyming "whens," "thens," and "whences" often fly around nearby. We earlier saw that Shakespeare some-times positions "shalls" in a poem that already has the full name "Henry Constable" spelled out. In turn, "hence" is sometimes included as a form of naming in a sonnet already laden with "shalls." Here are the opening lines of Sonnet 81, the poem con-taining seven "shalls." The very lines in which the word "hence" occurs direct the reader's attention to the fact that it is being used as a name:

> Or I shall live your epitaph to make,
> Or you survive when I in earth am rotten,
> From *hence* your memory death cannot take,
> Although in me each part will be forgotten.
> Your name from *hence* immortal life shall have,
> Though I, once gone, to all the world must die.

Sonnet 39 is the poem encountered earlier in which Shakespeare contemplates giving up his merged identity with his lover so that he can stand apart from him and praise him; but then, realizing that separation would be too painful, he devises a strategy whereby he remains merged with the beloved while merely pretending to be a distinct person. "O absence," the sonnet concludes, addressing the "sweet deception" of feigned separation:

> And that thou teachest how to make one twain,
> By praising him here who doth *hence* remain.

As *The Merriam-Webster Dictionary* indicates, "hence" (by designating this point outward into the future) is both here and there: it is derived from the "Middle English *hennes*, *henne*, from Old English *heonan*; akin to Old High German *hinnan* away, Old English *hēr* here." The triumphant argumentative force of "hence" as "therefore" reinforces the beloved's position "here": "By praising him here he doth [therefore] remain!" Simultaneously, it places the beloved in a separate, forever-to-be-praised space that stands apart: "By praising him here he doth [away from here] remain!"

"Hence" is as emphatic as "shall" is understated. Perhaps for that reason it occurs in only a handful of the beloved young man sonnets. There is not a single instance of the word "hence" after Sonnet 126. It has been reserved exclusively for the beloved man.

Despite the large difference between the vocal force of "hence" and the soft restraint of "shall," they work in similar ways. Like the word "shall," "hence" protects the beloved by embedding him in the future, sealing him off from time's clutches by enveloping him in what is guaranteed to be inconspicuous because it has never yet happened. Like "shall," "hence" always outpaces Time: the faster Time runs, the faster it propels what is hence into the future. Like that of "shall," its grammatical and semantic position is just below the radar of our attention. It is not a verb or noun that proclaims itself the major focus of attention.

"Hen" *is*, of course, also a noun—a noun that almost any other poet might avoid at all costs. For our hero, however, it provides one more occasion for tour de force virtuosity, the dazzling and dizzying Sonnet 143, in which a small sunny kitchen suddenly erupts into a zone of frantic motion, a hen flying through the air to escape the reach of a young housewife, her arms flailing as feathers fill the air, her swirling skirts pursued by a bereft screaming toddler, startled and pained to have lost her usually devoted attention. Although tyke pursues lady and lady pursues hen, the chase is not horizontal but vertical, the "feathered creature" in the upper region, the swirling lady in the middle, the small child in the realm of tossing skirts below. The sonnet is a tube of rushing motion.

Like the escaped feathered creature in the poem who must be reined back in, this is a sonnet that almost flies out of the overall sonnet sequence: the erotic trio has here devolved into such an unexpected swirl of protagonists that critics have sometimes come close to wishing it unwritten. Like the hen that is nominally domestic but actually wild, this seemingly most domestic of sonnets proves the hardest to domesticate; it dashes toward poetic violation and indecency. The three beings in the poem compete for who among them is most outrageous: that the beautiful young man should be a hen! that the dark lady should be a poultry-tending, child-tending housewife! that Shakespeare should be a toddler! The poem has occasioned among readers almost as much sweet-natured flailing, flying, indignation, and wailing as what takes place within the poem.

But if in real life the beloved's name was Hen, ah well then . . . all should be forgiven. In the final lines of the poem, calm is restored: the wronged cherub accepts the transgression of his household goddess, and we accept the poetic transgression and permit 143 back into the household. All three beings have their backs to us in the first eight lines; two of the three turn and face us in the sestet; the wailing child (nearest us, but still with his back to us) implores the young mother to "turn back" to him (the verb, as Helen Vendler notices, occurs twice). The feathered creature, now captured, is still in her arms, for the child does not wish her to give up the prize she has so ardently pursued. The volte, or formal turn, of the sonnet is materialized in the content of the poem: the turning toward us of the woman and her prize permits the poem as a whole to bestow features on beings who might otherwise remain faceless.

Equally ingenious is the appearance of "hen" as a noun at the end of *Venus and Adonis* when the goddess confers on her dead lover immortal life as an extraordinary flower.

> By this the boy that by her side lay killed
> Was melted like a vapour from her sight,
> And in his blood that on the ground lay spilled
> A purple flower sprung up, check'red with white,
> Resembling well his pale cheeks and the blood
> Which in round drops upon their whiteness stood.
>
> (lines 1165–70)

Only a single flower anywhere in Europe, the United Kingdom, or the Americas conforms to this description—the delicate, early spring flower with nodding maroon and white checkered blossoms *Fritillaria meleagris*, the guinea hen flower. Its tiny maroon checks sometimes darken into deep purple or black or may instead soften into hues of mauve and pink; its white checks sometimes appear white, sometimes silver, pink, or gray.[37]

No other flower is literally checkered, a geometric pattern that in combination with its decadent moody colors made it beloved by art nouveau and art deco artisans, and earlier made it beloved in the Renaissance, when it was thought to be both mysterious and beautiful. John Gerard writes in his 1597 *Herball*: it "consisteth of sixe small leaves, checkered most strangely . . . surpassing (as in all other things) the curiest painting that Art can set down."[38] He ends his chapter on the "Ginny-hen Flower" by reporting that these flowers "are greatly esteemed for the beautifieng of our gardens, and the bosomes of the beautifull."[39]

Past and present plantsmen, botanists, and herbalists all agree that the Latin name *Fritillaria meleagris* aspires to capture both its chessboard, checkered quality and its association with the feathers of the guinea hen. Gerard writes, "it hath beene called *Fritillaria*, of the table or boord upon which men plaie at chesse, which square checkers the flower doth very much resemble."[40] On a chessboard, either of the two colors can be seen as background or instead as foreground. So, too, in the account Venus gives, the flower is maroon with white checks, then a moment later is said to derive from what is white with maroon checks, the fallen youth, whose face is white with purple spots of color.

The term "*meleagris*" is from the guinea hen, whose feathers have the same checkered appearance and after whose plumage the tiny early spring flower derives its name. Gerard writes that each of the blossom's six petals resembles the feather of the guinea hen: "every leafe seemeth to be the feather of a Ginnie hen, whereof it tooke his name."[41] The 1576 English translation of Rembert Dodoens's *A New Herball, or Historie of Plants* provides the same

ɪ *Frittillaria.*
Checkered Daffodill.

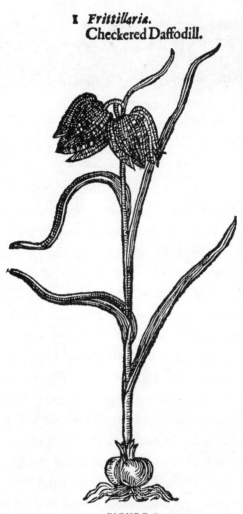

FIGURE 3
From Gerard's *The Herball*.
Chapter 79, "Of Turkie or Ginnie-hen flower"

derivation: "[It] is called of the Greeks and Latines, Flos Meleagris, and Meleagris flos, as a difference from a kind of bird
called also Meleagris, whose feathers be speckled like unto these
floures, but not with violet specks, but with white and black
spots like to the fethers of the Turkie or Ginnie hen, which is

FIGURE 4
Ornament recurring throughout Constable's 1592
Diana that contains checkered blossoms

called Meleagris avis."[42] It is worth noting that Henry Constable's 1592 *Diana* contained on its first page (and on a sequence of pages following) a blossom that appears to be checkered.

Unlike Shakespeare's Venus, neither Dodoens nor Gerard comments on the scent of the flower, nor is the guinea hen flower today esteemed for its scent. But Venus's brief celebration of its lovely smell (and the far lovelier smell of Adonis, which precedes and causes it) may come from the *Fritillaria*'s association with two other flowers—flowers present in Constable's poems—the lily and the narcissus. Gerard observes that the Dutch plantsman Mathias Lobelius (whose book appeared in 1581) called the ginnie hen flower "*Lilio-narcissus variegatus*, for that it hath the flower of a Lillie, and the root of *Narcissus* . . ." Dodoens groups the ginnie hen flower with tulips but, noting that "tulip" is a Turkish word, says that "we may call it Lilly narcissus."[43]

Constable's poem, encountered earlier, that thanks the beloved for sending the white narcissus—

> O beautiful Narcissus, O dazzling white lilies,
> gifts of my Hyella, presents worthy of a mistress,

—continues by describing the transformation of the pure white flower into a *Fritillaria meleagris*. After puzzling what godlike space the flower has come from—

What earth gave you birth?
With what sweet nectar and grassy odors
did the western breezes moisten your locks?
Did golden Venus nourish you in the Idalian woods?
Did Apollo feed you in the mountain glade of Pegasus?

—Constable describes its birth. When the purple mouth of the beloved touches the blossom in a kiss, the color transfers to the flower, spreading throughout its cup. But beneath the newborn purple resides the white of the original blossom, in a grid like a wicker basket (the Latin is *"calathus"*) of glowing white holding the purple in the open spaces of its weave:

O too blessed blossoms, touched by the right hand
when picked and by the purple lips when kissed.
Am I mistaken? Did the flower draw its redness from a
    red mouth?
Does the whiteness of a mistress' hand now reside in the
    petals?
This much is certain. Do you see how
the blush at the center now shines throughout,
so that the red glows in its milk-white wicker basket?
Over these I would prefer
neither those harvests which arrive from India
nor whatever the opulent Arab habitually sends.

The poet—like the botanists Gerard invokes—continues to address the transformed blossom as a narcissus:

May you live forever, Narcissi,
may heavy summer not scorch you
nor winter burn you with biting cold.

Live forever as a record of our passion;
And may that color always remain in you
as long as the soft west winds are suffused with your
   deep breathings.

·

Then I will everyday consecrate you in my song.
Then I will prefer you to the beautifully shaped violets:
The rose yields to you, the hyacinth yields,
even though one belongs to Apollo, the other to Venus.[44]

The alternating colors—analogous to the squares of a chessboard
or to the spotted plumage of the guinea hen—are here perceived
as one color glowing through the basket weave of a second color.
Images of the "*calathus*" from the Roman period show how closely
it resembles the blossom of the dainty flower.

But despite this beautiful conception of the geometry of the
blossom as the cross weave of a miniature basket,[45] the chessboard
associated with the name "*meleagris*" remains the most frequently
invoked template.

While Shakespeare's very early *Venus and Adonis* closes with
a salute to *Fritillaria meleagris*, so, too, does his final play, *The
Tempest*. The spirit companion of Prospero is the bird-like, airy

FIGURE 5
The *calathus* (or wicker basket) is like an inverted
Fritillaria meleagris blossom.

Ariel. His name so close to Harry, Ariel (like Hal, the root word for breath) is "but air" and "drink[s] the air" before him. As the play rushes toward its end, Prospero confers many names on him— "my dainty Ariel," "my tricksy spirit," "my diligence" (V.i.97, 229, 244)—but his final appellation, and the penultimate sentence of the play, conjures forth the intimate name "hen": "My Ariel, chick, / That is thy charge. Then to the elements / Be free, and fare thou well!" "My Ariel, chick" . . . might be rewritten, "My Harry-el, hen." This farewell is the next-to-last sentence of the play, a second away from the last act, the collective inhalation, then exhalation of all on the stage, as Prospero requests, "Please you, draw near," an inward contraction that is then followed immediately by the radiating outward dispersal: "Exit all."

The blossom of the *Fritillaria meleagris* is vividly present. Ariel in the closing moments tells us his residence: "Where the bee sucks there suck I, / In a cowslip's bell I lie / . . . Under the blossom that hangs from the bough." If it is not the guinea hen but a primrose that he names, he uses the dainty primrose's animal name: "cowslip." The latent presence of the guinea hen blossom may explain the otherwise puzzling emergence in these final seconds of the chessboard—the single place anywhere in Shakespeare where the word "chess" explicitly occurs. "Here Prospero discovers Ferdinand and Miranda playing at chess." This final tableau, a pair of lovers yoked to a checkered surface, is sacred: it is preceded by Prospero's call for a wonder—"At least bring forth a wonder"—and followed by the identification of it as more than a wonder: "A most high miracle," "Now all the blessings / of a glad father compass thee about," "O wonder!" (V.i.172–84). That Miranda and Ferdinand are in a gentle tussle over whether one has played the other false sets before us, once again, the enduring frame of love that can accommodate betrayal.

While it is indisputable that Shakespeare identified his male beloved as the creative genius inspiring the sonnets, is it plausible that many years later he should confer this honor on him in relation to his plays? Beyond Shakespeare's capacity for enduring love, there is another reason why he might have credited Henry Constable with his flourishing as a playwright. But to entertain this possibility we must turn away from Hals, Hyellas, and Hens to another subject, the identity of the rival poet.

5

—

THE RIVAL POET

George Chapman, Christopher Marlowe, Michael Drayton, and Edmund Spenser have long been among the candidates named for the position of the rival poet in the sonnets. Because Henry Constable was immersed in the contemporary poetry world, many—perhaps all—of these long-favored candidates remain candidates. But a new possibility also emerges. Sonnet after sonnet provides strong evidence that the rival poet is, in fact, Scotland's James VI.

Henry Constable not only attended King James at the court in 1589, but stood with the twenty-three-year-old sovereign on the coast as he waited on the shore for the arrival of the ships from Denmark carrying the fourteen-year-old Princess Anne, soon to be Queen of Scotland. The arrival was delayed by seven weeks of storms at sea. Both Constable and James wrote poems about that delay. Placing the two poems side by side helps us visualize the two men standing side by side, for more than a month, on that tempestuous coastline, before James decided to set sail himself to seek his bride.

A complaint against the contrary Wyndes that hindered the Queene to com to Scotland from Denmarke	To the K: of Scots upon occasion of a sonet the K: wrote in complaint of a contrarie winde which hindred the arrivall of the Queene oute of Denmark.

From sacred throne in heaven Empyrick hie

A breathe divine in Poëts brests does blowe

Wherethrough all things inferiour in degrie

As vassalls unto them doe homage showe

There songs enchants Apollos selfe ye knowe

And chaste Dianas coache can haste or staye

Can change the course of Planets high or lowe

And make the earthe obeye them everie waye

Make rockes to danse, hugge hills to skippe and playe

Beasts, foules, and fishe to followe them allwhere

Though thus the heaven, the sea, and earthe obeye,

If I durst sigh still as I had begun

Or durst shed teares in such abundant store

Yow should have need to blame the sea no more

Nor call upon the wind as yow have done.

For from myne eyes an Ocean sea should run

Which the desired ships should carrie o're

And my sighes blowe such winde from northren shore

As soone yow should behold yowre wished sun

But with those sighes my deare displeased is

Which should both hast youre joy and slake my payne

Yet for my good will (O Kinge) grant me this

Yett mutins the midde region of the aire.
What hateful Juno, Aeolus entiseth
Whereby contrarious Zephyre thus ariseth.[1]

When to the winds yow sacrifice agayne
Sith I desir'd my sighes should blow for thee
Desire thow the winds to sigh for me.[2]

Both poems credit the world-changing powers of the poet; both credit the power of nature to act, independent of any human wish or plea (including that made in poetry). Particularly striking in Constable's sonnet is line 9. While he has earlier contributed his sighs and tears to the welfare of the king's marital adventure, Constable's own beloved is pained that he should so dedicate himself: "But with those sighes my deare displeased is." As a result, Constable dare not continue his heartfelt efforts on the king's behalf. But he asks the king to credit his good intentions and to carry out a reciprocating act of compassion: "Desire thow the winds to sigh for me." Out of the coastline mist a triangle of three men begins to come into view.

The 1589 meeting was not the only meeting between Henry Constable and the king: there is inconclusive evidence that they might have met as early as 1583 and certain evidence of their periodic contact after 1598. But the 1589 period is registered in poems that each of them wrote to the other and will therefore be central to the description that follows.

Many phrases in Shakespeare's rival poet sonnets match features of James VI. In fact, it is hard to find in any of Shakespeare's rival poet sonnets a phrase that does not match, and match with precision, the features of the young Scottish king.

SHAKESPEARE'S SONNET 78

Sonnet 78—in which Shakespeare complains that "every alien pen" has now caught his practice of being inspired by the beloved—

identifies three kinds of persons. The first is "dumb," weighted with "heavy ignorance." This person is suddenly transformed by exposure to Shakespeare's beloved and becomes, for the first time, newly capable of song and flight. The second person starts out in a far better position than the first, for he is already "learned" and has "wings." Contact with Shakespeare's beloved gives him "added feathers" so that—with the assistance of the beloved— he soars still higher than he would independently. The third is Shakespeare himself: he starts out in as bad a position as the first (weighted with "rude ignorance"), yet he ends up soaring as high as the second (the learned flier who flies still higher because of added feathers). He achieves this feat because the beloved not only mends his style, as with the other two poets, but provides the subject matter of his poems.

> So oft have I invoked thee for my muse,
> And found such fair assistance in my verse,
> As every alien pen hath got my use,
> And under thee their poesy disperse.
> Thine eyes, that taught the dumb on high to sing,
> And heavy ignorance aloft to fly,
> Have added feathers to the learnèd's wing,
> And given grace a double majesty.
> Yet be most proud of that which I compile,
> Whose influence is thine, and born of thee:
> In others' works thou dost but mend the style,
> And arts with thy sweet graces graced be;
>   But thou art all my art, and dost advance
>   As high as learning my rude ignorance.

The phrase "alien pen" is consistent with the Scottish dialect of those in the northern court. The "dumb" and "heavy" creatures who "under thee their poesy disperse" may well include the Scottish court poet Alexander Montgomerie, since he dispersed Constable's window poem (translating it into the Scottish tongue) as though it were his own.[3] Constable's poem is about the "eyes"—it opens, "Thyne eye the glasse where I behold my hearte,"[4] as Montgomerie's opens, "Thyne ee the glasse vhare I beheld my hairt"—and Shakespeare's line stipulates that it is the beloved's eyes that have wrought this change in the formerly unsuccessful poet: "Thine eyes, that taught the dumb on high to sing, / And heavy ignorance aloft to fly." Montgomerie was the leading Scottish poet at that time.

The most prominent feature of the second person—he is learned—matches the young king, who was widely known for his learning. Adam Nicolson writes of James: "[He] became immensely intellectual, speaking 'Greek before breakfast, Latin before Scots,' . . . capable on sight of turning any passage of the Bible from Latin to French and then from French to English."[5] A French agent in 1584 describes the eighteen-year-old king as "this strange, spiky-edged, intellectualized, awkward and oddly idealistic king."[6] The Danish record of his marriage passage through Norway and Sweden and Denmark in 1589–90 observes with admiration that James visited Tycho Brahe at Uranienborg near Elsinore (he later wrote three poems to the mathematician and astronomer); and records his visit to the Royal Academy in Copenhagen, where he listened to several lectures and on parting said in Latin, "I have since childhood been given to the literary arts and have had joy in them—and I should like to declare that today."[7] James's account of his childhood is accurate: by the time he was eight years old, observers had noted with astonishment his unusual intellectual preoccupations; at the age of twelve, he already had the largest library in Scotland: six hundred books.[8]

King of Scotland from an early age, James VI years later became King James I of England. His words, spoken when visiting the Bodleian Library at Oxford, only confirm what was by then his lifelong aspiration—and reputation—for great learning:

Were I not a King, I would be a University-man. And I could wish, if ever it be my lot to be carried captive, to be shut up in this prison, to be bound with these chains, and to spend my life with these fellow captives which stand here chained.[9]

This same aspiration is audible in the residence he wished to be built for his son: "the forme of the Prince's house should rather imitate a colledge then a court."[10]

The recognition that James is the rival poet is invited not only by the crisp designation "learned" but by the royal idiom which follows:

> Thine eyes . . .
> Have added feathers to the learned's wing,
> And given grace a double majesty.

Sonnet 78 twice doubles grace (first here in line 8, then again in line 12) in a deft salute to Henry Constable's "Grace full of grace" poem—as we saw in chapter 2. But while that specific vocabulary alludes to Constable's signature poem, it also contributes to our recognition of the rival's identity. The designation of a king as "His Grace" or as "His Majesty" was widespread in the sixteenth century. It may therefore be that the rival poet possesses grace and majesty because, quite simply, that rival poet is a king. Sonnet 78 carries out a practice visible in many of the rival poet sonnets: Shakespeare uses a *literal* designation that everyone will mistake for "mere" metaphor or hyperbole. The person he speaks about here really is—in the social hierarchy of the day—full of grace and majesty; those already existing attributes are then magnified by his contact with Shakespeare's beloved.

What does Shakespeare mean by claiming that his beloved has "added feathers" to the learned flier's wings? The metaphor, Stephen Booth points out, is from falconry; it refers to the practice of "imping," in which feathers are literally added to the bird's wing to give it additional lift.[11] The metaphor is still at work when in line 11 Shakespeare says the beloved "mend[s] the style" of the other poets, since "imping" was a way of repairing or mending an imperfect wing; and, as Booth notes, "style" is from the word "stylus," a writing instrument, that was in this period usually a feather.

To understand what prompted Shakespeare to use this particular image, one need look no further than Henry Constable's own sonnet to James VI which—yes—endows the king with feathers. In Constable's eyes, the king flies not with the earthly feathers of Cupid or worldly time but with the feathers of angels:

TO THE KING OF SCOTLAND

When others hooded with blind love doe flye
Lowe on the ground with buzzard Cupids wings
A heavenlye love from love of love thee brings
And makes thy Muse to mount above the skie

Yonge Muses be not wonte to flye so hye
Age schoold by tyme such sober dittie sings
But thy youth flyes from love of youthful things
And so the wings of tyme doth overflye

Thus thow disdainest all worldlye wings as slow
Because thy Muse with Angells wings doth leave
Tymes wings behinde and Cupids wings below
But take thow heed least fames wings thee deceave
  With all thy speed from fame thow canst not flee
  But more thow flyest the more it followes thee.

HENRIE CONSTABLE

King James VI printed this sonnet (with the author's name attached) in his 1591 volume *His Majesties Poeticall Exercises at Vacant Hours*:[12] it is, in fact, the poem with which the book opens![13]

Adding feathers to the king's wings, Constable in this poem carries out poetically the equivalent of the act of "imping" in falconry. Although the added feathers come from an angel rather than from a bird, the sphere of falconry—unmistakable in Shakespeare's sonnet—is also unmistakable here in Constable's, as the opening description of a hooded flier makes clear: ". . . others hooded with blind love doe flye / Lowe on the ground with buzzard Cupids wings." A miniature hood is a key piece of equipment in the art of falconry, and Constable introduces it from the outset to differentiate novice fliers still undergoing training from those with expertise, restricted vision from open horizons, earthly flight from heavenly. James VI was from an early age a regular practitioner of falconry, as portraits attest that show him as a young child, holding on his left hand a falcon or sparrow hawk.[14] His falconry equipment (glove, pouch, hoods), exquisitely embroidered with silk and metal threads depicting blackberries, flowers, and mistletoe, can still be seen in the Glasgow Museums.[15] In addition to hawks and falcons, he trained ospreys to retrieve fish for him.[16]

Constable wrote a second poem to the king that "adds feathers" to him. The poet tells the king that he honors him not for his status and position as king but for his bearing as a poet:

> Bloome of the rose I hope those hands to kisse
> Which yonge a scepter which olde wisdome bore
> And offer up joy-sacrifice before
> Thy altar throne for that receaved blisse
>
> Yet prince of hope suppose not for all this
> That I thy place and not thy guifts adore

Thy scepter no thy pen I honoure more
More deare to me then crowne thy garland is

That laurell garland which (if hope say true)
To thee for deeds of prowesse shall belong
And now allreadie unto thee is due
As to a David for a kinglie songe
  The pen wherewith thow dost so heavenly singe
  Made of a quill pluckt from an Angells winge.[17]

Perhaps inspired by Constable's claim that James VI writes with a feather plucked from an angel's wing, Shakespeare in Sonnet 85 designates the rival poet's writing tool a "golden quill." Constable's praise of James's poetic talents may seem overstated to us today. So, too, Shakespeare's account—sometimes teasing, but on balance deeply respectful—may seem overstated. It is important to recognize that other famous poets of the era similarly credited the king. In his *An Apologie for Poetrie*, Sir Philip Sidney sees it as a tribute to poetry that kings not only credit poetry but themselves practice it: "Sweete Poesie, that hath aunciently had Kings, Emperors, Senators, great Captaines . . . not onely to favour Poets, but to be Poets. And of our neerer times can present for her patrons a Robert, king of Sicil, the great king Francis of France, King James of Scotland."[18]

SHAKESPEARE'S SONNET 80

King James VI's preoccupation with shipbuilding—grandiose shipbuilding—is possibly in the background of two of Shakespeare's poems about the rival poet, Sonnet 80 and Sonnet 86. Here is Sonnet 80, in which Shakespeare contrasts his own modest bark with the powerful ship of his rival:

O how I faint when I of you do write,
Knowing a better spirit doth use your name,
And in the praise thereof spends all his might,
To make me tongue-tied speaking of your fame!
But since your worth, wide as the ocean is,
The humble as the proudest sail doth bear,
My saucy bark, inferior far to his,
On your broad main doth willfully appear.
Your shallowest help will hold me up afloat,
Whilst he upon your soundless deep doth ride;
Or, being wrecked, I am a worthless boat,
He of tall building, and of goodly pride:
　　Then if he thrive, and I be cast away,
　　The worst was this: my love was my decay.

In the elliptical eleventh and twelfth lines, Shakespeare says it does not much matter if he is wrecked since his little boat is worthless; whereas if "He of tall building, and of goodly pride" be wrecked, a larger piece of civilization will go down. As though the thought of the king's catastrophe is too treasonous, he presents it in condensed phrasing where "being wrecked" modifies, in sequence, his own ship, then that of his rival with the consequence to the rival left unstated. Choosing not to complete the thought, he shifts in the couplet to the flourishing of his rival, and the catastrophe to his own saucy bark—sucked down by love beneath the ocean waves.

It might for a moment seem that the sonnet's central lines (5–11) position us at sea, and that in the twelfth line "He of tall building" carries us back to shoreline architecture. But Shakespeare is here surely still talking about the construction rising up on the surface of the ship's deck. By the time James was King of England, his preoccupation with maritime magnificence produced ships so oversized that two of them—the *Prince* and the

Trade's Increase—could not successfully make it out to sea because the berthing dock was too narrow to permit their egress. The *Prince* was the first English Navy ship to have three decks: "she was gorgeously decorated . . . with carvings, and 'curious paintings the like which was never in any ship before.'"[19] Though in their size the *Prince* and the *Trade's Increase* were extreme, the naval historian Michael Oppenheim says that under James there was a "tendency to overload ships, however small, with forecastle and poop superstructures."[20]

We have fewer concrete descriptions of the ships James constructed earlier as King of Scotland, but we do know that when he set out to Denmark to retrieve his bride, he sailed in a fleet of five ships; we also know that (despite his well-deserved reputation for pacifism) part of the dowry he requested of the Danes was "three men of war with all their equipment and appurtenances," as well as the loan of seven ships for the return voyage.[21] James, however, lacked the funds to pay for ships, and even in his venture to Denmark was dependent on the private wealth of John Maitland, Lord Thirlestane, one of the country's leading noblemen and a powerful individual at court.[22] By contrast, the first time James surveyed the navy he inherited when he assumed the English throne, he was looking at a fleet of thirty-seven ships.[23]

Long before he became King of England, a country whose ample forests and finances allowed him to carry out spectacular constructions, James was imaginatively preoccupied with extravagant ships. The astonishing three-day ceremony dedicated to the 1594 christening of his son Prince Henry culminated in a masque. The large assembly of guests included ambassadors from Denmark, Holland, Zeland, Scotland, England, Almaine, and Flanders. Now, toward the end of the festivities, there suddenly glided into their midst a dazzling vision: the radiant sails of a ship eighteen feet long and eight feet wide, riding on a skirt of artificial blue ocean: a "lively counterfeit" of seawater twenty-four feet in length.

The sails—yards upon yards of glistening white taffeta—were ornamented with colorful silk cordage, tackling, streamers, and
flags (one of them forty feet high). The hull was adorned with "the
riches of the seas, as Pearls, Corals, Shelles, and Mettalls, very rare
and excellent." Standing on the deck, dressed in silver and gold
taffeta, were Neptune, Thetis, and Triton. The lavish ship contained a yet-more-lavish cargo: there spilled forth from the decks
into the laps of the guests a banquet served on fragments of artificial seawater, "Christalline glasse, very curiously painted with
Gold and Azure," loaded with "Hearings, Whytings, Flookes,
Oysters, Buckies, Lampets, Partans, Hapitars, Crabs, Spout-fish,
Clammes." Where the actual species could not be supplied, its
form was imitated in sugar so that no known denizen of the sea
would go unrepresented. Spilling, too, from the decks was music:
"Arion sitting upon the Galley nose, which resembled the forme
of a Dolphine fish, played upon his Harp." He was accompanied
by fourteen musicians. Oboes played in five parts, then violas and
voice in counterpoint, then recorders and flutes. After the banquet
ended and thanks was given, "there was sung with most delicate
dulce voices, and sweet harmonies in 7. partes, the 128. Psalme,
with 14. voices."[24]

Why would a ship be the climactic spectacle at the extravagant
three-day event? The document detailing the baptismal ceremonies explains that the ship celebrated the king and queen's triumph over the 1589 stormy seas, a triumph that not only permitted
their wedding but led to the birth of the child. Indeed the Danish
record of Anne's attempts to reach Scotland, and James's attempts
to reach Anne, make us see that their eventual union was indeed
a romantic, courage-filled triumph (even if the marriage years did
not contain the same romance).[25] Was Henry Constable present—
either physically or in spirit—at this baptism? Present were guests
from many countries, but not from France, where Henry Constable was then living as part of the French court of King Henry IV.

If he was present, it is probable that he was present only in the thoughts of the celebrants.

But even here—at a 1594 masque in Scotland rather than a 1603–11 berthing dock in England—we still reside in the realm of material realization. To appreciate what Shakespeare may be speaking about, we need to go back even earlier, to the period of the 1580s and early 1590s when James's ships were primarily designed, built, christened, and commissioned inside lines of poetry. Here is one remarkable poem where James's vision of his court at sea equals—or surpasses—in maritime grandeur Shakespeare's phrase "tall building . . . of goodly pride":

> Whill as a statelie fleeting castle faire
> On smoothe and glassie salt does softlie slide
> With snowie sheets all flaffing here and thaire
> So deck'd and trim'd as she were Neptunes bride
> And no ways troubled with contrarious tide
> And shining Titan from his firie cart
> Smiles seing nature triumph'd of by art.[26]

James imagined his court not just as a ship-at-sea but as a castle-on-a-ship-at-sea, an elaborate edifice softly gliding in a happy delirium of liquid motion. The nine-stanza poem continues, describing the inhabitants of the court—"citiezens of Thetis sliprie grounde"—who, placing "setled trust" in the ocean's "unsetled grounde," are unaware that their sea paradise may suddenly be subject to a storm caused by the devastating departure of someone beloved by the king. Here are the adored person's attributes:

> Whose comelie beautie graced our Princelie traine
> Whose modest mirth express'd alluring grace
> Whose absence makes us lacke our light allace.

The Court as garland lackes the cheefest floure
The Court a chatton toome that lackes her stone
The Court is like a volier at this houre
Wherout of is her sweetest Sirene gone.
Then shall we lacke our cheefest onlie one?
No, pull not from us cruell cloude I praye
Our light, our rose, our gemme, our bird awaye.

To whom is the poem written? The title indicates a woman: "A Complaint of His Mistressis Absence from Court." But several features open the possibility that it is a man who is absent from the court. The person is described as the court's "sweetest Sirene" who, by departing, has reduced the court to an empty birdcage. James's many reflections on poets in the court never mention a female singer. Furthermore, James has here relentlessly positioned himself—or at least his court—as feminine: the court is the setting of a ring that has lost "*her*" stone; the court is like a birdcage that has lost "*her*" sweetest singer. If James, in other words, feminizes himself, it is possible, too, that he performs a feminine transformation on the missing person's gender.

If the addressee is indeed a woman, it is likely to be (as the scholar Allan Westcott argues) "Ladie Glammis," who in another poem of the same period is mentioned in the title by name: "A Dreame on His Mistris My Ladie Glammis."[27] But that poem, rather than settling us securely in the presence of a woman, at a key moment brings us into the presence of a man. According to the poem, the king suffers a hallucinatory dream in which an otherworldly being leads a lady to him. The king insists the dream is not an ordinary night dream, but a visitation by some god or supernatural creature who essentially delivers both the dream and the poem-about-the-dream to him. When he awakens, rather than the dream images vanishing (as happens, he says, with ordinary night dreams), two objects given to him during the dream—an amethyst jewel and a golden tablet—still hang around his neck. The heart-shaped jewel (we are explicitly told) stands for the king, the golden tablet for the missed person. The tablet has one surface that has not yet been filled in with the portrait of the missing person, a feature that suggests that the identity of the addressee is unclear. The locket has other interior surfaces specifying the person's virtues, one of which is her siren voice.

It might seem that this celebration of her "siren voice" contradicts what was said a moment ago—that James does not seem to think of poets as female. But here is the representation of that siren voice:

> One of the leaves on utter side
> A nacked man does beare,
> Whome Pheobus rosts with hote reflexe
> And stinging flees doe teare,
> Yett sitting in the forrest greene,
> As senceles of his harme,
> By harmonie of violl sweete
> He never irkes to charme
> The ravish'd foules and beast about,
> Esteeming so there joye,
> As makes him quite for to forgett
> His grievous sore anoye.
> This man not onlie represents
> Her Siren voyce divine,
> Wherewith she makes the dullest eares
> And hardest harts encline,
> Bot as his dittie sayes, To please
> The rest he suffers paine . . . [28]

Even here, then, in a poem about a named female mistress, that directly credits her with a poetic voice, that poetic voice is represented

as a young naked man, an Orpheus delighting all earthly creatures with the sounds he makes, even if they originate in his own
suffering caused by invisible agents (burning rays of the sun and
bites of microscopic insects).

If now, we return to "A Complaint of His Mistressis Absence
from Court" (or, as it was originally titled, "A Complaint of His
Mistris Absence from Court"), we see that as we progress through
the nine stanzas, the nautical castle on the slippery sea is making
relentless headway to repossess the absent beloved. The lines describing the missing person—lines that will climax "Our light,
our rose, our gemme, our bird awaye"—begin with the single line
in the poem that uses a female pronoun. This is then followed by
two lines each of which spell Henrie Constable's name (the "ie" in
"Henrie" is the way James spelled it in his own *Poeticall Exercises at Vacant Hours*).

Since she who did our Princelie Court decore
Is abs**ent**, **absent** d**oth** all**ace** r**emaine**
H   e   n   r   i   e   C   o   n   s   t   a   b   l   e
W**hose** **comelie** **beautie** gr**aced** our Pri**n**celie tra**ine** . . .
H   e   n   r   i   e   C   o   n   s   t   a   b   l   e

Is the presence of the name here an accident, a two-in-one-
hundred chance that just happens to have happened twice, in
consecutive lines, at the very moment when the identifying features of the beloved begin to be enumerated?

While it may be an accident, it is also possible that the name
is intentionally there. The lines (unlike Shakespeare's) do not announce that the name is present within the line; but they are about
the physical countenance of the person. The final stanza of the
poem is optimistic: I should be writing a dirge, says James, but
"my Muse" makes me sing so boldly, I take it as a happy sign that

FIGURE 6

Marriage portrait of James VI by Adrian Vanson, currently housed in Edinburgh Castle. James was twenty-three at the time of the 1589 marriage (and
the 1589 visit of Henry Constable). The portrait, which was sent to Denmark
as part of the wedding negotiations, was painted several years earlier, when
James was nineteen or twenty. While it therefore understates his age in 1589,
it is closer to the age of the three men in the triangle than the mental pictures
of the king and of Shakespeare we derive from portraits of them made when
they were in their forties or fifties. Shakespeare in the year 1589 was twenty-five
and Constable between twenty-three and twenty-seven. The various "Unknown Young Man" miniatures made by Hilliard in the late eighties and early
nineties also provide useful reminders of the youth of the three poets we are
here contemplating.[29]

the missing person will return. Was this poem—or one in the same genre—sent to Constable and seen by Shakespeare? Did it inspire the opening of Sonnet 86: "Was it the proud full sail of his great verse, / Bound for the prize of all-too-precious you . . ."?

SHAKESPEARE'S SONNET 86

The rival poet twice causes Shakespeare nearly to lose consciousness. In Sonnet 80, as we have just seen, he nearly faints when he considers the discrepancy between his small bark and the rival's ship: "O how I faint when I of you do write, / Knowing a better spirit doth use your name." Now in Sonnet 86 he nearly dies! The sonnet offers three possible explanations for this near-death experience, the first two of which he rejects in favor of the third.

> Was it the proud full sail of his great verse,
> Bound for the prize of all-too-precious you,
> That did my ripe thoughts in my brain inhearse,
> Making their tomb the womb wherein they grew?
> Was it his spirit, by spirits taught to write
> Above a mortal pitch, that struck me dead?
> No, neither he, nor his compeers by night
> Giving him aid, my verse astonished.
> He, nor that affable familiar ghost
> Which nightly gulls him with intelligence,
> As victors, of my silence cannot boast;
> I was not sick of any fear from thence.
> > But when your countenance filled up his line,
> > Then lacked I matter, that enfeebled mine.

The relevance of the first quatrain to King James VI has already been recounted. Like Sonnet 80, Sonnet 86 associates the rival and the rival's poetry with large-scale ships, a preoccupation of James's in his poetry of the 1580s, in the baptismal masque of 1594, and in his baroque British fleet of the 1600s. Vast as the rival's maritime aspirations are, the sonnet eventually assures us, they are not what nearly entombs Shakespeare's poetic voice.

In the second and third quatrains, Shakespeare introduces another feature of the rival that might explain why he is astonished into near-silence. The rival claims to be receiving poetic assistance from the supernatural world: he is "by spirits taught to write / Above a mortal pitch," spirits that Shakespeare describes now in the plural ("his compeers by night"), now in the singular ("that affable familiar ghost").

James VI's *Daemonologie* includes a section on the power that magicians have to call upon affable familiar ghosts. In the preface he alludes to a detail that later appears in the sixth chapter:

> Magiciens . . . can suddenly cause be brought unto them, all kindes of daintie dishes, by their familiar spirit: Since as a thiefe he delightes to steale, and as a spirite, he can subtillie & suddenlie inough transport the same. Now under this genus, may be comprehended al particulars, depending thereupon; Such as the bringing of Wine out of a Wall, (as we have heard oft to have bene practised) and such others . . . [30]

Arriving with dainty dishes, James's "familiar spirit" has much in common with Shakespeare's "affable familiar ghost." According to James, the familiar spirit will sometimes attend the magician as though his page. The magician will carry on his person "a tablet or a ring, or such like thing," enabling him to summon the spirit at will. The tablet (a "flat ornament with jewels"[31]) is a locket-like miniature such as the one we encountered in James's dream poem containing a locket containing, in turn, a siren-voiced naked boy. In addition to the familiar's "agilitie" and "speede" that endear him to princes by letting him deliver "faire banquets and daintie dishes, carried in short space fra the farthest part of the worlde," he can deliver all kinds of intelligence about "artes and sciences," "newes from anie parte of the worlde," including "secretes of anie persons" and "fore-telling [to princes] manie great things; parte true, parte false."[32] Thus James's account of the familiar in *Daemonologie* coincides with a second feature in Shakespeare's account of the rival's familiar spirit in Sonnet 86: the creature "nightly gulls him with intelligence." The spirit's affability, his gift giving, and his delivery of true-or-false intelligence are shared by James VI and by Shakespeare.

James published *Daemonologie* in 1597, but the views expressed in it were ones he had held for many years prior to the book. The parts of *Daemonologie* dedicated to witches record beliefs that James seems to have acquired only after his dangerous wedding trip in 1589–90.[33] But his keen belief in more "affable" spirits, and in particular in otherworldly presences that supply him with poetic intelligence, is there throughout the 1580s as well as in the 1590s. It will be helpful to see, first, James's early and ongoing belief in spirits; then, second, his belief in otherworldly contributions to his own poetry that correspond with Shakespeare's description of the rival poet in the second and third quatrains of Sonnet 86.

James's beautiful sonnet "The Azured Vault" celebrates the plenitude of sky, ground, and water. "Prodiges appearing in the aire" are among God's creations:

The azured vault, the christall circles bright
The gleaming firie torches poudered thair
The changing rounde, the shining beamie light
The sadd and bearded fires, the monsters faire
The prodiges appearing in the aire

The rearding [roaring] thunders and the blustering windes
The foules in hewe, in shape and nature rare
The prettie notts that wing'd musiciens findes
In earthe the sauourie flowres, the metall'd mindes
The wholesome herbes, the hautie pleasant trees
The silver streames, the beasts of sundrie kindes
The bounded roares, and fishes of the seas
    All these for teaching man the Lord did frame
    To honoure him whose glorie shines in them.[34]

The opening line of the second quatrain, "The prodiges appearing in the aire," presents a phenomenon distinct from all other phenomena in the poem: the word "prodiges" in Scots meant a supernatural or portentous occurrence. At the same time, the phrase radiates out in all directions, as though it names a category to which all the other wonders in the poem belong. The phrase "prodiges appearing in the aire" seems descriptive of the "monsters faire" that immediately precede it, and descriptive as well of the sun, stars, and inexplicable ignitions that fill the sky show of the first quatrain. But equally, the line has room enough to accommodate all that follows, for the fowls and birds in lines 6 and 7 (dazzling in color, shape, and musical artistry) are themselves "prodiges appearing in the aire," as are the claps of thunder and the alarming winds. When the third quatrain moves from fire and air to earth and water, the sounds[35] and flashing colors still seem, in part, "prodiges appearing in the aire."

The eeriness of "air-bourn prodiges" is more overt in James's *Short Treatise on the Rules of Scottish Poetry*. At one point he describes "tumbling verse" or verse appropriate for flytings, poetry contests entailing the ritualized exchange of insults. He provides for illustration a stanza about All Hallow's Eve, a twilight world of elves, fairies, and shape-transforming creatures which flit in and out of the green vegetable world:

In the hinder end of harvest upon Alhallow ene,
Quhen our gude nichtbors rydis (nou gif I reid richt)
Some bucklit on a benwod, & some on a bene,
Ay trottand into troupes fra the twylicht:
Some sadland a sho ape, all grathed into grene:
Some hotcheand on a hemp stalk, hovand on a heicht.
The king of Fary with the Court of the Elf quene,
With many elrage Incubus rydand that nicht:
  There ane elf on ane ape ane unsell begat:
  Besyde a pot baith auld and worne,
  This bratshard in ane bus was borne,
  They fand a monster on the morne,
  War facit nor a Cat.[36]*

James's sometimes "tumbling," sometimes reverential, crediting of the spirit world is compatible with Shakespeare's perception that his rival is on intimate terms with apparitions and unsettling forces. More decisive is James's constant annexing of the supernatural to his own poetic accomplishments.

Some instances of supernatural assistance have already become visible in the poems described earlier, such as the dream poem delivered to James by an otherworldly being. So, too, the end of his castle-on-the-sea poem marvels that when he should be writing a dirge, he instead feels elated confidence because some force ("my Muse") has enabled him to write poetry. Sometimes James says his genius is dull, his brain blunted ("my dull ingyne and blunted branis"),[37] and regularly invokes supernatural mending: "though my skill be small, / I pray then everie one of you to help his pairt."[38] In "The Translators Invocation" which James affixes to his rendition of "The Furies" by the French Huguenot poet Guillaume de Salluste Du Bartas, he addresses the gods or

*For translation, see note 36.

muses who, he says, regularly assist him in his attempts at heavenly verse, and whom he now asks for equivalent aid to his Spirit here:

> O now inflame my *furious* Spreit,
>   That *furiously* I may
> These *Furies* (mankinds plagues allace [alas]!)
>   With *furious* Pen display:[39]

At the end of the "Invocation," he calls on a force (now ambiguously that belonging to the poet he is translating and the supernatural agents who regularly assist his poetry):

> Then ô thou guider of my Spreit,
>   And leader of my pen,
> Graunt, that as he his subjects faire
>   Doth (liberal) to me len,
> That so he len his loftie stile,
>   His golden draughts, his grace,
> Wherewith in variant coulors he
>   Adornes the papers face,
> That I may vivelie [vividly] paint him forth:
>   Peace PAN, peace pratling Muse,
> Heare PHOEBUS in a borrowed tongue
>   His owne discourses use.

Twice in the passages just cited, James has called upon spirits to assist "my furious Spreit," "my Spreit," in a way compatible with Shakespeare's description in Sonnet 86, "Was it his spirit, by spirits taught to write / Above a mortal pitch, that struck me dead?"

Vivacity or furiousness—the incontestable "is-ness" of the thing being described—is the poetic quality James most cherishes; it is also the feature he hopes supernatural agents will supply. Among his earliest poems is a sequence of remarkable sonnets about the nature of poetic creation. In them he asks the classical gods for assistance. As summarized, it may sound as though these poems represent a commonplace act of invoking a muse. But James has a very special preoccupation in his petition to the otherworld. As a king, he of course has a keen sense of his own world-altering power in the civic realm, as well as an acute sense of the incredible constraints on those powers. James sees (from an early age) that in poetry, by contrast, one has almost no constraints on the world-alterations one may bring about; and he is continually astonished by that world-creating power. Yet he sees also that the world-altering mental images the poet generates succeed as a new world only if the images jump into the reader's mind as vividly and incontestably as they did into the poet's mind. And it is exactly here at the hinge between writer and reader that he requests supernatural intervention.

Four of the twelve sonnets ask Pheobus for help in carrying the seasons into the minds of readers. Should I write about spring, he says, "Graunt Readers may esteme, they sie the showris, / Whose balmie dropps so softlie dois distell, / Which watrie cloudds in mesure suche downe powris, / As makis the herbis, and verie earth to smell / With savours sweit . . ." When he writes about summer: "Let Readers think they fele the burning heat . . ." When he takes up his pen to describe autumn: "Let then the *Harvest* so vive [lifelike] to them appeare, / As if they saw both cornes and clusters neare." When winter storms unfold in James's mind, let the readers "heare the whiddering *Boreas* bolde, / With hiddeous hurling, rolling Rocks from hie . . . Yea let them think, they heare the birds that die, / Make piteous mone, that *Saturnes* hairis are spred."[40]

Of the twelve sonnets, the seventh invokes the assistance of Neptune should James undertake a description of the sea:

And when I do descriue the *Oceans* force,
Graunt syne [directly after], ô *Neptune*, god of seas profound,
That readars think on leeboard, and on dworce [starboard],
And how the Seas owerflowed this massive round:
Yea, let them think, they heare a stormy sound,
Which threatnis wind, and darknes come at hand:
And water in their shipps syne [next] to abound,
By weltring waves, like hyest towres on land.
Then let them thinke their shipp now low on sand,
Now climmes & skippes to top of rageing seas,
Now downe to hell, when shippmen may not stand,
But lifts their hands to pray thee for some eas.
   Syne [Thereupon] let them think thy *Trident* doth it calme,
   Which maks it cleare and smothe lyke glas or alme
     [crystal alum].

The eleventh and twelfth sonnets ask the muses for consistent help: "O *Muses*, let them thinke that they do heare / Your voyces all into my verse resound." These sonnets, like his short treatise about Scottish poetry, show someone thinking meta-poetically about the nature of poetry.[41]

Conversations with the spirit world, described in Shakespeare's Sonnet 86, were, then, an ongoing part of King James VI's daily life. But just as Shakespeare tells us it was not the "proud full sail of [the rival's] great verse" that nearly led to the premature burial of his poetic power, so he assures us it is not the existence of the spirits (pressing the rival into higher and higher levels of poetry) that nearly struck him dead.

The couplet now places in front of us the third—and this time, actual—cause of Shakespeare's evisceration and near-death:

     But when your countenance filled up his line,
     Then lacked I matter, that enfeebled mine.

Even "enfeebled" Shakespeare astonishes. The first line of the couplet contains the fourteen letters of Henry Constable's name, thereby ensuring that the beloved "fills up" Shakespeare's own poetic line at the very moment Shakespeare cries out against the rival poet.

There are at least three ways to understand this couplet, two of which we have already encountered. At some point, Shakespeare surely would have seen—either in manuscript or in printed form—King James's 1591 book *Poeticall Exercises at Vacant Hours*. It contains on its first page a poem by Henrie Constable; it is Henry's poetic countenance, not James's, that "filled up" that initial page. Opening this book might have delivered a powerful blow to our young Swan of Avon.

A second explanation is that James VI may have described Henry Constable in one of his published or unpublished poems. As we have seen, one published poem—"A Complaint of His Mistressis Absence from Court"—appears to spell out his name in two adjacent lines, and credits the missing person with features (physical beauty, a kind spirit, a siren voice) that coincide with the way others describe him. A poem James wrote in 1589 seems to describe his parting with Constable on the Scottish coast, a parting undertaken (as the third stanza reports) for the sake of another love (his bride-to-be); yet nonetheless an assault on this male friendship—and on Venus's boy:

SONG I

What mortall man may live but hart [yearn]
As I doe now suche is my cace
For now the whole is from the part
Devided eache in divers place
   The seas are now the barr
   Which makes us distant farr

That we may soone winne narr [succeed in arriving near]
God graunte us grace.

Full manie causes suire I have
Which does augment my woe and caire
Bot one more speciall nor the leave
When I doe thinke what joye was thaire
    What gladness and what greeting
    At our long wished meeting
    I can not well unwitting
    My cheekis declare.

And sine how we so soone were shedd
And loste our long desired joye
O what mischance, I never redd
That lovers hade such cause of noye [distress]
    For other lovers uses
    The one to make excuses
    Of absence, thus abuses
    Them Venus boye.[42]

One of Henry's poems to James VI expresses the same distress at their separation on the coast: "To the K: of Scots upon occasion of his longe stay in Denmarke by reason of the coldnesse of the winter and freezing of the sea."[43] The sonnet's first two quatrains describe the fire and pain of the poet's longing, torment he must suppress lest "she" (presumably, Queen Anne) be blamed; the third quatrain and couplet bravely pivot to salute the happy union of the wise king and his beautiful spouse.

There is another poem that we can be confident was written by James VI to Henry Constable. The poem Constable wrote to James crediting him with angels' wings—the poem cited above that James included in his own published volume of 1591—is answered by an anonymous poem that was almost certainly by James. In it, James accepts Henry's description that he (James) flies at the highest pitch on angels' wings. But he then says that in the very act of so describing him, Constable's Time-bound, Love-bound poetry has flown very near him. This act has so astonished the king that he has stood still in midair to witness the feat (thus jeopardizing his angelic position of superior speed and height). However, when the three (Angels, Time, and the Love-Muse) are flying in full sunlight, the second and third weary quickly and only the Angel-king continues on. Therefore, the king concludes, come to me; I invite you and your muse to lie upon my wings and I will carry us all to heaven. Here is Constable's poem (again) and the anonymous poem that can be by no other hand than that of King James:

To the King of Scotland

To H.C upon occasion of his two former Sonets to the K. of Scots

When others hooded with blind love
    doe flye
Lowe on the ground with buzzard
    Cupids wings
A heavenlye love from love of love thee
    brings
And makes thy Muse to mount above
    the skie

SWEET Muses' son! Apollo's chief
    delight!
Whilst that thy pen the angells quill
    doth prayse,
Thou mak'st thy Muse keeping with
    angells flight,
And angells wing the wing of Tyme
    doth rayse.

Yonge Muses be not wonte to flye so
    hye
Age schoold by tyme such sober dittie
    sings
But thy youth flyes from love of
    youthful things
And so the wings of tyme doth overflye

That he which chang'd blind Love for
    love of light,
And left Tyme's wings behind, and
    Love's below,
Amazed stands to see so strange a sight,
That angells wing nor tyme nor love
    outgoe.

Thus thow disdainest all worldlye
  wings as slow
Because thy Muse with Angells wings
  doth leave
Tymes wings behinde and Cupids wings
  below
But take thow heed, least fames wings
  thee deceave
  With all thy speed from Fame thow
    canst not flee
  But more thow flyest the more it
    followes thee.

The danger is least when the heate of
  sun
The angells and the other wings shall
  trye:
A highest pitch both Tyme and Love be
  done,
And only she find passage through the
  skie.
  Then rest thy Muse upon the angells
    winge,
  Which both thy Muse and thee to
    heaven may bring.[44]

HENRIE CONSTABLE

The poem is almost an erotic invitation: the poet invites the addressee to lie on top of his wings, filling up the line of his own wingspan with the countenance of the beloved. Could a lovesick third person looking on—Will Shakespeare—experience anything other than devastation, a sense that his own body had been emptied out of its own matter and subject matter?

A third explanation for Shakespeare's couplet in Sonnet 86—"But when your countenance filled up his line, / Then lacked I matter, that enfeebled mine"—carries us forward to the year 1594 and the baptism of Prince Henry. The infant's full name—Frederik Henry—honors Anne's newly deceased father, Frederik, and James's long-deceased father, Henry. The choice of the first name has struck historians as inevitable; the choice of the second, thought-provoking, even surprising.[45] In choosing the name Henry, the name by which the prince would be known, James might have had an additional reason beyond filial piety (as parents of every era often have multiple reasons for the names they confer on their children). If the king confided to his English friend his special fondness for that chosen name, and if Constable in turn reported the conversation to Shakespeare, Shakespeare's lament about the rival's "line" now "filled up" with the beloved's countenance could refer to the king's biological line rather than his poetic line.

Henry Constable—we should perhaps at this moment recall—was a distant relative on his father's side of the Stuart line and a descendant on his mother's side of the original Order of the Garter.[46] Less because of these family connections than his sweet charm and personal charisma, he seems to have been destined to act as midwife or godfather to King James VI's marriage and paternity. Not only did he serve as the king's companion on the first phase of his journey to Anne of Denmark, but at an earlier point when the king was entertaining the possibility of marrying Catherine of Navarre, the sister of Henry of Navarre (soon to be King of France), Henry Constable served as an intermediary in those negotiations.[47] A third prospective bride—England's Lady Arabella Stuart—was one whose eligibility was also sponsored by Henry Constable. He wrote a poem to James VI stating that both he and the "sweet dame" had chosen the king as their protector. Alluding to the king's famous poem "The Phoenix," Constable writes that he and Arabella will fly "Under youre Phoenix wing" to shield ourselves from "carrion beakes"; and he concludes, "O happie! If I might but flitter there, / Where yow and shee and I should be so neare."[48] Just as Shakespeare in his first seventeen sonnets urges the beloved to perpetuate his biological line, so Henry Constable was very much at work to ensure the perpetuation of James VI's biological line. It is not unreasonable to suppose that his own first name was honored in the first infant that resulted from a marriage union.

Many readers over the centuries have puzzled over Shakespeare's intricate and intimate knowledge of court life. Sometimes the magnitude of their puzzlement has led them—against massive evidence[49]—to deny Shakespeare's authorship: "There is . . . shewn in the plays the most perfect knowledge of Court etiquette, and of the manners and the methods of the greatest in the land, a knowledge which none but a courtier moving in the highest circles could by any possibility have acquired."[50] If an explanation is needed for Shakespeare's knowledge of court life, Henry Constable provides one: his intimacy with the Scottish court is just a sample of the relations he had with courts all over Europe, as he moved in and out of England, Scotland, France, Poland, Germany, Italy, and the Netherlands.[51]

SHAKESPEARE'S SONNET 85

Sonnets 80 and 86 describe the way the rival poet sabotages Shakespeare's poetic power, a complaint Shakespeare repeats in Sonnet 85. Shakespeare, who is "tongue-tied" in Sonnet 80, again in Sonnet 85 protests that his "Muse" is "tongue-tied." The rival's muse, no, *muses*—they are multiple!—have all stepped forward in unison to assist him with full-throated ease. Shakespeare adores the beloved but does not articulate that adoration; meanwhile the rival and his muses busy themselves writing hymns of praise.

> My tongue-tied Muse in manners holds her still,
> While comments of your praise, richly compiled,
> Reserve their character with golden quill,
> And precious phrase by all the Muses filed.
> I think good thoughts, whilst others write good words,
> And like unlettered clerk still cry "Amen"
> To every hymn that able spirit affords,
> In polished form of well-refined pen.
> Hearing you prais'd, I say, " 'Tis so, 'tis true,"
> And to the most of praise add something more;

But that is in my thought, whose love to you,
  Though words come hindmost, holds his rank before.
    Then others for the breath of words respect,
    Me for my dumb thoughts, speaking in effect.

Shakespeare is in a position of financial and educational humility: he is an "unlettered clerk" while the rival is steeped in a verbal
world of wealth and royalty: "richly compiled," "golden," "precious," "polished," and "well-refined."

The rival composes hymns; Shakespeare composes only feeble
supplements to those hymns, such as "Amen," or "'Tis so, 'tis
true." Here Shakespeare brilliantly conflates two features derived
from the world of James VI. The first is the king's dedication
to hymns. James had already translated from Latin into Scottish
meter one of the psalms—Psalm 104—by the time of the 1584
publication of his *The Essays of a Prentise*.[52] Twenty-nine other
psalms translated by James into Scottish meter appear, along with
Psalm 104 and a translation of the Lord's Prayer, in the manuscript
MS. Royal 18.B. xv. Though the king had a lifelong passion for
the psalms (and would later translate them into English meter),
James Craigie provides strong evidence for assigning these thirty
to the late 1580s.[53] Craigie also notes that the king "used no fewer
than twenty-eight stanza forms, most of them his own invention
and some of them of considerable complexity of structure."[54] Any
reader of James's 1591 *Poeticall Exercises at Vacant Hours* would
know about the psalms, since he there tells his readers he may
soon publish them. Word-of-mouth reports of the king's sponta-
neous recitation of the psalms would also acquaint a wide audience (including, presumably, our Swan) with his preoccupation.[55]

The second feature of Sonnet 85 that coincides with James
VI's world is the king's capacity to elicit admiring assent from
those around him. While the collective affirmation of a prayer
with the word "Amen" is a reverential act, as scripted in this sonnet

where it is placed in the company of "'Tis so, 'tis true," it comes across as unseemly deference. Kings in any era are inevitably surrounded by yes-men, an entourage of Polonius-like well-wishers who not only affirm but tsk and task over how wise, how insightful, how adorable the king's utterances are: ah, amen, 'tis so, 'tis true. Shakespeare in this sonnet combines James VI's love of psalm singing with the way executive power inspires admiring compliance: he carries off a brilliant sleight of hand, since he has to do all this while, simultaneously, appearing "tongue-tied" and "dumb," silent and stupid.

SHAKESPEARE'S SONNET 87

The last sonnet in the rival poet series is a heartbreaking poem. When two people compete for a beloved, it can seem in the heat of the struggle that the two aspirants are equals. But that intimacy, that alikeness, is just a delirious, middle-of-the-night, erotic illusion. The sonnet opens, "Farewell! Thou art too dear for my possessing," and it ends with the couplet:

> Thus have I had thee as a dream doth flatter,
> In sleep a king, but waking no such matter.

He had experienced himself as very like . . . a king? No, that's not quite it. He had experienced himself as very much like *the* king, King James VI of Scotland. Their shared love for the beloved, far from increasing Shakespeare's stature (as it seemed when they were locked in the embrace of combat), has instead invalidated any claim Shakespeare formerly had to him, exposed it as fraudulent, hence cancelled. Katherine Duncan-Jones points out that the lowercase "king" in the Folio version of the couplet is an uppercase "King" in the Quarto version, thus, in her words, suggesting that "he has enjoyed [the beloved's] presence in a way analogous to James I"![56] She also points out the haunting repetition of "king" in "waking" (line 14), "making" (line 12), and "mistaking" (line 10), as well as the ten-times repeated end syllable of "ing" in the poem's overall architecture.

The sonnet is an overlay of two charters: the original marriage charter between Shakespeare and the beloved, and the royal charter between the king and the beloved. Kings bestowed charters not only on entire towns (as when Æthelstan in the tenth century conferred a charter on the townsmen of Malmesbury in return for their assistance fighting the Danes) but on individuals, as a way of conferring honor or thanks. During his six months of wedding travels through Norway, Sweden, and Denmark, James VI, for example, conferred rewards on those who served him. The historian David Stevenson notes: "As a leaving present James issued [Vaus of Barnbarroch] a new charter for his lands, which in future were to be held from the crown for the nominal annual payment of one rose—the symbol of love."[57]

The rival's poems to the beloved are just such a charter, a conferring of royal honor and recognition. By now revealing to the beloved his true worth, the royal charter simultaneously reveals that the beloved is "too dear for my possessing." Thus Shakespeare releases him from their contract, or—more accurately—the now invalidated contract itself releases him. If this sonnet is painful when young Will Shakespeare's kinship with kings is understood to be metaphorical, it is devastating when recognized as literal. Here is that final sonnet:

> Farewell, thou art too dear for my possessing,
> And like enough thou know'st thy estimate:
> The charter of thy worth gives thee releasing;
> My bonds in thee are all determinate.
> For how do I hold thee but by thy granting,

And for that riches where is my deserving?
The cause of this fair gift in me is wanting,
And so my patent back again is swerving.
Thyself thou gav'st, thy own worth then not knowing,
    Or me, to whom thou gav'st it, else mistaking;
So thy great gift, upon misprision growing,
    Comes home again, on better judgment making.
        Thus have I had thee as a dream doth flatter,
        In sleep a king, but waking no such matter.

One man is a king; the other, merely a mistaking.

Yet, in the long run, the aura of equality was not delusory. The Todd manuscript of Henry Constable's poems ended with two poems addressed to him by other hands (these were published in the eighteenth-century *Harleian Miscellany* printing of the manuscript). Many poems had to have been written to Constable during his life: Why are these two, and these two alone, given pride of place at the end of his own poems? The first is the poem we have just encountered in which a poet—I believe James VI—writes to Henry Constable inviting him to rest his muse on the outstretched angel wings of the speaker. The second is the poem we encountered in the first chapter of this book, "England's Sweete Nightingale." It is worth listening to the voices of the two one more time, especially the haunting voice of the second, stranded between wit and yearning:

To H.C upon occasion of his two
former Sonets to the K. of Scots

SWEET muses' son! Apollo's chief
    delight!
Whilst that thy pen the angells quill
    doth prayse,

To Henry Constable Upon Occasion of
Leaving His Country

England's sweete nightingale!—what
    frights thee so,
As over sea to make thee take thy flight?

Thou mak'st thy Muse keeping with
 angells flight,
And angells wing the wing of Tyme
 doth rayse.

That he which chang'd blind Love for
 love of light,
And left Tyme's wings behind, and
 Love's below,
Amazed stands to see so strange a
 sight,
That angells wing nor tyme nor love
 outgoe.

The danger is least when the heate
 of sun
The angells and the other wings shall
 trye:
A highest pitch both Tyme and Love be
 done,
And only she find passage through the
 skie.
 Then rest thy Muse upon the angells
  winge,
 Which both thy Muse and thee to
  heaven may bring.

And there to live with native countryes
 foe,
And there him with thy heavenly songs
 delight?

What!—did thy sister Swallow thee
 excite
With her, for winter's dread, to flye
 awaye?
Whoe is it then has wrought this other
 spite,
That when as she returneth, thou
 should'st stay?

As soone as Spring begins she cometh
 aye;
Returne with her, and thou like tidings
 bring;
When once men see thee come, what
 will they say?
Loe, now of English poesie comes the
 spring!
 Come, feare thou not the cage, but
  loyall be,
 And ten to one thy Soveraigne
  pardons thee.

If the second poem is indeed by Shakespeare, it means that the two rival singers—at least in the space of this manuscript—stand shoulder to shoulder in the company of the beloved.[58]

 Before too many years would pass, James VI of Scotland would become James I of England. Shakespeare and James would go on to have almost as much proximity to one another as either of the two lovesick mortals would have with Henry Constable. By the time James I was in a position to choose a company of players to be designated—by charter!—the King's Men, he would have spectacular evidence of Shakespeare's prowess: *Romeo and Juliet,* *A Midsummer Night's Dream, Hamlet,* and twenty-two other plays. In hindsight, it may appear to us self-evident that James would select Shakespeare's company. But as the leading scholar James Shapiro writes: "Exactly how and why Shakespeare's company was elevated to the position of King's Men has never been satisfyingly explained . . . Mystery will always surround how Shakespeare and his fellow players were chosen to be the King's Men."[59] It is not impossible that his attention to Shakespeare was assisted by having heard about his genius long ago in Scotland, beginning in 1589 when a young courtier who recognized that genius—recognized it not with the evidence of twenty-five plays at hand but only a handful of sonnets—described him to the king in their daily conversations about poetry.[60] A decade later, Constable resided in the Scottish court for six months from March 1, 1599, to September 1599,[61] providing another period when the king might have heard admiring mention of the by-then highly accomplished playwright. If the king was wary of the tidal currents in Henry Constable's religious judgments, he could be certain that Constable's judgments about poetic genius ran deep and true.

6

LAST NAMES

If one's beloved has a surname that contains a noun or a verb, it is surely advisable to abstain from punning on that noun or verb when writing a poem to the beloved. This excellent advice neither Shakespeare nor Constable chose to follow. Their poems—which spell out each other's full name and invent intimate forms of first-name address—also memorialize their surnames. Despite the tonal peril of constables and shaking spears, the yearning to find yet one more way to caress "thy sweet beloved name" was apparently irresistible.

The name "Constable" is etymologically derived from "con" and "stable," "con" from the Latin for the preposition "with" and "stable" from the Latin verb "to stand." "Constancy," even in the frantic midst of two love triangles, is designated the key feature of the beloved. Shakespeare tells us that rare precedents exist for the astonishing beauty of his beloved: Adonis is one, Helen another, a ravishing spring day a third. But there is no precursor for his steadfastness: "But you like none, none you, for constant heart" (Sonnet 53, line 14).

Because "constancy" is the key feature of Shakespeare's beloved, the sonnets describing that beloved are of necessity also constant:

> Kind is my love today, tomorrow kind,
> Still constant in a wondrous excellence;
> Therefore my verse, to constancy confined,
> One thing expressing, leaves out difference.

While the energy of poetry usually springs from its freshness and newness, the delight of Sonnet 105 comes in varying the lines as little as possible. Thus the first line of the quatrain—"Kind is my love today, tomorrow kind"—opens and closes with the same word, making it, as Stephen Booth writes, "a model of constancy" (as well as an instance of a particular poetic figure called epanalepsis).[1] This is just one of several line designs that enable the poem to fulfill its claim: "one thing expressing, leaves out difference." Another line uses four phrases in a row to reassert a single idea: "To one, of one, still such, and ever so" (line 4). Still another line repeats a four-word phrase from the previous line: "Fair, kind, and true . . . / Fair, kind, and true" (lines 9 and 10), which is then repeated a third time in the couplet, "Fair, kind, and true." If the precious gift of constancy is the subject, consistency—even ingenious monotony—shall be the poetic form.

The name "Constable," with its aura of constancy, seems present even when the virtue is not explicitly named—even, in fact, when the virtue is contradicted. In Sonnet 95, Shakespeare writes, "Naming thy name, blesses an ill report" (line 8). The sonnet is about sexual waywardness or, as Katherine Duncan-Jones writes, "promiscuity";[2] yet people "Cannot dispraise; but in a kind of praise, / Naming thy name, blesses an ill report." His name is self-exonerating, since to report acts of inconstancy carried out by someone named Constancy seems to cancel out, to make right, the very wrong reported. It would be like saying "Sir Trusted Person today removed some goods from our house," in the course of which the disappearance of the furnishings seems transformed into a benign event.

How easily a poet might have been tempted to explore the irony of a discrepancy between a Name and an Act: such is the gentle charisma of the beloved and the alchemy of Shakespeare's poetry that the gravitas of love is maintained during the transformation of waywardness into a steadfast blessing.

The name "Constable" instigates and reinforces the poet's aspiration that the lovers be constant to one another: an ever-fixed mark, the star to every wandering bark. It is this meaning—rather than the "constable" who officiates in castles, towns, and prisons as an agent of the law—that is at the heart of Shakespeare's invocation of the beloved's surname. But that other meaning is not altogether absent from the sonnets. Shakespeare being Shakespeare, how could it be?

In England, the position of constable originated as a prestigious office within a castle, a fortress, or a large regional territory. The position was sometimes hereditary, but more often the person was directly appointed by the king and was usually of high social standing such as a baron.[3] The person often had a large staff and was responsible for upholding the law, maintaining the peace, overseeing the workshop in which peacekeeping armaments were made, and serving as keeper of the forest and parks.[4] Generations before his birth, Henry Constable's family took the name "Constable" from the position of constable held by one of its patriarchs.[5] The office was not restricted to economic heights. Just as law and peace were dispersed throughout the fabric of the country, so the office of the constable was dispersed across the widest spectrum from the highest to the lowest, from the elite (not just the constable of Windsor Castle or Dover Castle but the constable of England, the constable of Scotland) to the everyday (the constable of each town or village—a position held by Shakespeare's father).

By the sixteenth and seventeenth centuries, the word still retained—or had not altogether lost—its glamorous associations. During the first year of his reign as King of England, the state papers of James I are full of reports about prestigious constables both domestic and foreign. The constable of Castille, for example, makes many appearances in the official documents of 1604, now bestowing on the ten-year-old Prince Henry "a richly comparisoned pony,"[6] now in turn receiving from Queen Anne a pearl necklace for his wife,[7] now in conversation with the king for forty-five minutes of nonstop flattery: "The audience lasted about three quarters of an hour, and was entirely confined to compliments."[8]

But across the centuries, its meaning had gradually pivoted away from the villas to the villages: one historian, summarizing "the English village constable" between 1580 and 1642, credits the accuracy of Shakespeare's Dogberry in *Much Ado About Nothing*, and observes that the town officer was often perceived as "an incompetent agent of royal authority," "unprofessional," "lazy," and even "criminal."[9] If the 1604–1605 state papers of James I record the comings and goings of the constable of Castille, they also contain complaints from townspeople: "Finally, notice may be made of a complaint that the basest sort of the common people were being made petty constables and tithing men. This arose from an evil custom of late to make the tithing man by the house, never respecting the honesty of the man . . . with the result that [the post] usually alighted upon the poorer and baser sort of people 'that dare not say buffe to a goose.' "[10]

Stay away from this noun, friend Shakespeare, we might again counsel. Yet would a poet who permits a hen into his sonnet sequence close the door to a constable? Of course not. He permits the officer to enter at least twice. Here in the sonnets his constable is neither grand nor grandly silly: compared with his cousins who appear in the plays, he is status free; he simply performs his work of making—or abstaining from making—an arrest. However, of Shakespeare's two sonnets, one carries the regalia of the high officer of the castle; the other is one's neighbor from a nearby village.

Sonnet 58 is about Shakespeare's jealous inquiries into the beloved's whereabouts during his absence, and about the beloved's suppression of those inquiries. The poem uses the vocabulary of lord and vassal, master and slave (lines 1, 4). The beloved, as lord, is at liberty to act on his erotic pleasures and is accountable to no one—certainly not to the poet. Any request for an accounting is an illegitimate attempt to "control" him. The poet, as vassal, has no right to initiate an inquiry or level an accusation (lines 3, 8, 14). The aura of judicial inquiry surrounds the poem, for it is the power the poet lacks and the beloved has, thus summoning into the sonnet the figure of the constable.

Constable (let us here use his name) has discretionary power of prosecution: he has the right to discipline the poet, actively reprimanding him (lines 1, 2, 7, 8) and effectively "imprisoning" him (line 6), depriving him of motion, action, will.

> That god forbid, that made me first your slave,
> I should in thought control your times of pleasure,
> Or at your hand th'account of hours to crave,
> Being your vassal bound to stay your leisure.
> O let me suffer, being at your beck,
> Th'imprisoned absence of your liberty,

And patience tame, to sufferance bide each check,
Without accusing you of injury.

(lines 1–8)

Shakespeare assigns himself a crushing series of passive verbs that make him as motionless as a prisoner: "bound to stay," "let me suffer," "being at your beck," "imprisoned absence," "patience tame, to sufferance bide each check," "Be where you list," "I am to wait, though waiting so be hell." Many of these phrases contain internal feats of magnification. Both "bound" and "stay" are passive, but are compounded when slammed together in "bound to stay." "Suffering," already the extreme of a passive state, is made more so by requiring optative permission, "O let me suffer." The passivity of "waiting" is deepened by having to be carried out at someone else's direction, "I am to wait." Similar forms of magnification are at work in "tame, to sufferance," and "bide each check." The eight phrases in sequence march us forward into the ground. Shakespeare protests that it is not some action of his but his very existence, his very being—"being at your beck"—that is circumscribed by the harsh perimeter drawn by his lover.

(Poor Malvolio in his dark prison! Before we feel too indignant on Shakespeare's behalf, we should pause to remember that in many other poems it is Constable who suffers excruciating jealousy and is permitted little room in which to protest or question. What we survey at the moment is the way Shakespeare smuggles his beloved's last name into his account of the injustice he suffers at his lover's hands. If within the poem his accusation is silenced, the sonnet itself is a fourteen-line accusation that dances his beloved into a morally compromised corner.)

The beloved in Sonnet 58 has discretionary power of prosecution not only because he can initiate proceedings against the poet, but because he himself is immune from prosecution. Worse, he has the power to exonerate himself, as the sonnet's third quatrain makes clear:

> Be where you list, your charter is so strong
> That you yourself may privilege your time
> To what you will; to you it doth belong
> Yourself to pardon of self-doing crime.
>
> (lines 9–12)[11]

The generous account of the way the name "Constancy" "blesses an ill report" in Sonnet 95 here in Sonnet 58 has a legal equivalent in the power of a constable to clear himself of all crimes. Both sonnets are about sexual trespass. Both distinguish between the trespass (blameworthy) and the person who committed the trespass (blameless, morally and legally). Both use the beloved's last name to accomplish the decoupling of the bad act from the good person. Both use the last name to "clear" the person of wrongdoing. Yet the tonal effect could not be more distant. The alchemical forgiveness in the description based on moral virtue (Constable as Constancy) is here an angry account of the way class privilege (Constable as constable) works to obscure, and thereby multiply, harms.

A very different constable appears in Shakespeare's Sonnet 74. The poem is a direct response to a poem by Henry Constable which pictures Death as an inconsequential postboy:

> The light-foole lackie that runnes post by death,
>   bearing the Letters which containe our end,
>
> . . . .
>
> O Deere, this care no intrest holdes in mee.[12]

Death arrives at our door not with pomp, ceremony, and blaring trumpets, but as a light-footed messenger boy who means no harm: he is too silly for mean motives; his light head contributes to his buoyancy and agility, which together guarantee that he (and the fatal announcement he unwittingly carries) will make it to one's door. Constable asserts that postboy Death—who is carrying news only about the body, not the soul—is easy to disregard: "O Deere, this care no intrest holdes in mee."

Here in Sonnet 74 is Shakespeare's revised version:

> But be contented: when that fell arrest
> Without all bail shall carry me away,
> My life hath in this line some interest,
> Which for memorial still with thee shall stay.
>
> (lines 1–4)

Shakespeare replaces the lackey postboy with a not-so-easy-to-dismiss arresting officer. He counters the line "this care no intrest holdes in mee" with the line "My life hath in this line some interest."

His "life hath in this line some interest" for four reasons. First, because it is a modification of a line by Henry Constable. Second, because the line describes the cessation of life; Death has arrived at the door not with a message but with the means to execute the message. Life has been "arrested" not because it has been hauled off to prison but because it has been stopped altogether. Cruelty and the power to strike down make it not just an arrest but a "fell" arrest.

Shakespeare's "life hath in this line some interest" for a third reason: the arresting figure is a constable. This wildly "interesting" feature is heightened by a fourth. The punctuation in the opening line was added by the eighteenth-century editor Edmond Malone on the assumption that the original must have had a colon. Grammar requires that "contented" be followed by either a colon or a period. If the unpunctuated line was a printer's error, it is more

likely that he missed a colon than that he missed a period followed by a capitalized *W* beginning the next sentence at mid line.
Assuming, then, that the colon was in the original, Shakespeare
had a fourth reason for being interested in the line. It spells out
his beloved's name according to the beloved's signature—"Hen:
Constable."

> But be CONtented: wHEN that fELl ArreST
> H e n :   C o n s t a b l e

If one accepts the signed version of Constable's name as a "full"
version, Shakespeare's sonnet fulfills the two criteria set out
earlier: it both spells the whole name and directly instructs us to
inspect and treasure the line, which—he specifies in line 4—serves
as a memorial: "My life hath in this line some interest, / Which
for memorial still with thee shall stay" (lines 3 and 4). Like the soul
within the body, it is not the poem but what is inside the poem
that is the treasure. The final couplet reiterates the instruction to
perceive in the poem its hidden cargo:

> The worth of that, is that which it contains,
> And that is this, and this with thee remains.

As the sonnet arcs from its first to its final line, Constable as constable (line 1) returns to Constable as constancy: "this with thee
remains" (line 14). Care about the body is disdained by both
poems: Constable calls it "th'abortive bastard of a coward mind"
(line 4) and Shakespeare agrees, "the coward conquest of a wretch's
knife" (line 11). The soul remains, and you—Shakespeare tells his
beloved—have my soul; you are my soul.

The arc within Sonnet 74 also describes the motion across
Sonnets 74, 75, and 76, which address four sonnets by Constable
in which the lackey postboy occurs. Constable's four sonnets form

an interlocking sequence, since the last line of each provides the first line of the next. The poet describes being in a state of spiritual agony about his separation from his lover and says the severe pain he suffers makes him unpleasant to be with. The poems will alternate between distance and bodily intimacy. He is not "a modell" or a "signe" of care, but its "consuming essence," its "quintessence." Thus when he is held in his lover's arms, the lover can smell the care like a perfume, taste it in his tears, touch it on his skin.

> Within thine armes sad Eligies I sing,
> > unto thine eyes a true hart love torne lay I,
> > thou smell'st from me the savours sorrowes bring,
> > my teares to tast, my trueth to touch display I.
> Loe thus each sence (deere faire one) I importune,
> But beeing care, thou flyest mee as ill fortune.[13]

His distress—as the couplet reports—makes itself felt on each of his lover's senses, causing him to "flyest mee as ill fortune," this final line then providing the opening line of the postboy sonnet, which ends, "Deere to my soule, then leave me not forsaken."

The next sonnet, the eighth in the sequence, again has a scene of bodily intimacy, since the poet dreams he is in bed with his lover, only to awaken and find that he has fallen out of his arms once again:

> And on the shoare of that salt tearie sea,
> > couch'd in a bed of unseene seeming pleasure,
> > where, in imaginarie thoughts thy faire selfe lay,
> > but being wakt, robd of my lives best treasure.[14]

In the ninth and penultimate sonnet, the pain-filled care, the "slaine-hopes," the "feast of sorrow" turns at last to the "blacke night" of "Dispaire." The second quatrain of the poem is a miniature digest of themes that will surface in *Hamlet* and *Love's Labour's Lost*.

> No Tymbrell, but my hart thou play'st upon,
>   whose strings are stretch'd unto the hiest key,
>   the dyopazon love, love is the unison,
>   in love, my life and labours wast away.[15]

In almost the only positive image of himself in the four poems, Constable describes his heart as a stringed instrument from which his lover extracts a chord comprised of three notes, love, love, and love: "the dyopazon love, love is the unison, / in love . . ." "Dyopazon" is from the Greek—*dia pasōn chordōn*—meaning "through all the strings" and conveys an enlisting of the full scale, the full octave.[16]

Shakespeare across his answering sonnets says, Fear not death. Rest easy. Be contented. My spirit is yours, now, yesterday, and tomorrow. Like Sonnet 105, which confesses he is to constancy confined, Sonnet 76 says his lover is his only subject. He plays not upon his heart (not upon strings, not chords or "compounds"), but, like Pan, upon "a noted weed," a simple reed flute with a single note at a time or a single melodic line of notes that are the sonic equivalent of spelling "Henry Constable."[17] The phrase contains a lovely aural pun: the classic phrase "oaten reed" has become the almost sonically identical "noted weed"—a pun that would surely have delighted the person to whom the poem was addressed, who would know both the classic (Virgil) and contemporary (Spenser) love of the phrase "oaten reed." In Shakespeare's *Love's Labour's Lost*, "shepherds pipe on oaten straws" (V.ii.904), and Titania in *A Midsummer Night's Dream* tells of Oberon seducing a young woman by disguising himself as a shepherd and "playing on pipes of corn," the stalk of the maize plant (II.i.67).

The phrase "noted weed" is often—in scholarly commentary on the poem—glossed as referring to livery or clothing, a reasonable interpretation, especially since the word "dressing" occurs later in the sonnet. But the reading of the "weed" as a flute, lovely and true to the spirit of the sonnet, seems an alternate or additional meaning the poet would not miss. Shakespeare used the word "weed" more than sixty times in his plays and sonnets, three times as often to refer to plants as to clothing. Sometimes the "weed" is an unwanted plant, but often it is a colorful blossom, wildflower, herb, or reed. It may be that in Sonnet 76, as in some of the plays, he intends a conflation of the two meanings (dress and plant), as when wildflower weeds become the weeds Lear "fantastically" wears (IV.iv.1–6; IV.vi.80), or again wildflowers and "fantastic garlands" become the "coronet weeds" and "weedy trophies" worn by Ophelia (IV.vii.168–74). Weeds as clothing and weeds as plants once more nearly coincide when Romeo sees a man in "tatter'd weeds" who is an apothecary-herbalist (with roses and seeds in his arsenal, V.i.39) or again in *The Merchant of Venice* when Portia reveals the plan to be secretly "accoutered like young men / . . . And speak between the change of man and boy / With a reed voice" (III.iv.63, 66). If the two meanings are in play in Sonnet 76, the weed Shakespeare wears and by which he can be recognized is the simple weed-reed pipe inside of which he and his narrow invention reside.

As in Sonnet 105, here in Sonnet 76 he exuberantly celebrates the monotony of his constancy to constancy:

> Why is my verse so barren of new pride?
> So far from variation or quick change?
> Why with the time, do I not glance aside
> To new-found methods and to compounds strange?
> Why write I still all one, ever the same,

> And keep invention in a noted weed,
> That every word doth almost tell [thy] name,
> Showing their birth, and where they did proceed?
> O know, sweet love, I always write of you,
> And you and love are still my argument:
> So all my best is dressing old words new,
> Spending again what is already spent:
> > For as the sun is daily new and old,
> > So is my love still telling what is told.

Constable's black night of despair has given way to Shakespeare's forever rising morning sun.

The word in brackets—"thy"—is elsewhere printed "my," a printing which (though true to the Quarto and subsequent editions) is, if not totally incoherent, nearly so.[18] Most commentators bypass, or give modest attention to, the phrase. Only those who believe Shakespeare's works were written by someone other than Shakespeare can make use—and seeming sense—of it, since only if the author's name is not the one on the title page is there a motive for worrying "that every line doth almost tell my name." In contrast, the line "That every word doth almost tell *thy* name" is completely consistent with the rest of the poem. It seems possible, then, that "my" is a printer's error for "thy" (just as the previous word in the line, "tell," was misprinted as "fel" in the Quarto edition).[19] It is also worth noticing that the very next line does "almost tell" Henry Constable's name, since it contains all letters except the *l*. That a line can have the full name minus one, two, or three letters is not remarkable; it is the normal state of a line to have many or even most of the letters. What is striking is that a line that *nearly spells* the name is preceded by a line that specifies that state of approaching without accomplishing the act of naming: "That every word doth almost tell thy name,"

<u>Sh</u>ow<u>ing</u> <u>the</u>ir <u>b</u>i<u>r</u>th, <u>and</u> where the<u>y</u> did pr<u>oc</u>e<u>e</u>d?
H   e   n   r   y   C   o   n   s   t   a   b [   ]   e

It is also possible that this was not a printer's error, but that the poet himself withdrew "thy" at the moment of publication. Shakespeare often gives within an individual sonnet an announcement that the name lies within this very line in this very sonnet; he does so in many different individual sonnets, always referring only to what is in that one poem. Perhaps he considered the instance in Sonnet 76 an all-encompassing admission—an overt, sweeping, and accurate description of all the sonnets, not just that one poem; and so at the last moment, sacrificed it to near-nonsense. Whether line 7 is "my" or "thy," every line of the sonnet confirms that the poet writes about a single subject, his beloved.

For two lovers obsessed with one another, it may seem a given that their only poetic subject is one another (and therefore nothing to crow about). But what if one of the two lovers inhabits an aristocratic world of privilege and compliment? What if his poems are often about, or to, other persons, the jet set of the day? Ladie Rich, Ladye Arbella, the Countess of Essex, the Countesse of Shrewsburye, Queen Elizabeth, King James, Mr. Hilliard, Sir Philip Sidneye. These are the men and women to whom Constable addressed many of his poems. That Shakespeare, as far as we know, did not write or publish sonnets to the many people who populated his world—his neighbors, his children, his parents, his patrons, his fellow actors—is, then, perhaps something "to note."

The delight in one-notedness (or a single melodic line) is reinforced by the fact that end rhymes across lines are supplemented with rhymes internal to individual lines, joining words that begin and end a line, or words coming in sequence or at brief intervals: the *I-I* sound of "Why . . . pride" in the first and final words of line 1; the *I-I* sound of "Why . . . aside" in the first and final words of line 3; the triple *I-I-I* sound of "Why write I" in line 5; the *ES IS*

ES of "best is dressing" in line 11. Appropriately, the line with the most internal rhyme is line 9: "O know, sweet love, I always write of you." The line begins with the *OH-OH* in "O know"; then comes the *I-I* of "I . . . write," a phrase framed on either side by the *OV-OV* in "love . . . of." "*OH* kn*OH*, sweet l*OV*e *I* always wr*I*te *OV* you." His noted reed has at least three notes. These internal rhymes echo across other lines. So the opening *OH-OH* of line 9 rhymes with the opening word of line 2 (s*O*), the opening word of line 8 (sh*O*wing), the opening word of line 11 (s*O*), and the opening and closing words of line 14 (s*O*) (t*O*ld). In effect, Shakespeare gives the sonnet not end rhymes but start-and-end rhymes.

Though Shakespeare plays his music one note at a time and almost the same note each time, in line 9 he reproduces the chord of love—"the dyopazon *love*, *love* is the unison, in *love*"—that Constable introduced, giving three iterations of love: "O know, sweet *love*, I always write of you, / And you and *love* are still my argument: / . . . So is my *love* still telling what is told."

Of course, no one needs to be persuaded that Shakespeare constantly writes about constancy. We need only see, in addition, that Shakespeare's writing about constancy is one of many ways he coaxes each sonnet into saying his beloved's name.

What about Henry Constable's incorporation of Shakespeare's surname into his poems? The question tells us we are near the end of this book because it circles us back to the book's beginning. We there encountered three poems in which Constable perceived in Shakespeare and in his name a lightning bolt whose jagged zigzag places a shaking spear high in the sky. One poem compared Constable's inability to suppress his lover's name to the inability of a bird's nest to contain a bolt of thunder. A second poem described a bolt of fire flashing from his lover's eyes: "a flame of fire did from thine eye lyds goe, / which burnt my hart through my sore-wounded side." The third poem—the Latin poem given on the opening page of this book—described the felt experience of being made love to: "Beneath a double night with double light, / you pressed down on me, wayward love seizing me from exile. / Struck by twin thunderbolts, our eyes hurl light, / they tremble and flash like a star-filled night."

In that last poem, does the poet describe an actual, or instead an imagined, act of lovemaking? As noticed earlier, both Constable and Shakespeare in their poems celebrate their power to place the phantom of the beloved in front of their eyes. The passage cited is framed on either side by lines which indicate that the poem describes an overwhelming capacity—at least when assisted by Venus and Cupid—to hallucinate the beloved. It also describes the devastating outcome of such a mental experiment.

CARMEN XV

The winged boy glides down on silent feathers
to carve your bright image deep in my heart.
Your eyes, my Life, have lifted up my heart
which holds your picture high in the air.
Unable to find a shadow of you,
        a shadow of me,
I wandered lost, without a guide.
Beneath a double night with double light,
you pressed down on me,
wayward love seizing me from exile.
Struck by twin thunderbolts, our eyes hurl light,
they tremble and flash like a star-filled night,
they ignite a torch—like the Northern Star
that sailors seek when the storm is through—
so that I might find traces of me,
        traces of you.

> But Venus, her wings shorn, does not fly,
> so naked Love stays behind in the ravished heart.
> Scorched on every side by the heat of the heart,
> the goddess, magnified, soon disappears.
> Now bereft of any guide,
> one will look for but nowhere find
> the boy within the woman, the woman within the boy.[20]

The poem seems to describe the mental act of creating a phantom: the Latin word "*umbram*"—here translated as "shadow"—can also be translated as "phantom." Once the missing image is carved in the poet's heart, the heart-with-its-picture rises high in the air, then bears down on him in the lightning love act. The heat is so high that Venus and her son, caught in the conflagration, are unable to depart, "consumed with that which it was nourished by."

In another poem—this time four lines long in the Latin—Constable again describes being struck by lightning.

> Given that a man besieged by fire
> May gather himself,
> His stiffness enhanced by his opponent;
> Is it any miracle that my limbs
> Struck down by lightning from on high[21]
> And ablaze with the heat of my own heart,
> Are knocked senseless, rigid, as though encased in ice?[22]

Assuming this poem is about Shakespeare, no one can say that none of Shakespeare's contemporaries noticed his special power.

The lightning in Henry Constable's poems describes the felt experience of being in the beloved's presence: this no reader is likely to doubt. But does that lightning really pronounce Shakespeare's name?

The kinship between a lightning bolt and a spear—both lethal, both slender, both flashing, both flying through the air—requires no elaboration, since writers themselves so often asserted their similarity. If, additionally, the association of lightning with the verb "shake" turns up only here and there throughout Elizabethan and Jacobean writings,[23] it frequently and consistently turns up in the works of one writer in particular: William Shakespeare. Titus Lartius says to Coriolanus: "with thy grim looks and / The thunder-like percussion of thy sounds, / Thou mad'st thine enemies **shake**, as if the world / Were feverous and did tremble" (I.iv.60–62). Cleopatra says of Antony, "But when he meant to quail and **shake** the orb, / He was as rattling thunder" (V.ii.84–85). Lear says to the storm: "And thou, **all-shaking thunder**, / Strike flat the thick rotundity o' th' world" (III.ii.6–7). And in *The Tempest*, where Ariel's entries and exits take place in flashes of lightning, both he and his master attach the verb "shake" to lightning and to a "spear-like" object, a trident in Ariel's case, a staff in the case of Prospero. Together their lightning speeches open and close the play.

The very first lines Ariel speaks are his account of the lightning storm at sea he has just produced. He boasts (as, here at the end of his career, Shakespeare might well say of the visions he has produced), "I flamed amazement . . . I flame[d] distinctly":

> . . . now on the beak,
> Now in the waist, the deck, in every cabin,
> **I flamed amazement**: sometime I'ld divide,
> And burn in many places; on the topmast,
> The yards and bowsprit, would **I flame distinctly**,
> Then meet and join. Jove's lightnings, the precursors
> O' the dreadful thunder-claps, more momentary
> And sight-outrunning were not; the fire and cracks
> Of sulphurous roaring the most mighty Neptune
> Seem to besiege **and make his bold waves tremble,**
> **Yea, his dread trident shake.**
>
> (I.ii.197–207)

Shaking confers motion on what it shakes (a cedar tree, a pine, a cliff, a grave, a house), causing it either to rise and fall or to swing rapidly from side to side. If it does both at once, the motion zigzags. Perhaps waves and a ship on a rocking sea are already rising and falling, moving side to side, but these are motions that Ariel's lightning drastically magnifies, confuses, and accelerates. Crucially, lightning not only shakes the surfaces it hits; it itself shakes; it rushes up and down and side to side in a zigzagging motion so well enacted by Ariel's darting arrival now on the boat's beak, now waist, now deck, cabin, topmast, yard, bowsprit. This is the zigzagging motion we have come to associate with lightning, powerfully depicted in the frontispiece of the 1709 edition of *The Tempest* (figure 7).[24] A zigzag is the way a slender shaking wand is depicted if arrested in time.

Late in the play, Prospero bids farewell to his art. After celebrating his cosmic powers of creation and transformation, he (like Ariel) takes up residence within a lightning bolt.

> . . . to the dread rattling thunder
> Have I given fire and rifted Jove's stout oak
> With his own bolt; **the strong-based promontory**
> **Have I made shake,** and by the spurs pluck'd up
> The pine and cedar: graves at my command
> Have waked their sleepers, oped, and let 'em forth
> By my so potent art. But this rough magic
> I here abjure. And, when I have required
> Some heavenly music, which even now I do,
> To work mine end upon their senses that
> This airy charm is for, I'll break my staff,
> Bury it certain fathoms in the earth,
> And deeper than did ever plummet sound
> I'll drown my book.
>
> (V.i.44–57)

FIGURE 7
Frontispiece of *The Tempest* in Nicholas Rowe's
1709 collected and illustrated Shakespeare

The breaking of the staff heightens, rather than obscures, the zig-zag motion of the wand. Shaking, arrested in time, becomes a broken line, its segments alternating direction.

According to the *Oxford English Dictionary of Etymology*, a zigzag, or, as it was originally named, ziczac (*zigzac* in French, *zickzack* in German), takes the form ᴧᴧᴧᴧ, which is a "symbolic formation suggesting alternation of direction." While the word itself seems to surface only in the eighteenth century to describe fortifi-cation walls, the recognition of the phenomenon, whether in waves, walls, hills, or a wayward path, was available without the word and certainly recognizable in the lightning bolt's abrupt shifts of direction, interrupting its proceeding down with a swerve to the left, resuming its downward thrust, then veering back to the left, then down again. It is because of its quick turns and swerves that Shake-speare again and again calls the lightning "nimble." It is "sight out-running," as Ariel notes, and speech out-running, as Juliet proclaims:

> . . . too rash, too unadvised, too sudden;
> Too like the lightning, which doth cease to be
> Ere one can say "It lightens."
>
> (II.i.160–62)

It disappears even before one can point to it and say "Behold!" as Lysander complains in *A Midsummer Night's Dream*: "So quick bright things come to confusion." Rather than the word "zigzag," Shakespeare uses the language of crisscross, as when Cordelia speaks of "the most terrible and nimble stroke / Of quick cross lightning" (IV.vii.33–34), or when Cassius in *Julius Caesar* says "the cross blue lightning seemed to open / The breast of heaven" (I. iii.53–54). The crisscross, like the zigzag, registers the shaking of the narrow lance.

So we return to the question: Can we presume that Constable's constant riffs on lightning in part salute the beloved's last name? Does the lightning really pronounce Shakespeare's name? In all the plays, the person most often recognized as a straightforward stand-in for Shakespeare is Prospero. Astonishingly, Shakespeare has the thunder—lightning's voice—pronounce Prospero's name! Alonso, the father of Ferdinand, provides the account:

> O, it is monstrous, monstrous!
> Methought the billows spoke and told me of it;
> The winds did sing it to me, **and the thunder,**
> **That deep and dreadful organ-pipe, pronounced**
> **The name of Prosper . . .**
>
> (III.iii.95–99)

The passage begins with the last syllable of Prospero's name, "O," and ends with the first two, "Prosper," enfolding the lightning description in between as though to lodge it inside Prospero. Yet lightning has much less in common with the whispering, hopeful name "Prospero" than with his authorial sibling "Shaking Spear." We need not ask from whom Shakespeare learned to think of his surname as a lightning bolt, for the answer lies close at hand.

Two other poems by Constable compare being in the presence of the beloved to being in the presence of lightning. The following sonnet survives only in Latin, here translated back into English. Across the night sky a thousand lights—ambiguously stars or lightning strikes—flash and dance. Entitled "Song 18" ("Carmen xviii"), it might be called "Jewel of the World":

> Look closely: the jewel of the world
>   breaks into dazzling lights
>   scattered across the starry plains.
> You see flashes from every direction
>   trembling radiance, a thousand torches
>   pulsing in the sky, a thousand torches in your eyes.
> Look deep within the innermost heart;

you will say its coldness is more extreme
    than the frost-filled breast of Saturn.
If his countenance is calm, he makes all things serene
    in the manner of Jupiter;
But when he swells, he hurls from his eyes
    the weapons of Mars.[25]

Look deep within the innermost heart of what or whom? Perhaps the innermost heart of the universe, as though to penetrate outer space and find it laden with snow crystals like those we will find at Olympus at the end of the poem. Or perhaps the innermost heart of the beloved that, like Olympus, is lined with ice. Or perhaps the speaker's own heart (like the vows of chastity Constable will be overheard to take in his later life after leaving England).

The opening lines contain the word "shake"—"*tremulo*"—in line 3 of the Latin (line 5 in the transcription above) and a phrase close to "spear"—"*Martia tela jacit*" (hurling weapons of war)—in line 8 of the Latin (lines 12 and 13 of the transcription). Constable has other poems in which the two words, or synonyms for the two, are put in much closer proximity.[26] But more important than the yoking of the two words is the conceit of seeing the countenance of the beloved dispersed across the vast plains of the night sky.

The poem then moves to a striking conception. Across the sky, the multiple golden lights—stars or strikes—look like tresses of hair, jagged locks.

His golden hair, long flowing, would grace
    even the forehead of Venus, yielding
      nothing to Apollo.

This transition to the sensuous beauty of the beloved, his lightning locks, prepares for the powerful final account of the chosen terrain of erotic and poetic power.

> He who is swept along with Mercury
> > finds only the unreliable trust of a woman.
> In the end it is Diana who measures out Olympus,
> > joining radiance to ice.

As in Walt Whitman's elegy for Abraham Lincoln, Constable sees the face and figure of the beloved traced out in the night sky. Published in the Netherlands in 1591, this poem was probably written in the mid to late 1580s: at this early date, it cannot be the scale of his friend's playwriting accomplishments but his felt presence as a poet and a lover that is being described.

Here, finally, is a sixth, and for the time being, last, sonnet—though we will encounter a seventh at the end of the afterword. Like some of Constable's English sonnets quoted throughout this book, it is a poem that did not appear in the first printing of *Diana* in 1592, only in the 1594 second edition. This poem has been relegated to the "Doubtful Sonnets" category because (as explained earlier) it along with its companion sonnets are homoerotic and use a Shakespearean stanza.[27] Yet Constable's love for a male friend, and his voicing of that love in the poetic form of that friend's voice, each follows from the other.

In this poem, the comparison of the beloved to lightning occurs in the climactic third quatrain. It shares a feature we have encountered in the other lightning poems, but one we have not yet fully enough appreciated. The revelation of the friend's erotic power lasts less than a second but it is so decisive it leaves permanent certainty in its wake.

> What view'd I deere when I thine eyes beheld?
> > Love in his glory? no, him Thrysis saw,
> > and stoode the boy, whilst hee his darts did draw,
> > whose painted pride to baser swaines he tell'd.
> Saw I two sunnes? that sight is seene but seld, [seldom]

> yet can their broode that teach the holy law
> gaze on their beames, and dread them not a straw,
> where princely lookes are by their eyes repeld.
> What saw I then? doubtlesse it was Amen,
>   arm'd with strong thunder & a lightnings flame,
>   who bridgroome like, with power was riding [them][28]
>   meaning that none should see him when he came.
> Yet did I gaze, and thereby caught the wound
> Which burnes my hart, and keepes my body sound.[29]

Two people look at one another. One of them is ravished by what, within a microsecond, flashes from the other's eyes. Perhaps a moment earlier, they had been having a normal conversation, about, say, verse forms . . . or about poems they have read . . . or about the Arden Forest in Warwickshire. Suddenly, though, in the midst of excited talk and laughter they, just for a split second, lock eyes.

Is this event like the darts emanating from the boy that Thrysis saw and was "struck" by? Constable asks in the first quatrain. In the second quatrain, he moves away from the nakedly erotic to the religious, the celestial: Was looking into his eyes like the moment when a priest saw two suns in the sky? Now the erotic from the first quatrain and the celestial from the second combine to provide the answer that is right. What he saw was "a man" so otherworldly he might be described by the reverential "Amen," armed with lightning and thunder, but armed not in his arms but between his legs, not holding or hurling the bolts but riding them, his true self carried on, coming into being, standing revealed, then just as quickly disappearing with each strike.

The sky clears. The lightning disappears. Normal conversation resumes. But the world of the two—and maybe it is even fair to say the world—has been changed forever.

AN AFTERWORD
ABOUT AFTERWARD

It is tempting to end this book with the year 1591, the year in which Henry Constable, by now a devout Catholic, departs for France, where he lives in exile for many years. It seems probable that by that year most of Shakespeare's poems to his beloved and Constable's poems to his beloved were written, though some of Shakespeare's were revised in later years and a number of new ones came into being.[1] It may be that after 1591 the two men never saw one another again, or it may be that their love and loyalty endured throughout their lives. Because we do not have a *second* sonnet sequence from each, either of these two futures is equally possible; whatever happened happened outside the poetic record.

While chapters 1–6 are factual—based almost solely on the words each spoke to his male beloved—this afterword that describes the period *afterward* is suppositional. It gives an account of Henry Constable's post-1591 life (based on many available facts), in which Shakespeare—and it is here that we begin to guess—may or may not have been included. Documents and records track Constable's public life but no record tracks his private life.

Do Shakespeare's plays help us? Yes, fourteen of Shakespeare's thirty-eight plays are about a person who suffers exile: the number is higher than fourteen, Jane Kingsley-Smith writes, if one includes exile endured by minor characters.[2] The condition of exile haunted Shakespeare—as James Joyce observed—from the early play *The Two Gentlemen of Verona* to his final play, *The Tempest*.[3] Details of individual plays are equally inviting. Shakespeare in *As You Like It* transports Arden Forest to France, as though to say, where my love goes, there goes Arden. Shakespeare's early play *Love's Labour's Lost* is about Henry of Navarre, the very man on whose behalf Constable traveled to France to support his eventually successful claim to become King Henry IV; because this play concerns a school for men, it is relevant to know that one of Constable's ongoing projects while in exile was founding a college for English Catholic exiles in Paris. Shakespeare's plays appear to be conversant with intricate details about the manners and mannerisms of royalty (at a time when fellow playwrights were writing not about royalty but about the merchant class);[4] Constable across these many years lived close to royalty. So, yes, Shakespeare's plays are helpful. But, no. The plays are so rich that evidence on behalf of almost any imaginable life story can be constructed out of them, so that avenue will be invoked sparingly.

There is, of course, one strong incentive for looking at the post-1591 period—the fact that Shakespeare published the sonnets in 1609. That will be our starting place, though we will eventually contemplate not this year alone but the major phases of Henry Constable's ardent life, a life centered on his love of God and the saints (as one can hear in his beautiful "Spiritual Sonnets," written in the transition from his life in England to his life in France) and on his tireless aspiration for world peace. Here, before beginning, is a map of his next twenty years. Henry Constable lives in France, in close proximity to King Henry IV of France from 1591 to 1598, where he is supported first by the king himself, with whom he is said to be a "great favorite," and then by the king's sister, Catherine. From 1598 to 1600 he resides off and on with King James VI in Scotland, where he appears to be partially responsible for Queen Anne's conversion to Catholicism (overriding her Danish upbringing as a Lutheran; and overriding any fear she or her husband might have about the way that conversion might imperil them physically or politically). By 1600 he is back in France, again supported by Catherine and again engaged in ardent projects on behalf of Catholicism. As he had earlier worked on behalf of King Henry IV's ascension to the throne in France, so throughout this period he constantly defends in writing the claim of James VI to the throne in England. It is fair to say that Constable's life is centrally dedicated to the problem of succession and so are Shakespeare's plays. Once Queen Elizabeth dies and King James VI of Scotland becomes King James I of England, Scotland, and Ireland, Henry Constable reenters England, where he lives for seven years, from December 1603 to 1610. In England, James courts him, twice imprisons him, and eventually sends him back into exile. Banished, he lives in France from 1610 to 1613. A false report of his death circulates in 1611; a more reliable—but possibly false—report of his death comes in 1613 when he travels from Paris to Liège to visit a fellow exile, an English priest.

AN INCENTIVE AND AN ORNAMENT

Shakespeare may have published the sonnets simply because he recognized their exquisite poetic merit: when they had circulated in manuscript in the 1590s, they had been celebrated, as is clear in Francis Meres's 1598 observation that "the sweet, witty soul of Ovid lives in mellifluous and honey-tongued Shakespeare . . . in his sugared Sonnets."[5] This welcoming reception alone might have prompted Shakespeare to publish the sonnets in 1599, 1600, 1601, or 1602, but it did not. Not only did he abstain from publishing them, he also limited the number of friends among whom they circulated in manuscript.[6] Perhaps the 1609 publication was prompted by a new, additional incentive: the desire to hearten a man twice imprisoned, weary with travel, deeply worried about religious divisions and the threat of impending religious wars. On an earlier page, we contemplated the ornament that appeared on the title page of the sonnets. What we now see below is the ornament that graced the opening page of the poems themselves, the page on which Sonnet 1 and Sonnet 2 are printed.

It will be helpful if the reader—before proceeding to the next paragraph—stops and contemplates this ornament and determines, in particular, what letter or letters of the alphabet are visible in the design.

The use of this same ornament in other late sixteenth- and seventeenth-century publications tells us that the letters could be, and were, sometimes construed as a pair of *As*, indicating the first letter of an author's name or, more often, indicating the general idea of a "starting place" or "beginning." But other letters are

FIGURE 8
In the first edition of Shakespeare's *Sonnets* (1609), this ornament appears at the top of the page containing the opening poems, Sonnets 1 and 2.

easily discernible in the ornament: a pair of exuberant *H*'s immediately stands forth. Prominent and, for us, most important are two pairs of letters: *HC* resides on the left and its mirror image, *CH*, on the right. Though (because of the mirroring) we are given the pair in two orders, the priority of the *HC* sequence is established by variations in shading: the open face of the *H* is most prominent in the left pair and the open face of the reversed *C* most prominent in the right pair. The printing house of George Eld made countless ornaments, almost always containing a letter if the ornament's destination was the opening paragraph of a book or chapter, seldom containing a letter if it was destined for the top of the first page. Usually when Eld did include a letter (whether for paragraph or page) it was, unlike the ornament in front of us, a stable single letter: a sturdy *A* or a *G* or an *S* remained, unambiguously, an *A* or a *G* or an *S*; it did not, as here, cartwheel into other letters.

Where was *HC* when the book appeared in 1609? The answer: Fleet Prison. On February 1, 1608, Henry Constable had been imprisoned but within a few days he had been released with the understanding that he would remain under the watchful eye of the Earl of Shrewsbury and appear before the Archbishop of Canterbury whenever summoned. Within a few days he was so summoned. Shrewsbury assured the Archbishop that there had been no subterfuge in Constable's conduct: "he hath beene dyvers tymes seene in publique places boath in London and in the Country."[7] On February 9 Constable appeared before the Archbishop in response to a summons that his biographer George Wickes believes originated with James; by February 11 the king had put him in prison, where he remained until July 31, 1610. He resided there for two and a half years; by the time the sonnets are published he has already been in prison a full year.

Imagine, then, Henry Constable, now in his forties, receiving this small book in prison and turning to the first page that contains the ornament along with Sonnet 1 and Sonnet 2. The ornament has the same Ovidian playfulness as the Cupid ornament on the title page: at the top left- and right-hand edges a bird and a bell-shaped blossom stand face-to-face. Is the bird a *meleagris* guinea hen? Is the blossom a *Fritillaria meleagris*? Perhaps not, but the bird is certainly a hen rather than a songbird, and the blossom, like the *Fritillaria*, has a bell shape; if the thin stems that ring the letters come from the flower, these are compatible with the slender, grass-like leaves of the guinea hen flower. (Among the ornaments that grace Constable's own 1592 book of sonnets one recurs that contains a checkered bell-shaped blossom.) Would HC smile to see his initials embedded in the ornament? The opening sonnet, describing his beautiful countenance twenty years earlier, calls him "the world's fresh ornament" (line 9).

The second sonnet—still on the opening page—would remind him that the degraded state in which he now finds himself was something they both saw coming, saw coming because it is an inevitable fate for any human being. It begins, "When forty winters shall besiege thy brow, / And dig deep trenches in thy beauty's field . . ." The sonnets relentlessly acknowledge the demise every human being will suffer. Seamus Heaney has spoken of the moving use of the word "brave" in Sonnet 12, a word that means both courageous and beautiful (as when in Ireland people greet each other under blue skies by saying, "It's a brave day"):[8] "When I do count the clock that tells the time, / And see the brave day sunk in hideous night; / When I behold the violet past prime, / And sable curls all silvered o'er with white . . ." Among the many letters passing back and forth between France and England reporting on Constable's dangerous conduct is a jeering description of his gray hair and small stature, a stab by one who probably had heard of, and wished to puncture, the once-celebrated beauty of this delicate man. Shakespeare again and again predicts that the beloved man's physical countenance will be savaged by time but, as we saw throughout the first six chapters, also promises the beloved will, by residing inside the sonnets, outpace time, a promise he makes come true. The poems, even in the midst of hideous night, work to keep their reader brave.

Even without Shakespeare's assistance, Henry Constable stands as a model of courage. We will see that the details of his imprisonment in April 1604 and again in February 1608 register his intense wrestlings with James I. The section that follows will enable us to appreciate the momentous project in which Henry Constable and his two kings—Henry IV and James VI and I— were all three engaged: the arduous labor of bringing about religious toleration in a world continually torn by religious strife.

But it is difficult to step away, even briefly, from Shakespeare's sonnets without one last postscript on the HC ornament that graces its opening page. A nearly identical ornament had appeared in James's 1591 *Poeticall Exercises at Vacant Hours* (figure 9).

The ornament is present on the book's opening page, "The Authour to the Reader," after which the reader turns the page to find "Henrie Constable's" poem to the king (looked at earlier in chapter 5, "The Rival Poet"). The ornament reappears later in the book on the title page of "The Furies," James's translation of the poem by the French poet Guillaume de Salluste Du Bartas; it occurs again on the "Author's Preface to Lepanto," James's own epic poem about the Mediterranean battle between Christians

FIGURE 9
Ornament at the opening of and at intervals throughout James VI's 1591
Poeticall Exercises at Vacant Hours

FIGURE 10
One section on the title page of James's
Poeticall Exercises at Vacant Hours

and Turks; then again, on Du Bartas's French translation of the king's poem "La Lepanthe de Jacques VI Roy d'Escosse."[9] Given the alternative readings of the ornamental letters as either a pair of *A*'s or instead a pair of *HC*'s, we can be certain the king intended the *A*'s: the apex of the letter (where the two vertical strokes close in an *A* but remain open in an *H*) is more visibly closed than in the variant in Shakespeare's sonnets. More important, the ornament occurs in James's earlier book of poetry, the 1584 *Essayes of a Prentise, in the Divine Art of Poesie*, as it also occurs later in the 1594 record of the extravagant festivities surrounding the baptism of James's son Prince Henry.[10] But all this confirms that the ornament was a kind of "signature" ornament for James's work, a detail Shakespeare was unlikely to have missed. Furthermore, the fact that it was originally selected by James for its *A*'s does not mean that the king—or a reader such as Shakespeare— would miss the double play of letters in a book whose very title page contained, in one of its sections, an *HC* design (figure 10), and whose very first poem was authored by, and openly attributed to, Henry Constable.

1591 TO 1603: HENRY CONSTABLE IN FRANCE AND IN SCOTLAND

Historians credit both the French king and the English king with large-scale aspirations to bring about peace in the small window of time that stands between two periods of slaughter. Their leadership is bookended on one side by the St. Bartholomew's Day massacre (in which thousands of French Huguenots were killed by Catholics on a single day) and on the other side by the Thirty Years' War, in which Catholics and Protestants practiced mutual carnage for eleven thousand days. The tool each king reached for—a tool not yet available for use unless each could himself rapidly hone and perfect it—was toleration.

The tool of toleration the French king created—the Edict of Nantes—is justly celebrated as an extraordinary achievement. He labored both on its design and on its passage from 1594 until April 1598, when he issued the proclamation at the small French town that bears its name.[11] It is, as Noel Gerson writes, a revolutionary document, one of the first written legal instruments ensuring equal civil rights for a religious minority. Included in its provisions were the right of Huguenots to hold office; the right to attend French universities (formerly exclusively Catholic); the right of Huguenot towns to defend themselves by building walls and fortifications around their communities (at the country's expense!); the right to build a house of worship in towns with large minority populations; in areas of sparse population, the right to build a house of worship at a place where people from multiple villages could converge.[12] The Catholic Henry IV, who as Henry of Navarre had himself been a Huguenot and had himself been nearly slain, would have had no trouble sympathizing with the minority; but there is a vast distance between sympathy and the creation of a legal instrument of protection; and it is the second, not just the first, that he achieved.

Did Henry Constable help the king with his thinking? Does the assembly of faces in the Dutch etching of the Edict of Nantes honor Henry Constable by including his countenance (figure 11)? These questions are not meant to imply that he was the single leading advisor (were that the case, the record would mention his

FIGURE 11
Ratification of the Edict of Nantes. Print on paper. Jan Luyken.
Amsterdam Museum

name); nor that he was the primary intellectual influence. But even if he were just one of a hundred voices urging the creation of such a document, that would be momentous. We know by his writings that he was, at the very least, one of the hundred—if not one of the eighteen or eight or five.

In 1589 there appeared in France Henry Constable's *Examen pacifique de la doctrine des Huguenots*. In the sixth and final chapter, he calls his book "this Treatise of Pacification"—and indeed, its primary aim is peacemaking (its secondary aim is to show that Henry of Navarre's Huguenot faith should not be construed as an impediment to his position on the throne of France). Constable addresses the prevailing verbal assault on the Huguenots as heretics, rebels, and traitors. The capacity for condensed argumentation visible in the sonnets—the pivot across quatrains or from the octave to the sestet—here manifests itself in rhetorically powerful single sentences, elegantly structured chapters, and the relentless sweep of the work as a whole. The Huguenot faith, he shows, is as consistent with Christianity and with the Church of Rome as is French Catholicism, as practiced both by elites and by the wider population. So either Huguenots are not heretics or French Catholics are.

The book appeared in multiple editions in French, and once translated into English and Latin went through multiple reprintings. Francis M. Higman, an historian of the French civil wars (1562–98), writes that three publications helped create "new ways of perceiving and thinking" and so provided a way "to put a stop to the apparently unending civil wars in France." Of the three, he singles out one for "particular emphasis" because of its "novelty": that work is Constable's *Examen pacifique*.[13] "The significant thing is . . . a new manner of arguing . . . a radically new, open path—opportunist, agreed, but a path which enables progress to be made."[14] In fact, Higman thinks the quality of both the argument and the French is so high that a person of Constable's youth (he notes his age as twenty-seven)[15] could not easily have written the book, and he "suggests" that Jacques Davy Du Perron—the French priest who a short time later converted Henry of Navarre to Catholicism and served as his spiritual advisor—might have dictated it to Constable (the two were close associates over many years). Since Constable's authorship is generally accepted by his biographers and other historians of the French civil wars (all of whom are aware of the two men's collaborative friendship),[16] Higman's skepticism is revelatory primarily as an expression of high regard for the quality of the treatise and appreciation of its influence.

While, as its title indicates, the Edict of Nantes is an executive order issued by the King of France, it required formal ratification by the Parliament and informal ratification by the population at large. Coaxing consent from outraged Catholic justices, Sorbonne faculty, parliamentarians, and Parisians was a backbreaking labor. Henry IV's sister, Catherine (herself a Huguenot), often stood near the center of the turmoil: her religion intensified the alarm of Catholics while it reassured the Huguenots, who, following the king's conversion, no longer regarded his protection as certain. As a member of her circle and recipient of a stipend, Henry Constable may have witnessed some of the carefully designed meetings with recalcitrant groups. He certainly came to regard himself (as we will see once we turn to his interactions with James) as someone gifted in the art of persuasion—as carried out both by a single individual, himself, and by an assembly of people holding a conference.

No sooner was the Edict of Nantes completed than Henry Constable shifted his efforts from France to the British Isles: while in France it was the Protestants who needed protection, here it was the Catholics. The writing of the Edict was finished by late November 1597;[17] work to secure its provisions was carried out from December 1597 through March 1598; it was issued at Nantes on April 13, 1598. By the following September, Constable's ambitious plans for securing religious toleration in Scotland were already being mentioned in the letters of contemporaries; but the French project was not yet complete. The Parliament in Paris at last ratified and registered the Edict of Nantes on February 25, 1599. Five days later—March 1, 1599—Constable arrived in Leith, Scotland. By March 24 he was dwelling at court, where he stayed through September, possibly returning again in 1600.[18] As he had been visible to onlookers as "a favorite" of Elizabeth, and as he had been visible to onlookers as "a favorite" of Henry IV when he first arrived in France, now his appeal to the Scottish king was striking enough to prompt observers to comment on it: "Boniton ys much made of by the King and so ys Constable who he carried wt hym ahunting and was seen to have great conference wt hym aryding."[19] Throughout 1598, James VI wrote *Basilikon Doron*, a book on the ways of a monarch addressed to his four-year-old son Prince Henry; when it was published in 1599 it opened with a poem sometimes thought to be by Henry Constable urging that spiritual virtues, rather than power, made a king a king.[20]

The poem's first quatrain opens by affirming the God-given position of the king but, in the space of just four lines, makes it clear that the effect of this divine-right authority is less the population's obligation to serve the king than the king's obligation to serve God. The second quatrain argues that "a happie raigne" will come by observing heavenly statutes, deriving earthly laws from God's law, and serving as God's lieutenant. The third quatrain and couplet describe the carriage and direction of the true Prince:

> Reward the just, be stedfast, true, and plaine,
> Represse the proud, maintayning aye the right,
> Walke alwayes so, as ever in his sight,
> Who guardes the godly, plaguing the prophane:
> And so ye shall in Princely vertues shine,
> Resembling right your mightie King Divine.[21]

When one enters the Palace of Holyroodhouse in Edinburgh today, one sees a portrait of James in which, as the curator notes, the accouterments of power have been set aside; his armor lies on the floor, his scepter and crown on the table; he wears no heavy robes; his simple black dress expresses his wish to be seen as a scholar and intellectual. His right hand caresses the medal that indicates his membership in the Order of the Garter, the honorary aristocracy that reveres spiritual virtues of courage, kindness, and courtesy.[22]

The king, who was invested with the insignia of the Order of the Garter in 1590, would have been acutely aware in 1599 that the man riding a horse by his side and possibly writing the prefatory poem summarizing his book was a direct descendant—through his mother, Christiana Dabridgecourt—of one of the twenty-four original Knights of the Garter. Three years earlier, in 1596, King Henry IV of France had been invested with the Order of the Garter in a ceremony in Rouen, in northern France.[23] Henry Constable was present at that ceremony, which was conducted by the Earl of Shrewsbury (Constable's cousin by marriage)[24] and William Segar, who in 1606 would become Garter King of Arms and grant Henry Constable's request for a certificate confirming his direct descent from the founding knight Sanchet D'Abrichecourt.[25]

Though Constable had without hesitation given up property and privilege on behalf of his Catholic faith, his application for a certificate of descent shows he wished to retain his citizenship in an aristocracy of the spirit. He later wrote a prefatory sonnet to Edmund Bolton's 1610 *Elements of Armories*. The sonnet describes a coat of arms as a radiant hieroglyph ("HIEROGLYPHICKS"), a condensation of all the arts: *"All* Arts *conjoin'd in this* Art *do appeare,"*[26] since it is a distillation of "Phylosophie," "GEOMETRIE," "ARITHMETICK," and "OPTICK *Colours.*" In its compression, a crest is like a sonnet, especially in Shakespeare's hands, where, like his sonnets, it provided a surface on which to transcribe a name. Modern readers often express puzzlement at Shakespeare's desire to obtain a family crest. Constable helps us to understand the spiritual and aesthetic aspiration of such ornaments. The one Shakespeare designed—gold, black, and silver—produced a radiant hieroglyph. It contains a picture for the word "spear" and a picture for the word "shake": the bird on the crest lifts his wings, an act preparatory to flight that in falconry is designated "shaking."[27] The elegant humility of the understated motto—"Not without right"— enlists a word that (invoked less often in the sixteenth century than in our own day) recurs throughout Constable's writing, and the three words become even more beautiful once transcribed into the soft trisyllable of the medieval French: "*Non sans droict.*"

But it was not horseback riding or courteous kingship or aristocratic hieroglyphs that had motivated Henry Constable to travel to Scotland in the spring of 1599. It was instead the civil rights of religious dissidents. Catholics in Scotland and England were no more heretics and traitors than were the Huguenots in France. Surviving documents register Constable's two very specific aspirations for his 1598–1600 visits.[28] First and most important was securing a policy of toleration for Catholics in the British Isles (where, he hoped, James VI would soon become the sovereign). Second, he hoped to convert both King James and Queen Anne to Catholicism.

While securing toleration was his major goal, biographies give more attention to the second goal, in part because it entails a vivid personal narrative of simultaneous success and defeat. Henry Constable had announced his hope of converting Anne as early as 1595 when he wrote to Essex expressing his hope of reconciling the two churches, converting Anne with the help of Father Du Perron, and converting James single-handedly.[29] His announced intention to convert Anne surfaces again in October 1597 when a man named John Petit writes, "One constable, a fyne poetical wytt that resideth in Paris has in his head a plat to draw the Queen (of Scots) to be a cathol[ic]."[30] Because Anne did in fact convert during the period of Constable's residence in Edinburgh (1598–1600),[31] it may be reasonable to surmise—as his biographer Joan Grundy does—that Constable's influence was felt.[32] Queen Anne had other Catholics close at hand: Anne's biographers note her close friendship with Henrietta Stuart, who had been raised in France, was sympathetic to the Jesuits, and whose husband, George Gordon, 1st Marquess of Huntly, was Catholic; it was Henrietta Stuart who recommended to Anne that she speak with the Jesuit priest Abercromby, who undertook Anne's formal Catholic training in 1600. But Henrietta Stuart had been Anne's close friend since the early-to-mid 1590s and Father Abercromby had been in Scotland from the outset of Anne's arrival there in 1590: so it is reasonable to look for an additional catalyst to explain the event that took place between 1598 and 1600.[33] Henry Constable seems a leading candidate.

Constable even more ardently hoped to convert James VI. There he failed. He left Scotland in September 1599 pained by the failure; but he planned to return the following spring, after traveling to Rome to secure Pope Clement's support, a project without success. He would try once more when James was finally on the English throne and he himself was—at last—openly residing in England. This constantly renewed attempt at conversion is sometimes pictured as Constable's stubborn refusal to accept defeat, but Joan Grundy wisely surmises that James acted as a theological flirt, inviting and rejecting his succession of attempts: "The craftiest of political coquettes, James constantly invited Catholic wooing, only to draw back when it became too ardent."[34]

While today we may think of the enterprise of conversion as a self-interested desire to bring another person over to one's own side, Constable's goal was deeply pacific. He believed that only by acknowledging the unity of all Christian religions, their path back to the Catholic Church, would unity be achieved and bloodletting stopped. Throughout Europe, people of goodwill were looking for a solution to what was becoming a continent-wide network of powder kegs waiting for a match to be lit. Constable's correspondence with Pope Clement VIII, with the nuncio in Paris, and with the nuncio in Flanders shows that over a period of years he felt confidence in his power to convert James.[35] Each time he embarked on the project of conversion, Constable defended the sincerity and philosophic intelligence of James to these religious authorities who questioned the king's spiritual sensitivity; each time afterward, he expressed to those same correspondents the very disparagement and distrust of James he had earlier parried so confidently.

But if Constable failed, and failed repeatedly, to convert James, he was far more successful in achieving—or more accurately, reinforcing—the primary goal: toleration. James VI already had a record of leniency toward Catholics: in Queen Elizabeth's letters to James throughout the 1590s, she often berates him for failing to punish Catholics, even in instances when they had carried out conspiracies against him. But the vision toward which both James VI and Constable aspired was not an ad hoc—case-by-case—tolerance but the establishment of principles that could be enacted and hold sway, and ultimately, the creation of a framework for theological discussion and shared understanding. One of James's first acts on becoming King of England in 1603 was eliminating the harsh penalties against Catholics; another was his making of a peace treaty with Catholic Spain, ending the high anxiety between the two nations that had been in play since 1599, when England feared the arrival of a second Spanish Armada.[36]

Recent historians have come to see how dedicated James was to the project of peace. In *King James VI and I and the Reunion of Christendom*, W. B. Patterson documents James's record as "a shrewd, determined, flexible, and resourceful political leader who had a coherent plan for religious pacification aimed at resolving urgent problems in the wake of the Reformation and Counter-Reformation."[37] Key to James's concrete proposals for establishing a framework for peace was his embracing of conciliarism, the idea of a regularly meeting assembly for peaceful disputation and debate. So steeped was James in this tradition that he was "ready to propose a general council to advance the cause of a broad religious pacification soon after his accession" to the throne of England.[38]

Patterson shows the many conciliar influences on James: fourteenth- and fifteenth-century Continental writers such as Nicholas of Cusa; the Scottish tradition of conciliarism centering on John Major; contemporary works by the British writer Richard Hooker.[39] But special emphasis is put on the French diplomat and Huguenot Jean Hotman, who compiled and circulated a bibliography of writings on this subject from many different countries (it was unpublishable in France, but was many years later published by Hugo Grotius in Strasbourg). Included in the *Syllabus* was Henry Constable's *Examen pacifique*. Hotman had sent a "gift of books" to James in 1593: given the prominence of Constable's book in France in the early 1590s,[40] it seems highly likely that *Examen pacifique* was among them, though there are many paths by which James could have received this book,[41] just as he periodically received other books written by Constable. English state papers tracking events in Scotland record King James VI receiving a book by Henry Constable on December 29, 1595 (we do not, at present, know what the book was or why the king was offended by it); and again receiving a book written by Constable on July 22, 1600.[42]

Here is an excerpt from *Examen pacifique* that puts forward the conciliar theory that would be so discussed by the French court throughout the 1590s and so embraced by the British court once James occupied the throne:

> Let us then have patience a while; and when wee shall perceive the times of peace to be the fittest for our purposes, let us (a Gods name) offer the same conditions unto the Huguenots, which they propounded unto us before; which was, *to assemble the best learned men in both Religions, to discusse friendly the points in controversie; to the end, that the quiet of the Common-wealth, may goe along with that of the Church*: which if the Huguenots shall accept of, (as I make no doubt but they will) I perswade my selfe, that there may be such a course taken in the Conference, that discovery may be made of many things, which have beene

concealed hitherto from both of us. Not that I imagine any noveltie can be found out in Religion, (God forbid that I should ever thinke so) but that *the meaner questions in controversie, being reconciled, the impertinent ones omitted, the greater may be insisted upon, to be cleared by more evident demonstrations.*[43]

Constable then offers—"though I be the meanest of a Million"—to lay out, when the time comes, the key points in dispute, which he regards himself as both theologically and aesthetically able to do; he cannot do so in the present treatise, he explains, because there can be no disputation if one side perceives the other side to be "already condemned for Heretikes."

So far, our primary focus here has been the years 1591 to 1603, in which Henry Constable resided in France or in Scotland but not in England. Before proceeding to the later years, it will be useful to ask if Constable was ever present in England during this interval.

Constable was without question intellectually and artistically present in England throughout the 1590s. His influential sonnet sequence *Diana* was published in 1592, a year after he had gone into exile. The second edition of *Diana*, containing many more poems, appeared in 1594. A third edition was entered in the Stationers' Register in 1598.[44] By this time, the manuscript of Constable's "Spirituall Sonnettes" had already been in existence for several years, though it is unclear how widely the poems circulated. Philip Sidney's *A Defence of Poesy* was published in 1595; it opened with four sonnets by Henry Constable. In 1600 appeared the anthology *England's Helicon*, which contained poems about shepherds believed by contemporaries to be (and talked about as though they were) by Shakespeare and Constable.[45]

Three anonymously written *Parnassus* plays also appeared at the turn of the century: *Pilgrimage to Parnassus, Return from Parnassus Part I*, and *Return from Parnassus Part II*. In them, Constable is explicitly mentioned by name and poetic achievement—

JUDICIO: Sweete *Constable* doth take the [wandring] eare,
And layes it up in willing prisonment.

And Shakespeare is just as explicitly mentioned by the figures he created—

JUDICIO: Who loves not Adons love, or Lucrece rape?
His sweeter verse contaynes hart throbbing line,
Could but a graver subject him content,
Without loves foolish lazy languishment.[46]

—and at a later moment by name—

KEMP[E]: Why heres our fellow Shakespeare puts [the university playwrights] all downe.

If recent scholars are correct in believing that Shakespeare is portrayed in the central character of Studioso, it would be tempting to wonder if the other central character, Philomusus, is Henry Constable. Or perhaps the two roles should be reversed: *Return from Parnassus Part I* ends with Studioso announcing he will leave England and go to Rome and Rheims; Philomusus immediately agrees to accompany him. By the end of *Part II*, they have decided to leave society and the fruitless profession of writing to become shepherds,[47] perhaps an allusion to the fact that each was (wrongly) thought to have had recently published a poem about a shepherd in *England's Helicon*.

Constable was a presence in England throughout the decade

not only in poetry and plays but in argumentative prose. *Examen pacifique*, though not yet translated into English in the nineties, may have circulated in French. Constable also wrote at least two other small books, the first of which, a theological treatise, appeared in manuscript form in 1596.[48] In 1600 he published a defense of James's right of succession to the English throne, *A Discovery of a Counterfeit Conference Held at a Counterfeit Place, by Counterfeit Travellers, for the Advancement of a Counterfeit Title by One (Person) that Dare Not Avow His Name*, a work present enough in England that modern scholars think it may have contributed to Shakespeare's account of the succession controversy in *Macbeth*.[49]

But the question is not whether Constable was a cultural presence—he emphatically was—but whether he was a physical presence. It seems almost certain that he would not during this period have entered England using his own name. While he often voiced his longing for England (longing expressed in his own letters or recorded in the letters of those who had heard him speak), he also voiced his terror of England: a correspondent reports that in October 1593 Constable was present at a country house gathering in France, but that he suddenly rode off at dawn out of fear that he would be seized and returned to England;[50] another letter-writer reports that when Constable was in Scotland in 1595 about to embark for the Continent, he expressed fear that the ship would make an unscheduled landing in England (as might occur in a storm or adverse winds).[51]

But is it possible that Henry Constable was during this period sometimes in England under another name? That this is by no means impossible is suggested by five factors. They are enumerated not to show that Constable traveled to England but to show that no physical or existential impediment eliminated that possibility.

First, Constable appears to have been an inexhaustible traveler. While we have summarized his residence in these twelve years as a large block of time in France and smaller block of time in Scotland, he was in fact often zigzagging around both country and Continent. Twice he traveled to Italy, for example, while dwelling in France in the 1590s.[52] He visited Scotland in 1595. When he moved to Scotland in 1599, his wayward path took him from Paris to the Netherlands, back to Paris, then onward to Scotland. His reported departures from Scotland during this period took him twice to Denmark, once to Antwerp, and once to Italy—as well as, of course, to France. Aragon also turns up briefly in his itinerary. A high tolerance for travel had been true even in the 1580s, when he resided in England but journeyed to Scotland, France, Poland, Germany, and Italy.

When Shakespeare's sonnets describe the beloved being away for many months at a time—in Sonnet 97, for example, the friend is away throughout the summer and early autumn; in Sonnet 98, he is absent the entire spring[53]—the poems may refer to his ambassadorial[54] travels before 1591 or instead after 1591. It seems more likely that they were written before 1591; but if, in fact, they were written later, it would confirm Constable's return to England during the nineties, since the beloved is described in these sonnets not only as being away, but as returning. For the moment, what is crucial to recognize is that the record, both early and late, confirms that Henry Constable was capable of indefatigable travel.[55]

Second, the number of ships traveling to England during the 1590s was huge. Let us say, for example, that an exile on the Continent wished to enter England through the west coast port of Bristol. In one two-year period in the nineties, 103 ships traveled to Bristol, with 37 from France alone. Their ports of origin included Bayonne (two ships), Bordeaux (ten ships), La Rochelle (nine ships), Nantes (one ship), St. Jean de Lux in the Pyrennes (three ships), St. Malo in Brittany on the English Channel (four ships), and Toulon (three ships).[56] All this traffic was destined for one British port, Bristol. But England had many ports. Take, for example, just those ships originating in Bordeaux that were carrying wine: in addition to six venturing to Bristol, fifty-two sailed to London, nine to Hull, eight to Guernsey, eight to Ipswich, six to Lynn, six to Southampton, five to Yarmouth, three to Poole, three to Newcastle, three to Brightlingsea, two to Falmouth, and two to Dartmouth. This is, once again, the tally for a two-year period originating from a single port and carrying a single cargo.[57]

Third and equally relevant are the descriptions we have of unregistered boats and skiffs sailing (or being rowed) under cover of night carrying priests and other Catholics from the northern coastland of France or Flanders to the southern coast of England. Here is a June 13, 1592, entry from the state papers during the reign of Elizabeth: "*There are eight priests to come to England from Rome* . . . The ordinary ways of sending to England are *Flushing, Calais, and Dunkirk; both letters and priests are set ashore far from towns.*"[58] The vision of Catholics slipping into the country at night continued throughout the decade so that by 1601 we find in the papers of Elizabeth an account of the dangerous array surrounding one Father Parsons: ". . . [H]e must have secret friends at Calais, for they have a stipendiary bark that passes across Jesuits, priests, and traitors by night, and sets them on shore far from any town. They repair to Catholic houses in Kent, or to London, disguised as seamen."[59]

A fourth factor is the important part played by the coastline of the Continent. Where, according to this 1601 letter, are these traitorous fugitives residing before they set out on their night crossing? They line the coast of the English Channel: "600 or 700" are in Flanders; the "most dangerous" are in Douay College, a seminary for English Catholic exiles in northern France; or in Brussels, where there resides a man who sifts and distributes "daily intelligence from England"; or the isle of Wight; or Dunkirk, seventeen miles from Dover; or the Jesuit English seminary, St. Omer, twenty-four miles from Calais.

Douay College—where "the most dangerous" reside—is not only a key station on the way to entering England but on the path of exiting. A 1599 letter to Elizabeth's secretary of state, Robert Cecil, warns Her Majesty that currently six hundred priests and Jesuits have infiltrated England and are moving from house to house for nourishment and shelter, that they feign allegiance to the queen in order to elicit compassion, that they often enter northern England from Scotland before embarking at Gravesend ("whence there com dayly *young Men over*") to sail to the College at Douay.[60] So dangerous are these colleges that a month later the same letter-writer—Henry Neville, the English ambassador to France—writes to Secretary Cecil urging that the King of France be asked to agree that he "shall not suffer any *College*, or *Seminary* of our *English Fugitives*, to be erected, or continued here."[61]

Henry Constable was part of the Douay College network. In his work to establish Mignon College, a seminary for English exiles in Paris, he was named in 1598 as one of two leading advocates; the other was Dr. Richard Smith, the first chancellor of Douay College.[62] In that same year, he received a long letter from Father Robert Persons, the founder of St. Omer's College, in which the Jesuit priest discusses Mignon and signs himself "Your lovinge frende and servant in [Christ]."[63] Dr. Barrett later became the rector at Douay; Henry Constable wrote to him in 1600 expressing the aspiration to have Catholic France, rather than Catholic Spain, working to bring about religious toleration under Elizabeth.[64] We also know that Henry Constable spent time in Rouen, thirty-eight miles from the port of Dieppe on the English Channel. Rouen was home to a Benedictine abbey, an order to which Constable was more consistently sympathetic than to the Jesuits, against whom he sometimes worked. Constable was present in Rouen not only when King Henry IV was installed into the

Order of the Garter on October 20, 1596; he appears to have resided there for a much longer period, from January to October
1596. Was he in Rouen continuously for those ten months? Or
was he there at the two terminal dates and somewhere else—such
as England—in between? Did he make his way to Stratford for
the August 11, 1596, burial of Hamnet Shakespeare?

In some of his reported geographies, we have letters from the
location itself, either from Constable or from someone else who
describes seeing him there. More often, the geography is simply
mentioned as his destination; so it is perfectly possible that the
statement "Constable has gone to X"—Rome, Antwerp, Rouen,
Denmark, Aragon—simply means "He is currently absent from
Paris and is said to be headed toward X."[65] Were he out of Paris
(or out of Scotland) because of a trip to England, he would certainly not mention that destination, nor would he abstain from
providing an alternative destination that would account for, and
camouflage, his absence.

A fourth consideration is the frequency with which aliases
and substitute names were used in the political and the religious
sphere. If it is easy to imagine Constable moving through the
English countryside or London streets with an adopted name,
we might attribute that ease to our familiarity with Shakespeare's
Viola becoming Cesario, Sebastian becoming Roderigo, Rosalind
becoming Ganymede, and an array of others—Celia, Portia, Ne-
rissa, Edgar, and Kent—becoming, one by one, Aliena, Balthazar, a
law clerk, Poor Tom, and Caius. Constable himself, however, might
have been less comfortable with the theatricality of the practice,
even if as a student in St. John's College at Cambridge University,
he had played several small roles in *Richardus Tertius* (a production that had a long afterlife in the conversation of Londoners).[66]

If the practice of assuming an alternative identity strikes us as
theatrical, it need not have done so to anyone living in the 1590s,
since both official state papers and religious papers are saturated

with examples of men—not onstage but in the real world—
adopting aliases or disguised in letters by a name written in cipher. In, for example, the *Records of the English Province of the
Society of Jesus*, the index of names contains many pages that
each specify between twenty and thirty *aliases*. Here is one such
page: "Rogers, John, *alias* Bamfield, Fr. S.J. . . . Rogers, Thomas,
Fr. S.J. *alias* Rochester . . . Romsey, Benedict, *alias* Williams
(priest) . . . Rone, Jerome, *alias* Crossland (priest) . . . Rookwood,
Ambrose, *alias* Gage (student) . . . Robert, *alias* Rauley . . . ," and
so on; eighteen other instances occur on this one page alone.[67]
The conditions of a person bearing an alias sometimes approach,
in this Jesuit record, the extremity of the conditions borne by
Shakespeare's Edgar/Tom O'Bedlam. One aristocrat had will-
ingly served as a valet to endangered priests, providing them with
shelters and lavish costuming. As a result, "All manner of snares
were set to entrap him, so that he had to take shelter for days together in caves, to go about disguised as a poor man, and to live
as an outcast in his native land."[68] (The Jesuit records are cited
here not because their faith is the closest to Henry Constable's[69]
but because their documentation during this period is more complete than that of the Dominicans or Benedictines.) A roll call
from the Catholic record conveys the thick texture of fictional
persons—the deep stream of double names and double lives—
through which Constable would be traveling.

The *Calendar of State Papers* for the reigns of Elizabeth and
James is less laced with *alias*es than the Catholic papers but they
still have a visible presence; a single volume, for example, contains
sixty-five instances, some merely indicating alternative spellings
but others incognitos.[70] Aliases are a close cousin to the phenomenon of written codes and ciphers, a well-developed practice in
the political activities of the day. Constable himself is included
in lists of those who are spoken about in cipher: the ambassador
to France, Henry Neville, writes to Secretary of State Cecil describ-

ing his success in tracking Catholic designs by falsely enlisting the trust of a friar with access to intimate letters: "In perusing the Names for the which he useth Speciall Characters in the Ciffre, I fynd of *Englishe* these contayned in the Note enclosed: Her Majestie, your Honor, my Lord of *Essex* . . . *Sir Walter Raughley*, . . . Mr. *Bacon*, Father *Parsons*, . . . Henry Constable, *Bishop* a Preest, Mr. *Pagett*, the *Englishe* College at Rome."[71]

A fifth consideration when contemplating whether Henry Constable ever touched down on English soil is that he possessed intelligence about the well-being and state of mind of Catholics in England. This country was, of course, just one of several geographies about which he was knowledgeable: he kept his correspondents in Rome informed about the Scottish king's state of mind (his letters on this subject are still relied on by twenty-first-century historians);[72] in turn, he kept Scotland's king informed about Rome's regard for him (including the Pope's offering James ten thousand crowns a month to support Catholic tolerance and perhaps conversion);[73] and he also reports to James on other heads of state (assuring him that all the Catholic princes of the Continent will support his right of succession to the British throne, primarily to be accomplished with French and Italian help, not Spanish);[74] at another point, he reports to James about papists in Aragon.[75] He of course reports on the state of English exiles in France to those at home, as when he writes to Robert Devereux, Earl of Essex, assuring him of their loyalty to England.[76]

But, along with these other geographies, the spiritual state of English Catholics in England is one of his areas of knowledge. In 1595 Essex receives a letter from Edward Wylton in Paris saying Henry Constable's "intelligence [is] good with the Papists both in England and on this side of the seas."[77] In 1597, Constable tells Essex that he has written to Rome "to dissuade the Pope from believing that in England Catholics are in favor of Spain's designs against Queen Elizabeth."[78] The Pope's later message to James that English Catholics are ready to support his efforts against Elizabeth with twenty thousand pounds and twenty thousand men appears to be intelligence about the British relayed to Rome by Constable.[79] In 1600, Constable notices that in England the Order of the Benedictines is on the edge of extinction, and he successfully intervenes on their behalf to Rome and is credited with having brought about their continued existence in England.[80] His papal contact in this endeavor was Cardinal Federico Borromeo in Milan, a strong exponent of conciliarism and a patron of the arts who first met Constable in 1593 and held Constable in high and warm esteem.[81] (Borromeo was the cousin of Archbishop Carlo Borromeo, who authored the "Spiritual Testament" that somehow made its way to Stratford, England, and into the roof tiles of Shakespeare's house; signed multiple times by Shakespeare's father, this document initiated the ongoing research into Shakespeare's possible Catholicism.)

Given the many directions in which Constable was receiving and dispersing information, it seems accurate to say he resided at the center of the Catholic nervous system. He was certainly so regarded by Catholics themselves: we know from a diplomat's letter to Secretary of State Cecil that when a synod of clergy met in Paris in July 1602, they "made a Levye of six hundred Crowns, to be bestowed upon the *English* Catholicks who live here. *Henry Constable* hath for his share 200, and so much hereafter of annuall Pension."[82] One third of the total levy, in other words, was bestowed on our hero. The question is not whether he gathered information about Catholics in several countries (the answer to that is certain), but whether the information he possessed from England was gleaned from contacts on the Continent or through his periodic presence on his own home ground.

If an English exile did return home, he would certainly work to keep it out of the public record, which also places the information wholly beyond our reach four centuries later. Constable, in fact, took care to document just the opposite, the fact of being starkly "away." But when he put his "awayness" on record by proclaiming his acute homesickness aloud so others would transcribe it, or when he announced his terror of setting foot on English soil, was he telling us true that he had not, and would not, return there, or was that the nimble record of a traveler who in truth made his way into England with some regularity?

In any event, once James VI of Scotland became James I of England, Henry Constable did return to England—formally, openly, and in his own name. It is to this homecoming that we now turn.

During most of Shakespeare's years in London, we have only a vague sense of the neighborhood or house where he resided. In the small set of years between 1602 and 1605, in contrast, we are able—thanks to the remarkable scholarship of Charles Nicholl—to picture with precision the place where he lived. At the moment Henry Constable stepped onto English soil in December 1603, Shakespeare's dwelling had three key features, each more striking than the one before.

First, the exterior neighborhood. Shakespeare is living in a rented chamber above a shop on Silver Street across from a small church called St. Olave's. The neighborhood contains many trees and a sequence of "secretive walled gardens," including (Nicholl infers) a physic garden designed by the botanist Gerard. In addition to the peal of St. Olave's bells, "birdsong mingles with noises of trade, the aroma of medicinal herbs vies with chimney-smoke, cooking-smells, and cesspits."[83] Shakespeare began his residence here either in 1602 or in 1603.[84]

Second, the interior. The shop is an island of activity that resembles what might take place in the fairy kingdom of *A Midsummer Night's Dream*. It hums with intricate and exquisite workmanship, wheels and wires; gauze, silk, satin, and taffeta; lace and feathers. Christopher and Marie Mountjoy are "brilliant

craftsm[e]n and designer[s]" who make delicate headpieces purchased by people across the social spectrum, up to and including
Queen Anne, whose royal account books document her purchases
of "head tiers" from this very shop. The room bristles with the
work of two to five people at a time. "It is a scene of small-scale,
miniaturist work: repetitive and delicate."[85]

Third and most astonishing, the interior of the interior.
The artisans—Shakespeare's landlord and landlady and their
daughter—are French Huguenots. Shakespeare has chosen to live
in a world where the language that floats up to his chamber from
the shop below is sometimes French, sometimes English with a
strong French accent. He has marooned himself with exiles. The
world he coinhabits is populated by a family that had to flee their
home, people who do not enjoy, indeed cannot even apply for, the
rights of English citizenship; they can apply only for "denizenship."[86] The Mountjoys would probably know of—possibly even
own—Constable's treatise on the equality of Huguenots and the
necessity of religious toleration. Far more compelling than this or
any other one detail, however, is the overall psychic architecture.

Out of a thousand nooks and crannies in London, Shakespeare
had chosen to dwell in an inverted silver mirror of Constable's
expatriate world of language, loss, and estrangement. How did
Shakespeare now welcome the exile home?

1603–1610:
HENRY CONSTABLE'S RETURN TO ENGLAND

Henry Constable's Homecoming and
Shakespeare's Sonnet 107

Among Shakespeare's many sonnets, one in particular is always
singled out by scholars as the most "topical" and therefore the most

"datable"—Sonnet 107. While most of the sonnets incite us to think about the poet's intimate life—his love for the young man or his mistress-wife—this sonnet incites readers to think about the historical era. Though many different dates have been proposed, the leading contender by a wide margin is 1603–1604, the era in which the reign of Elizabeth ended and the reign of James began. This is also the year in which Henry Constable returned to England: he came ashore in December 1603; was welcomed by James, Anne, and everyone at court; continued to live peacefully throughout the winter and spring; then was suddenly confined to the Tower on April 14, 1604. He was released on July 9, 1604;[87] he recovered and, before many weeks had passed, described himself as in even greater favor with the king than he had been before.[88] (His second imprisonment in 1608 and eventual banishment in 1610 were, at this point, far in the future.)

It seems reasonable to guess that Sonnet 107 was written during the three months of Henry Constable's first imprisonment, three months in which no one knew whether he would ever be released, or whether the punishment might be intensified: long imprisonment, torture, and banishment were all outcomes that other prisoners endured, but so, too, were sudden reprieves and unexpected releases.

In the opening quatrain of Sonnet 107, Shakespeare says that neither his own private fears about the future nor the careless predictions of the culture at large will determine when his love will end, despite the "confined doom" of the beloved that one might suppose would ensure an end to their union:

> Not mine own fears, nor the prophetic soul
> Of the wide world dreaming on things to come,
> Can yet the lease of my true love control,
> Supposed as forfeit to a confined doom.

King James had not only imprisoned Henry Constable; he had
suspended his right to have any visitors. This prohibition was not
unique to Constable: James seems to have treated the Tower as his
own playground, sometimes prohibiting, sometimes permitting
visits, and sometimes himself making sudden appearances there.[89]
Constable wrote a letter imploring that one exception to the prohibition be allowed: he urged that his cousin "William Constable"
and his uncle be permitted to visit.

The cause of his imprisonment was a reckless piece of writing.
During his early months in England, he had once again undertaken James's conversion to Catholicism and had once again
failed. As in his earlier attempts in Scotland, his meeting with
James was preceded by letters to papal officers expressing his
confidence in the undertaking, premised on the spiritual magna-
nimity of the man about to be converted. James's largesse had in
fact been recently in evidence, not only toward Catholics in general (whose punishments instituted under Elizabeth he had revoked
shortly after he became king) but toward Constable in particular:
James had not only granted Constable's written request to reenter
the country but cancelled some encumbering debts imposed on
Henry's father, Sir Robert Constable, by Queen Elizabeth.

But when Constable approached James on the subject of conversion, he received a cold slap. Recoiling from the event, Constable
now wrote to the papal nuncio in France—describing James's
spiritual and intellectual capabilities with something approaching derision. He had written this way about James in the aftermath of previous failures, but those earlier notes had not been
intercepted. This one was. The official account summarizes Constable's letter: "he held it for certain that the King had no religion
at all, and that everything he did was governed by political expe-
diency."[90] From the Tower, Constable wrote to the secretary of
state saying his regard for James was well-known and he hoped
any moments of "double construction" would be read in light of

his loyalty.[91] His letter to the papal nuncio—at least as it is summarized—does not appear to admit of double construction: its style is unequivocal ("held it for certain"), totalizing ("no religion at all," "everything he did"). Perhaps Constable's actual words were less decisive. A report made in an earlier year, however, following a failure to convert James, shows the same lack of delicacy and double construction—"he speaks of [the King] as little better than an atheist, of no courage nor judgment."[92] So either Constable had very bad luck in the accident of whoever twice provided the summaries of his words or, more likely, he was, once his overtures were rejected, just as high-handed as James feared he was.

We know what Henry Constable felt at the moment he walked away from the failed meeting with James. Remarkably, we may also know what James felt. As icily as he had treated Henry Constable, as soon as Constable left, James produced a sonnet: either he wrote it afresh or he reanimated a previously written sonnet, rescuing it from oblivion. The poem assures his addressee that though he has just treated him with haughty coldness, that treatment was merely a prelude to all-the-greater heat. The following sonnet turns up in James's state papers—without an addressee specified—during the same time period when the two had met, early 1604.[93] That Constable was someone with whom he had an established pattern of speaking in verse increases the chance that he is the person addressed. He also had a practice of rejecting Constable's initial overtures, then accepting them—which is the subject of the poem.[94]

In what is arguably one of James's best sonnets, he gives five analogues for what has just happened and what is to come: an archer slackens the bow string as prelude to its taut and powerful launch; a smith, to carry out his craft, now and then throws cold water on his blazing furnace; a husband and wife argue, only to discover a deeper union; two brothers debate, but are locked in love for life; Cupid, amidst "dissensions hot and rife," lets fall "sudden summer showers." By the final analogue the poem has not only moved to open physical desire, but the positive and negative have merged, so that the cooling down is as erotic as the phase of heat.

> Full many ane tyme the archier slakkis his bow
> That afterhend it may the stronger be:
> Full many ane time in Vulkane's burning stow [*stove*]
> The Smith does water cast with careful ee.
> Full oft contentions great arise we see
> Betwixt the husband and his loving wife
> That sine they may the fermlyer agree
> When ended is that sudden choler strife.
> Yea, brethren loving uther as their lyfe
> Will have debates at certain tymes and hours.
> The wingéd boy dissensions hot and rife
> 'Twixt his lets fall like sudden summer showers.
> Even so this couldnes did betwixt us fall
> To kindle our love as sure I hope it shall.
>   Finis J.R.[95]

During their meeting, Constable had been ardent, hopeful; James, distant and frigid. After their meeting, Constable was distant and frigid; James, urgent and reassuring. Each reported in writing his psychological state during the aftermath: James read what Henry Constable had written, a letter that would surely have been different had Constable only known what the king had written. But the king would not have written what he wrote, had he (in turn) first read Constable's letter. James, of course, had the option of comprehending Constable's action in the light of his own five analogies, a moment of hauteur to be followed by renewed loyalty and warmth.

Meanwhile, we have permitted Shakespeare to stand unattended, locked outside the prison, stranded in the first quatrain of Sonnet 107. Having opened the poem by asserting his own and the larger population's inability to prophesy the duration of his love for his imprisoned friend, Shakespeare then goes on to a general account of failed prophecy during the present era.

In the next four lines, the sonnet describes the error of extrapolation: unable to see any direction other than the one in which current events are headed, humankind is seduced into magnifying a present moment into an eternal outcome. When the world is dark, humans extrapolate and predict the end of the world. When peace comes they disavow their earlier predictions, then trip forward into exactly the same error of extrapolation, this time in the direction of endless grace. Now, in moving to the third quatrain, Shakespeare makes an odd swerve: though he has just exposed the hollowness of any prophecy based on the error of extrapolation, he here himself enacts that very practice. Since the present times feel so balmy, moist, and alive—or simply, because I suddenly feel so alive—let me succumb to the seduction of extrapolation and assert I will live forever. This is not only an odd turn within the confines of this one sonnet; it is odd within the entire sonnet sequence, since it is the only time he announces his own immortality, rather than that of the friend.[96] His other sonnets promise that the poems will long endure in order to ensure the beloved's ongoing survival, not their author's.

Two features make this seemingly odd celebration of himself comprehensible and quite beautiful. Having just exposed the infantile character of extrapolation, he does not want the friend's asserted immortality to be mentioned here. He instead lets himself stand in the way. He takes the hit of any residual derision, and the blow is not very strong: the lines are so buoyant they purge the poem of that derision. The light and lovely quatrain frees the poem to go on in the couplet to announce, with no shadow of scorn, the eternal life of the beloved. The sonnet critiques prophecy, then twice practices it, the first time in a risky, wry way, the second time with full confidence.

Here are lines 5–14, the sonnet's second quatrain (the error of extrapolation), the third quatrain (in which Shakespeare asserts his immortality by himself practicing extrapolation), and the couplet (in which Shakespeare asserts his friend's immortality):

> The mortal moon hath her eclipse endured,
> And the sad augurs mock their own presage;
> Incertainties now crown themselves assured,
> And peace proclaims olives of endless age.
> Now with the drops of this most balmy time
> My love looks fresh, and death to me subscribes,
> Since spite of him I'll live in this poor rhyme,
> While he insults o'er dull and speechless tribes.
>   And thou in this shalt find thy monument,
>   When tyrants' crests and tombs of brass are spent.

The two moments of extrapolated prophecy—the one falsely dark and now exposed as wrong (lines 5 and 6), the other falsely light (7 and 8)—have been seen by scholars as referring, respectively, to the last years of Elizabeth's reign and to the opening year of James's reign.

Elizabeth's final years were dark in part because of her refusal to permit any discussion of her successor. Throughout James's letters to Elizabeth in the late 1590s, he asks her for some sign of assurance that he will be her successor. Not only does she refuse his request; she accuses him of planning her funeral.[97] While we have already gotten some glimpse of the distress this absence of a named successor caused James, the repercussions were felt upon the pulses of everyone in England. Elizabeth had passed a law in 1581—the Act Against Seditious Words and Rumours—

prohibiting anyone from discussing the subject: Article V speci-fied that it was a felony punishable by death for those who "not only wished her Majesty's death, but also by divers means prac-ticed and sought to know how long her Highness should live, and who should reign after her decease, and what changes and altera-tions should thereby happen."[98] This meant that English men and women had to live each day with acute uncertainty about what would happen when the throne was at last vacant: Would the successor come from Scotland, from England, from Spain? As James Shapiro observes, the 1599 threat of a *second* Spanish Ar-mada meant that anxiety about succession was compounded by the fear of external conquest.[99] Shakespeare's *Hamlet*—where there is both internal distress in court and an external army ap-proaching the country—would certainly address these fears when the play arrived in 1600.[100]

The intricate plot of *Hamlet* was many centuries old before Shakespeare wrote his version of it, so he had no need of contem-porary events to inspire its narrative design.[101] But certainly he would have recognized the analogy between the position of Ham-let and the position of James: both in the year 1600 were in their early thirties; both were less statesmen than scholars; both had a parent murdered by the person now on the throne (Hamlet's father killed by his brother Claudius; James's mother executed by her cousin Elizabeth); both had their own path to the throne opened up (by the death of the parent) and obstructed (by the vil-lain's occupation of the throne) by the same hand; both were connected to Denmark (Hamlet directly, as his homeland; James through his marriage to Princess Anne of Denmark).

Hamlet's indecision about whether to act was mirrored in James's indecision about whether to wait for the seemingly immor-tal queen to die or to act before that event. James's relations with Constable show that both men were deeply committed to peace; both men spoke out against violence—Constable, for example, in

A Discovery of a Counterfeit Conference wrote that succession rightfully belonged to James but that it must not be solved by bloodshed, a point restated many times. Nonetheless their correspondence shows occasional forays toward violence, as when Constable tells James that the princes on the Continent will all support him, or when he numbers the troops inside England who will rally to his cause. At such moments, with a phantom army standing behind him, one might wonder to see "so delicate and tender" a person as Henry Constable now "with divine ambition puff'd."[102] The aspiration for peace and the practice of military solutions were not, however, during that historical era mutually exclusive: Constable had, after all, while working for toleration, minority rights, and nonviolence in France, served as a soldier to bring about by military means Henry IV's ascension to the French throne; and even after his father's death in 1591, his young manhood was illuminated by the glow of Sir Robert Constable's knighthood (earned for military service in Scotland) and high position in the war office. That his own military service meant something to him is indicated by his wish to be granted the Cross of Malta, an order of knighthood that combined religious and military virtues, as well as an oath of chastity. The aspiration for chastity also surfaces in his "Spirituall Sonnettes" as well as in a letter from prison to his relative the Earl of Shrewsbury: "whether I remayn in prison, or go out, I have lerned to live alone wt god."[103]

When Elizabeth at last died in 1603, the succession was as straightforward and conflict-free as it had been predicted to be dire. Scholars read the moon in Sonnet 107 as Elizabeth, who has, by dying, endured—that is, undergone—her own eclipse; or alternatively, as England, which has endured—that is, survived—her eclipse during the death of Elizabeth, and emerged, not into the predicted chaos, but into light. A country ruled by an aging, angry, and stingy queen had suddenly become a country ruled by a young king whose twenty-eight-year-old queen was pregnant with their sixth child. "England was full of newness and potential . . . London growing like a hothouse plum," writes Adam Nicolson, who, in his account of the writing of the King James Bible, describes James's springtime entry into London on May 7 amidst gardens, meadows, and riverbanks full of flowers: in bloom were Persian black fritillaries (the sibling of *Fritillaria meleagris*); tulips from Turkey and Crete; globe flowers from Greece; pennywort, royal ferns, foxtail grass, meadow saxifrage; in the greenhouses, too, were the new shoots of melons, marigolds, endives, and lamb's lettuce.[104]

Art, like nature, was alive and flourishing. Already in that same month of May, Shakespeare's acting company had become the King's Men. By the following December, the poet Henry Constable was permitted to reenter the country; if his meeting with the king and queen was delayed, that, too, was the result of art—it was Queen Anne's all-consuming involvement in a masque that slightly delayed the royal welcoming of Constable to court; by January 9, Constable had met with the king and queen; on January 12, the king assembled at Hampton Court the first meeting of the biblical scholars who eventually created the King James Bible.[105] Attention to art did not mean inattention to international relations. James would soon dispel the black cloud of feared conquest that had hung over the country for the previous five years by beginning peace negotiations with Spain and completing them by August 1604. He was also beginning to sketch his plan for the unification of England and Scotland.

Needless to say (since Sonnet 107 says it), the widespread euphoria—the feeling of peace, aliveness, and a fresh start—was for Shakespeare greatly heightened by the daily presence in the country—in or out of prison—of his newly returned friend. His temptation to believe in his own immortality in the third quatrain is, first and foremost, a way of expressing how newly alive he now felt.

A Rival Date for the Composition of Sonnet 107

While the composition of Sonnet 107 is most often attributed to 1603–1604, the year 1588 is the second-most-favored candidate. It may well be that the poem was first composed in the earlier year and revised in the later. Like the year 1603, the year 1588 was filled first with dark panic, then with euphoria. Henry Constable was in England during most of this year.

The 133 ships of the Spanish Armada were famously arrayed in a crescent shape. The final line of Sonnet 107, "When tyrants' crests and tombs of brass are spent," is believed by many scholars to allude to this "crescent" or "crest" shape. The Armada did not set out from the coast of Spain until May 1588, but panic about its arrival in the English Channel was already in full sway by early March. Elizabeth's state papers bristle with daily preparation:

March 6: "The supply of great masts is a matter of much importance, and requires the utmost speed";

March 10: "The whole Navy to be ready to go out of the Thames by the 10th of March. Soldiers to be in readiness upon the coasts";

March 11: "The Spanish fleet reported to consist of 210 sail, carrying 36,000 soldiers, and to be ready to sail on the 20th. Fears Sir Fr. Drake will not be ready in time";

March 12: "The arrival of the Lord Admiral . . . A new shift of sails for the *Rainbow* . . . [He] is preparing twenty great anchors. Desires . . . the hastening of the four great ships";

March 18: "The Lord Treasurer to take order for the supply of cordage and canvas and providing the great masts";

March 20: "The names of the four great ships are,—the *Elizabeth Jonas*, the *Triumph*, the *Bear*, and the *Victory*";

March 27: "Three ships discovered off the coast near Yarmouth taking soundings";

March 30: Sir F. Drake needs "*500 musketts, and at least 'one thousand arrows for them*' ";

March ? "Defence of the city of London";

March ? ". . . defence of Portsmouth and completion of the works there";

March ? "An army to be sent into the North to act on the defensive against Scotland in case the forces of Flanders should land there."[106]

Woven throughout these state preparations is the name of Henry Constable's father, Sir Robert Constable: "their Lordships have at this present written unto Sir Robert Constable, Lieutenant of th'Ordinance, to send two thousand pikes and two thousand burgenettes . . ." for the Essex levy;[107] "Note of the powder and munition delivered out of Her Majesty's stores in the Tower, for which J. Powell and Sir Ro. Constable have received payment;"[108] "Lord Burghley . . . [r]ecommends that Sir Robert Constable . . . survey the Thames;"[109] "Note of powder . . . taken to the Tower by Sir Robert Constable, Lieutenant of the Ordnance."[110]

While Henry Constable and William Shakespeare may have had an especially acute awareness of these daily preparations through their connection to Henry's father, the experience of alarm was universal and affected ordinary people throughout England. In the state papers we hear the daily roll call of towns and counties where muster exercises are held—Somerset, Wiltshire, London boroughs, Huntingdon, Warwickshire—but it is in the towns and counties themselves, not in the state papers, that the training is taking place. So, too, it is men and women all over the country who are making and mending the sails, cordage, anchors, and timbers for the ships named in those state papers: *Dainty, Disdain, Revenge, Swallow, Swiftsure, Scout, Antelope, Violet,* and *Lily.* Some towns provided their own ships (as Lynn provided the *May-Flower* and Bristol provided *Great Unicorn, Minion,* and

Handmaid)[111] or the needed mariners (Southampton contributed 110). New work meant new rules: laws were passed in Bristol licensing carpenters to purchase more candles so they could continue working after dark.[112] Town residents fortified town walls; citizens of coastal towns provided lookouts along the beaches; inland, the dread was felt by men and women alike, as we know from the birth in Malmesbury of Thomas Hobbes, whose mother's terror of the Armada led to his premature arrival: "For Fame had rumour'd, that a Fleet at Sea, / Wou'd cause our Nations Catastrophe; / And hereupon it was my Mother Dear / Did bring forth Twins at once, both Me, and Fear."[113]

The March dread about the anticipated entry of the Spanish Armada into the English Channel was deepened by another event: on March 3, 1588, England experienced a total eclipse of the moon.[114] "The mortal moon hath her eclipse endured"—the fifth line of Sonnet 107—has the ring of a literal event. Astronomers in the early modern period differentiated not only between partial eclipses and total eclipses but also between total eclipses that were light and those that were dark—that is, between total eclipses where enough light remained to enable the viewer to recognize the moon's location in the sky, and total eclipses so profoundly dark that the moon's location could not be discerned. The astronomer Tycho Brahe, watching the March 3, 1588, eclipse in Denmark, placed it in the second category.[115] We know from NASA astronomical data that England, like Denmark, endured a profound eclipse. Tracts from the period remind their readers that a total eclipse is coming and is likely to be followed by dire accidents.[116]

But—as the second quatrain of Sonnet 107 reports—the dire prophecies soon had to be retracted: later in the summer the Spanish Armada was decisively defeated, so weakened that it could not backtrack to Spain through the English Channel but had to sail around the northern peninsula of Scotland and the west coast of

Ireland, where storms wrecked many more ships, finishing what English mariners had begun. Now the euphoria was as widespread as earlier the panic had been.

Had every town celebrated England's new freedom from fear on a single day, the euphoria might have lasted only a short time. But the celebration went rolling through England across a succession of weeks and months. A national Thanksgiving was held on August 20, 1588, at St. Paul's Cathedral; on August 26 a celebratory "review of the troops" took place; September 8 brought another Thanksgiving at St. Paul's after the Armada suffered the additional losses off the coast of Ireland; in later weeks the churches of Salisbury and Lincoln, at the instruction of the Privy Council, had sermons and prayers of Thanksgiving; in churches such as Hastings and Lewes, bells were rung and guns were fired on November 19; the city of Bristol held its Thanksgiving on November 24.[117] "Incertainties now crown themselves assured, / And peace proclaims olives of endless age."

Sonnet 107, then, may be a palimpsest of the two different dates, first written in 1588, rewritten in 1604. Certainly the second quatrain—with its moon in eclipse and its announcement of panic followed by peace[118]—seems to have a compelling home in the earlier year.[119] But if one had to take a single period of composition, the greater weight falls on 1603–1604. The second quatrain is almost as descriptive of this later year as the earlier year; and the first quatrain, third quatrain, and final couplet fit the later year with greater precision. Shakespeare's friend suffered a "confin'd doom" in 1604, which neither of the two friends, as far as we know, suffered in 1588. Stylistically Sonnet 107 has struck scholars as different from the other sonnets, which reinforces the idea that it was written, or rewritten, at a different period: its lexicon "is extremely ornate and Latinate," according to Helen Vendler;[120] Stephen Booth notes that several critics have nominated it the single "most difficult of the sonnets" (whether because of the complex syntax, overly compressed history, or some other feature).[121] Booth himself observes that its odd combination of emphatic historical allusion and stubborn opacity reenacts the quality of "prophecy" that is the sonnet's subject.

The sheer euphoria of aliveness in the third quatrain seems motivated not just by public events—the rolling cascades of Thanksgivings in 1588 or the streams of flowers in 1603–1604—but by something intensely personal such as the return of a friend from whom the poet had been long separated.

Shakespeare picks up the liquid sound of the public euphoria at the end of the second quatrain—*lay, liv, less*—

And peace proclaims olives of endless age

—allowing the fresh and wet world of restored aliveness to spill like a fountain into the third quatrain—*lah, loo, ile, li*—

My love looks fresh . . .
. . . I'll live . . .

—with the beautiful sonic rhyme (noticed by Stephen Booth) of "olive" and "I'll live," identical sounds that may both be inspired by Shakespeare's neighborhood of St. Olave's. By the final line of the quatrain we have only *l*'s like the youthful sounds of a newborn: *ile, ull, ull, le*:

While he insults o'er dull and speechless tribes.

Because the dead have neither voice nor vivacity, they are "dull and speechless tribes," but the stream of *l*'s works to cradle and defend them. Here again are lines 8 through 12 (the last line of the second quatrain, followed by the immortality quatrain):

And peace proclaims olives of endless age.
Now with the drops of this most balmy time
My love looks fresh, and death to me subscribes,
Since spite of him I'll live in this poor rhyme,
While he insults o'er dull and speechless tribes.

Why, given the prominence of the *l* sound in the lines leading up to the couplet, does Shakespeare, once he moves to the couplet, deprive the final line of its *l*? This concluding couplet is one—like those we encountered throughout chapter 1—that seems to say, "Look at these lines and you will see the name of my beloved"—

And thou *in this* shalt find thy monument,
When tyrants' crests and tombs of brass are spent.

And indeed the final line "doth almost say [his] name": h-e-n-r-y-c-o-n-s-t-a-b-e, withholding only the *l*. Perhaps the *l* sound was so present from the earlier lines, where it recurs sixteen times, that Shakespeare mistakenly thought he had included it; or perhaps the "crest" of the final line—like the plume on a helmet—was intended to serve as a visual looped *l*; or perhaps—revising in 1603–1604—he decided that the spelling of the name was an act of love play precious to their early years and could not in good faith be recorded here, though it could be summoned to memory. The incomplete spelling when it might have been so easy to complete is again an argument for the later of the two dates. That later date is also suggested by the word "shalt" rather than the prayer-like "shall" (line 11); here again Shakespeare resists enlisting (hence, desecrating) a practice from their youth that was almost holy.

Constable lived in England from late 1603 to 1610—as a private person in the first four and a half years and as a prisoner for the next two and a half. Almost nothing is known about his actions at this time other than those already cited: that he applied for and received a certificate of his descent from the College of Arms in 1606; that he may have received a copy of Shakespeare's sonnets in 1609 while in Fleet Prison; that he wrote a poem on heraldry for a 1610 publication. To these facts biographers add that he served as a reference for a young relative seeking to enter the College of Rome in 1607—a seemingly small detail but one that will return with surprising force.

Because we know Shakespeare's precise whereabouts on specific days during this period, it is tempting to wonder about the likelihood or unlikelihood of Constable's presence at those same events. For example, the Catholic Queen Anne and the Catholic Southhampton arranged for a performance of *Love's Labour's Lost* at Southhampton's house in January 1605, a performance at which Shakespeare was of course present.[122] Since Constable knew all three, and since the play is about Henry of Navarre and the founding of a male-only college, one must wonder if he was present. But even if we had a positive answer to this question, this would give us just one day out of two thousand. The fact that we know he was in England in the first decade of the new century but have very little documentation of what he was doing has one positive implication: just as the absence of detail in this decade does not mean he was himself absent, the absence of documentation in the 1590s does not mean he was himself wholly absent during that earlier decade.

On July 31, 1610, Henry Constable was formally banished from England. His biographer Joan Grundy suggests—optimistically but unconvincingly—that rather than banishment, the royal sentence might be construed as a pass enabling him to get out of Fleet prison and leave England:

A passe for Henrie Constable to depart out of his ma^ties dominions, and not to returne without speciall directions and warrant in that behalf and to take with him one man and 100li in mony &c and that he dept wthin x dayes after the date hereof.[123]

Where Constable went on the Continent is unknown. Some of those who had earlier welcomed and financially supported him were no longer alive. Henry IV's sister, Catherine, had died in March 1604, a few months after Henry Constable returned to England. Henry IV himself was assassinated on May 14, 1610, a few months before Constable's banishment and return to France. Constable left London in early August; one biographer surmises that he eventually resided at the College of Arras in Paris, an institute set up both for priests and for polemicists in 1611.[124]

Once Constable was living in France we know only three pieces of information.

First, a false report of his death—November 27, 1611—circulated in France.[125] Unknown is whether Constable himself or, more likely, a third person initiated the false report. His death and return to life summon to mind Shakespeare's *Winter's Tale*, first performed in 1611 (perhaps the two had conversed about staged deaths before Constable left England), as they also summon to mind the staged deaths in *Romeo and Juliet* and *Much Ado About Nothing*.

Second, on September 4, 1612, he along with Ben Jonson listened to a theological debate between a French Catholic bishop and an English Calvinist chaplain about Christ's bodily presence after the resurrection. The debate took place in Paris at the home of an Englishman.[126] Published twenty years later, the opening section identifies the presence of "Ben: Jonson" and "Henrie Constable" but says that only the disputants were to speak, the others not to "entermeddle."[127] Because Constable and Jonson did not "entermeddle," their names do not reappear in the report of the debate which follows.

Third, Henry Constable died in the autumn of 1613, an event to which we turn below.

The Deaths of Henry Constable and William Shakespeare: Two Mysteries and One Solution

There is a mystery at the end of Constable's life and there is a mystery at the end of Shakespeare's life. We will end by proposing that maybe the two are really a single mystery—with a single solution. This proposal may be just wishful thinking. For a few pages, however, let's indulge the wish. The two mysteries are factual, as are the details brought forward on behalf of the solution.

The mystery at the end of Shakespeare's life is widely known and uncontested; so it is here that we should begin. Shakespeare always lived frugally in London: as far as we know, he only rented a room. In 1597, he bought for himself and his family in Stratford the second most expensive house in the town: the three-story-high New Place had five gables, ten fireplaces, more than ten rooms, two barns, two orchards, and a garden that (once supplemented with a later purchase) was three-quarters of an acre and contained an additional cottage. Successful in making money, he lavished it not on himself, in urban isolation, but on his family and his home ground, which became renowned for its vines and trees.[128] So far, there is no mystery.

The mystery begins with his much later real estate purchase. He bought a residence in Blackfriars in London: astonishingly, he lavished more money even than he had on the ample Stratford residence. He did not buy it so that he could live there; he had already retired and returned to Stratford.[129] He bought it so that a man named John Robinson could live there. While this person was only renting it, Shakespeare's will—which bequeaths the London residence to his daughter Susanna—actually identifies the dwelling by, or with, the present renter, John Robinson, as though establishing his right of occupancy into the unrestricted future. Bequeathing to Susanna the New Place house as well as "my barns, stables, orchards, gardens, lands, tenements . . . within the towns, hamlets, villages, fields, and grounds, of Stratford-upon-Avon, Shopton, and Welcombe . . . ," the will continues, "and also all that messuage or tenement with the appurtenances, wherein one John Robinson dwelleth, situate, lying and being in the Blackfriars in London, near the Wardrobe . . ."

Other than New Place ("wherein I now dwell") and the home of his sister ("wherein she dwelleth"), no piece of property is designated by its resident. The properties being willed are assumed to endure for some generations—passing (as the will explicitly states) from Susanna to her children, and from there to other descendants; so it would be odd to describe any of those properties by a temporary resident. But that is exactly what Shakespeare has done with Blackfriars Gatehouse, perhaps suggesting that he did not intend that designation to be understood as a "temporary" feature.[130] Susanna seems not so much owner as steward of the residence.

Recent scholarship on Shakespeare's possible or probable Catholicism often links this residence—and therefore also John Robinson—to the Catholic underground: the Blackfriars residence had doors and passageways leading to the Thames River that permitted secret entry into and out of London. There is also evidence that it was a location where Catholic Church services were held. In 1623, seven years after the death of Shakespeare, during a Catholic service the third floor of one of the buildings collapsed under the weight of the three hundred worshippers gathered there, killing approximately ninety people.[131] Quite apart from such services, the Catholic Church encouraged Catholics—as well as those sympathetic to the plight of Catholics—to purchase formerly monastic property, even though it might seem they would be personally benefiting from the dissolution of the monasteries. Their reasoning was that should England be restored to the

Catholic faith, Catholic owners of monastic property could then return it to the Church.[132] By purchasing such property, they were, in effect, holding it on behalf of the Church.

The oddity of this purchase and designation of a permanent renter is compounded by the fact that when Shakespeare was sick and on the threshold of death, John Robinson was with him in Stratford. John Robinson signed the will; he was one of five people—the only person from London—to do so. His signature was not needed; only three were required (as biographers note). Because no legal necessity required him to be there, it seems reasonable to assume that it was the press of friendship that had brought him there. John Robinson's name, then, occurs twice in the will, once as signatory, once as the man who dwells in Blackfriars Gatehouse.[133]

The mystery at the end of Shakespeare's life is not whether he bought the expensive London residence (this is certain) or whether he arranged for John Robinson's ongoing dwelling there, or whether John Robinson was in Stratford at, or close to, the time of Shakespeare's death (again, certain). But simply: Who was John Robinson?

And now, the mystery at the end of Henry Constable's life.

Once banished, Constable went to live in Paris. In late September or early October 1613, he went to Liège to meet with Benjamin Carier, who had served as one of James's court chaplains until he had undergone a conversion to Catholicism. Upon discovering his own Catholicism, Carier fled to the Continent. James pursued him, sending an emissary with a letter demanding his immediate return. Rather than comply with the king's orders, Carier instead wrote a reply—addressed to the king but also published both in England and in Flanders, where it circulated widely—explaining why he would by no means return: laws written under Elizabeth and confirmed by James would license the state to execute him and, worse, to say he was killed not for his "Catholic Religion, but for Felony and Treason."[134]

The treatise was published in December 1613, and has elements of Constable's argumentative style in it. Conceivably, it was to assist him in the writing of this reply that Constable went to Carier's Jesuit refuge in Liège. In fact, nine years earlier, while Constable was still in London, he had written to the nuncio in France that James had two chaplains, one of whom was on the verge of conversion.[135] If this letter refers to Carier (who was indeed James's chaplain by that year), it seems reasonable to surmise that Constable may have assisted him in his conversion, as well as in the later writing of his published letter to James.[136]

According to all modern biographical accounts, Constable died in Liège on or about October 9, 1613, roughly ten days after arriving at Carier's residence and two months before Carier's tract was published. But there is reason to wonder whether this death report is true. Constable's death does not seem to have been anywhere reported at the time it is said to have occurred. Nothing is heard about Henry Constable's death for two years. When Carier published his treatise and sent it to James, he did not mention the death of this famous poet and courtier, even though he would be acutely aware of their long and complex association. His silence seems remarkable—unless, of course, Constable had not actually died, in which case it would be prudent to circulate the information only orally and let someone else commit it to writing.

Who, then, did report his death? Two years later, George Hakewill—the chaplain to James's son Prince Henry—wrote a rebuttal to Carier's treatise, assuring King James that he, Hakewill, would not have stooped to refute the "foule" and "malicious" treatise had it been restricted to James's eyes. But since it has been widely distributed, read, and admired, it must be rebutted. In his dedicatory epistle to the king, he mentions—with satisfaction and in a subordinate clause—that Henry Constable had traveled to Liège to confer with Carier and died "a fortnight" later.[137] (We also learn in the same sentence that Carier himself died the following summer in Paris—both deaths, as far as Hakewill is concerned, a confirmation of Carier's "vaine project.") Henry Constable's only death certificate, then, seems to be this cruelly dismissive announcement, though the sentence ends by acknowledging that "the speach of dead men commonly proves more effectuall, more profitable, or more dangerous than that of the living."

So Henry Constable, whose every move sometimes seems to have been tracked by religious and state leaders for several decades, and whose poetry continued to be widely known, and whose putatively dangerous acts a short time earlier had earned him imprisonment in and banishment from England, dies without being mourned—almost without being mentioned. He exits from the world in a twenty-one-word subordinate clause in an eighty-four-word sentence.

It is tempting to suppose that Henry Constable did not die, that he went to Liège, where many fewer people than in Paris would notice him (or would notice his sudden vacating of the city should he leave), that from there he slipped back into England, that no one formally committed his supposed death to writing but allowed it to retain the status of oral rumor until two years later, when Hakewill obligingly reported it as a stark fact, after which its truth seems never to have been questioned (even when its oddity was noted).[138] If the 1616 report of his 1613 death was knowingly or unknowingly false, it would be the second time: a false report of Henry Constable's death had circulated in 1611, and may well mark an earlier attempt to go back to England.

We earlier saw that the habit of acquiring aliases was robustly practiced by Catholics, that in Jesuit records for the period (which are more thorough than those of the other Catholic orders), the number of aliases is so high that index pages sometimes contain twenty to thirty instances on a single page. When one sees the swarms of aliases on such pages, a question naturally arises. How did people in the Catholic underground remember all the false and true names? Did they need to remember only the false name or did they need to remember both names? The fact that the indexes in the *Records of the English Province of the Society of Jesus* so carefully stipulate both true and false names suggests that one had to keep track of the yoked pair.

Like any memory system, there were paths to assist this work. One shortcut seems to have been that people with the same surname were sometimes given the same alias: for example, Michael Jenison, Thomas Jenison (a priest), and Thomas Jenison (a student) all have the alias surname "Gray"; Francis Salkeld and John Salkeld both have the alias surname "Anderton"; Edward Thimelby, Henry Thimelby, Richard Thimelby, and William Thimelby all have the alias "Ashby"; Robert Thwing and Thomas Thwing both have the alias surname "Palmer." In some cases this continuity of aliases reflects family ties: Edward and George Wakeman are brothers and both have the alias surname "Gifford"; Henry and William Warren, brothers, share the alias "Pelham"; members of the Poulton family are all called "Brookes"; the Fazakerly family are called "Ashton"; the Harcourt family, "Lane."[139]

But the biological connection is not necessary: the number of same surnames with same aliases that are not family appear to outnumber those that are family. An alias used for a family member will also be used for a non–family member if he has the same last name: Edward Scarisbrick, James Scarisbrick, and Henry Scarisbrick all have the alias surname "Neville," but only the first two are related. Conversely, a family member was in some instances given a surname different from the one assigned to his siblings.

None of the Constables—even the *Henry* Constable—listed in the index of this same Society of Jesus volume is our Henry Constable: the persons named here traveled from England to the

Continent at just about the time our banished hero traveled to France, but they are the next generation, just beginning their Catholic studies at St. Omer and the English College in Rome.[140] But because of the continuity of alias surnames across true surnames, their designated aliases deserve our attention. Here is the index entry:

Constable, Henry, Esq.
   Henry, *alias* Robinson (priest) and Robert, *alias* Salvin, Fr. S. J. and William, *alias* Robinson, (student) and their parents 260, 268, 275.[141]

"Robinson" is not the only surname given to a Constable in the index; but that it occurs at all—and multiple times—is important. The two youths with the Robinson alias were, in fact, closely related to our Henry Constable: their grandfather, Marmaduke Constable, was the uncle of our Henry Constable, the brother of Henry's father, Robert.[142] A fuller account of "Constable, Henry, alias Robinson" is given in a recent study—*The Seminary Priests*—that compiles Catholic records from many sources from the late 1590s and early 1600s.[143]

If a fellow Catholic crossed paths with another Catholic, and if he were expected to remember both names, it is not hard to imagine that a scrambling could occur, a potential confusion not only of false and true names, but of first and last names. William Constable, alias William Robinson, could easily become Robin Williamson or Robin Constable. If this hypothetical seems needlessly complicated, consider the following actual historical instance included in the *Records of the English Province of the Society of Jesus*: a man with the name Edward Robinson who has the alias "Edward Rodney" is traveling to England with a Henry Constable who has the alias "Henry Robinson."[144] A third person crossing their path might have a difficult time addressing them correctly.

Something like this may explain the odd event in 1593 when a Catholic imprisoned in England sought to lessen his sentence by giving information to English officials about other recusants on the Continent. Although he claimed to know our Henry Constable well—to have spoken with him "diverse times"—he misremembers his name, possibly shuffling *alias* and *vere*, and *first* and *last* as well. Here is the English official's report sent to Robert Cecil (a powerful minister and eventually secretary of state in Elizabeth's court):

> The 8 day after supper we had some talk and he demanded of me if I did know one Robin Constable, son to Sir Robert Constable. And I told him I did not know him. Why, quoth he, he was a while here up and down in the Court, and, quoth he, I have divers times talked with him and he was the rankest heretic that you should talk withal. But I will tell you, quoth he, what is become of him. He went into France with my lord of Essex and when he came there he got him to the other side and became a good Catholic. Therefore, quoth he, a man may see God can call one in the middle of his mischief.[145]

It seems likely that any alias Henry Constable used during the 1590s would be the same alias he would use after 1613. Since "Robin" was then (as it is today) the diminutive of "Robert," the often repeated identification of Henry as "Sir Robert's son" could also explain the appropriateness of originally choosing the alias "Robinson." Though Robin is only one of hundreds of names in Shakespeare's plays, it is a privileged one.[146] Most relevant is the final line of Ophelia's beautiful song: mourning the death of her father and spring violets, she delivers, out of nowhere, a piercing non sequitur, "For bonny sweet Robin is all my joy."

In looking at the mystery connected with Shakespeare's death, we already saw that the Blackfriars purchase is cited by scholars as evidence (along with many details from his immediate and his extended family) that Shakespeare may have been Catholic or, in the spirit of toleration, may have assisted the Catholic underground, if only by providing a place to meet. If, instead, we were to learn that Shakespeare purchased Blackfriars to assist his friend Henry Constable, that account would in no way undercut the other account, since Constable was certainly at the center of the Catholic underground.[147]

The location of Blackfriars Gatehouse is identified (from Shakespeare's will forward) as near the "Wardrobe," where "Wardrobe" means not theatrical dressing room but royal storage. It was a neighborhood that one scholar calls "excellent" and another "pricey."

Blackfriars would have been as utopian an abode for Henry Constable as the orchards and gardens of New Place were for Shakespeare's wife and children. First, as a former monastic abbey, its architectural tone would have been as close to the French Catholic colleges as would be available in London. Second, it was a free space: when the Dominican monastery was dissolved in 1538, it was designated a liberty zone independent of the city authorities, and therefore hospitable to foreigners and immigrants.[148] Third, it housed at least one associate of Henry Constable, Ben Jonson, with whom (as we saw earlier) he spent an evening in Paris.[149] Fourth, it was part of the Catholic underground.[150] And fifth, it was part of the ambassadorial world. The Blackfriars house where the third floor collapsed—which was part of the same constellation of buildings as the Gatehouse—housed the French ambassador to England (who was not himself harmed that October evening, because he was out visiting the Venetian ambassador). His occupancy is confirmed by multiple sources, including a contemporary book called *The Doleful Even-Song* that describes the church gathering in great detail, and a contemporary letter written a week after the collapse.[151] So, too, state papers for earlier years—the 1590s and opening decades of the 1600s—record the dwelling in Blackfriars of the English agent to France, as well as many members of Parliament.[152] Nothing we know about Henry Constable would make it strange to find him living in close proximity to the ambassador of France or ambassadors from other foreign countries. The very first time he turns up in state papers is 1583, when, after participating as a very young man in an embassy to Scotland, he is then spoken about admiringly by Francis Walsingham, Elizabeth's secretary of state, in a letter recommending him to the English ambassador in Paris.[153] Throughout the history of his time in France, Italy, and Scotland, as the foregoing pages have chronicled, he is an official or unofficial emissary, courtier, or courier, living in the company of ambassadors, clerics, and kings from Catholic countries.

Our story, then, has two possible endings. In one (the most likely), Constable, banished, leaves England in 1610 and dies in 1613; in the interim, Shakespeare does not see him again; in fact, it may be that months or even years pass before Shakespeare learns that his friend is dead. In the other ending, Constable undergoes an illness and false death, and returns to England in October 1613 to a London dwelling Shakespeare had already purchased for him by the previous March and had made a second payment on by September 29, discharging that part of the balance that enabled him to take possession. (The "due date" or possession date of September 29 had been stipulated in the original purchase contract; September 29 is also either the exact day or nearly the exact day that Constable is believed to have arrived in Liège, thus inviting the possibility that the two participated in a coordinated plan.) As Shakespeare serves and protects him, enabling him to continue his work on behalf of Catholics, Constable cares for Shakespeare; he is present and possibly nurses him during his final illness. Shakespeare scholars sometimes surmise that John Robinson was Shakespeare's servant[154] and nurse.[155] Constable, despite his aristocratic lineage, would have welcomed these appellations.

This second story seems almost too good to be true. But its being almost too good to be true does not mean that it isn't true. These are two people who undertook many difficult projects in their lives and produced many wonders. This would be just one more.

To die is to join the "dull and speechless tribe" over whom Death presides. The first version of the story is certainly that, with Henry Constable's death not even mentioned for two years; no gravestone (as far as we know) marking his grave; and an eventual eulogy at Westminster Abbey that contained inaccurate dates and locations, announcing his having lived at Lyon for twelve years and itself appearing in a volume for events that occurred twenty years earlier, 1586–94. This error-ridden sequence marks the path along which a person sleepwalks forward to join the dull and speechless tribe.

But the other story is not wholly free of this silencing. One of the reasons humans want graves with names on them is because the name is like a kite over the grave announcing that the person lying there was once someone who spoke: though the person cannot say much, he at least, for a time, can keep saying his own name. (In very rare cases, the gravestone might even perform an additional speech act: naturally, Shakespeare's gravestone provides a powerful instance.) If a harsh political climate requires one to mime one's own death, to forfeit one's name, to take an alias, to countenance slips, erasures, and shuffled alternatives, the alien, even in the safest of safe houses, has already stepped onto the path toward death.

Shakespeare's contemporary Edmund Spenser wrote a beauti-

ful quatrain about the ease with which the name of a beloved can
be erased:

> One day I wrote her name upon the strand,
> But came the waves and washèd it away:
> Again I wrote it with a second hand,
> But came the tide and made my pains his prey . . . [156]

Shakespeare gives even more powerful voice to this dread in Sonnet 64, where the hungry ocean erases the shore, and the shore in
turn distresses the waters in a lethal exchange that demonstrates
the disintegration of all things into rot and ruin:

> When I have seen the hungry ocean gain
> Advantage on the kingdom of the shore,
> And the firm soil win of the watery main,
> Increasing store with loss, and loss with store;
> When I have seen such interchange of state,
> Or state itself confounded to decay,
> Ruin hath taught me thus to ruminate,
> That time will come and take my love away.
> > This thought is as a death, which cannot choose
> > But weep to have that which it fears to lose.

The blurred and beautiful modulation of "ruin" into "ruminate"
seems the mumbling that takes place on death's highway. Not fury
but the "crackeing" of the heart is what Shakespeare suffers when
he contemplates the ruin Time will bring to his beloved and to
their love. The very modesty of the verbs—"gain advantage,"
"win," "increasing," "confounded"—magnifies the sense of sin-
ister cruelty, a cruelty that requires no fanfare or curtain call or
ornamented imperatives but only its own relentless operation
through the largest of agents, ocean and land. As the power of

Shakespeare's opponent is expressed through understated actions, the acuity of his pain is expressed in the poem's almost
unbearable metrical control.

But despite the dread of Sonnet 64, the achievement of the
sonnet sequence as a whole is precisely the opposite of what that
one sonnet so fears. Reading the sonnets is like walking along a
shoreline; whatever the scale of the breakers coming in, by the
time they approach us they have become row upon row (usually
fourteen) of etched white crests, trim and luminous lineations;
and the one that breaks at our feet leaves two words in the sand,
Henry Constable. We walk further and turn to watch: Henry
Constable. Again we walk and watch: Henry Constable.

Naming his name, Shakespeare enables us to hear Constable's
voice—his ingenious metaphors, his reverence for his beloved, his
recognition of his friend's much greater poetic genius, his silence
when his friend steals from him, his ability to reason his friend
out of his stormy denunciations, his physical desire, his trueness.
England's sweet nightingale. And hearing Constable's voice in
turn enables us to hear Shakespeare's voice more clearly, not a
soliloquizer talking to himself, not a lover speaking to a mute
beloved (incapable of returning a single sentence), but a poet in
conversation, speaking and listening, writing and writing back.
Have there ever been two people who liked listening to each other
more or who listened more closely, modifying an iamb into a tro-
chee, a marigold into marjoram, a postboy into a constable; or
who steered each other through more nuances of passion, scold-
ings, feints, apologies; or who derived more acute delight from the
youthful practice of saying, spelling, praying, shouting each other's
name: "Forgive mee, Deere, for thundring on thy name"?

We have already encountered in these pages six poems in which
Constable speaks of his friend's effect on him as a lightning strike.
Here is a seventh, in which, after the bolt has struck, the delight
in one another's voice survives. This final poem is the poem with

which every printed edition and every surviving manuscript opens:

> Resolved to love, unworthy to obtain,
> I do no favor crave but humble wise
> To thee my sighs in verse I sacrifice;
> Only some pity and no help to gain.
>
> Hear then, and as my heart shall aye remain
> A patient object to thy lightning eyes,
> A patient ear bring thou to thundring cries;
> Fear not the cracke, when I the blow sustain.
>
> So as thine eye bred my ambitious thought,
> So shall thine ear make proud my voice for joy:
> Lo, Dear, what wonders great by thee are wrought
> When I but little favors do enjoy.
>> The voice is made the ear for to rejoice
>> And your ear giveth pleasure to my voice.[157]

The love of talking and talking back was their present. This, too, is their afterward.

NOTES

Introduction

1. Henry Constable, "Carmen xv," lines 5–10, "Adumbratum de Anglico Henrici Conestabilis," in Jani Dousae Filii, *Poemata*, ed. Gulielmo Rabo, J.U.D. (Rotterdam: Adrianum van Dijk, 1704), p. 158. Janus Dousa the Younger's book of poems was first published in the Netherlands in 1591. It contained fifteen poems by Constable, five translated into Dutch, ten into Latin. I am grateful to the classicist Richard Thomas for his kind and expert help in translating into English "Carmen xv," as well as several other Latin poems. My translations sometimes diverge from a literal transcription and all errors are my own.

2. Constable, "Carmen xx," in Dousa, *Poemata*, p. 161. Richard Thomas points out that in the Latin, this four-line poem is in elegiac couplets, a form often used by Ovid, where a line of dactylic hexameter is followed by a line of dactylic pentameter:

> *Narcissum tepedi mitto, lux, munere Veris,*
> *Junctaque narcisso carmina nostra tibi:*
> *Ut mihi pro libro reddas humentia labra,*
> *Proque meo florem des mihi flore tuum.*

A literal transcription reads: "I send, Light, this narcissus to you by the gift of warm spring, and I send our poems joined to the narcissus. I do this so that in return for the book (*libro*) you may give back to me moistened lips (*labra*), and in return for my flower you may give your flower to me."

I follow other scholars in assuming Constable wrote the poems in English and Dousa translated them into Latin (just as Dousa almost certainly provided the Dutch translations). See J. A. van Dorsten, *Poets, Patrons, and Professors: Sir Philip Sidney, Daniel Rogers, and the Leiden Humanists* (Leiden: Leiden University Press, 1962), p. 83. It is certainly possible, however, that Constable himself composed the poems in Latin: at St. John's College, Cambridge, he would have written as often in Latin as in English. Nor is there any question that Shakespeare would have been able to read the poems in Latin. In her study of sixteenth-century schoolchildren, Jean Vanes says students in the lower schools learned grammar while reading Aesop and Cato; in upper school their Latin and Greek readings included, among others, "Terence, Virgil, Martial, Plautus, Lucian, Horace, Cicero, Plato, Homer, Aristotle, and Aristophanes" (*Education and Apprenticeship in Sixteenth-Century Bristol* [Bristol, U.K.: Bristol Historical Association, University of Bristol, 1982], p. 11). The Shakespeare biographer Samuel Schoenbaum enumerates a similar list of Latin authors—adding Ovid, Erasmus, and modern Latin poets—whose writings were used to teach the children both reading and speaking Latin (*William Shakespeare: A Compact Documentary Life* [New York: Oxford University Press, 1987], pp. 67–70).

3. Joan Grundy, ed., "Introduction," *The Poems of Henry Constable* (Liverpool: Liverpool University Press, 1960), pp. 34, 64, 65. See also William Carew Hazlitt, "Biographical Notice," in *Diana: The Sonnets and Other Poems of Henry Constable, now first collected and edited, with some account of the author, by William Carew Hazlitt, to which are added a few notes and illustrations by the late Thomas Park* (London: Basil Montagu Pickering, 1859), pp. xv, xvi, xvii.

4. Grundy, "Introduction," *The Poems of Henry Constable*, pp. 26, 36, 40. In his earlier biographical study, George Wickes also records the correspondence observing the respect and affection three monarchs gave to Constable (*Henry Constable: Poet and Courtier, 1562–1613*, in *Biographical Studies 1534–1829*, vol. 2, no. 4 [Bognor Regis, U.K.: Arundel Press, 1954], pp. 276, 279, 283, 285, 286).

5. Samuel Schoenbaum writes, "From 1585 . . . until 1592, . . . the documentary record presents a virtual blank. This is the interval that scholarship has designated the Lost Years" (*Shakespeare: A Compact Documentary Life*, p. 95). Katherine Duncan-Jones dedicates a section of her biography—*Shakespeare: An Ungentle Life*—to what she, too, labels "The Lost Years": "we should not be at all surprised that the earliest part of Shakespeare's adult life is 'lost' from the documentary record" (London: Methuen Drama, 2001). Some writers widen the time span: Joseph Pearce in *The Quest for Shakespeare* says that with the exception of the record of Shakespeare's marriage in 1582 and the birth of his three children in 1583 and 1585, the "impenetrable fog of the so-called lost years" extends from 1579 to 1592 ([San Francisco: Ignatius Press,

2008], pp. 63, 64, 88). Shakespeare's marriage and fatherhood are, on the other hand, large-scale pieces of information.

6. George Wickes writes that "for almost three years [1585 through 1588] we have no news of Henry Constable," and when he next appears it is only for us to learn that he attended a funeral (*Henry Constable: Poet and Courtier*, p. 274). Joan Grundy writes, "his movements after [1585] are a tantalizing succession of 'fallings from us, vanishings'" ("Introduction," *The Poems of Henry Constable*, p. 23). While the record of the 1580s is sparse, we have many more glimpses of Constable during this decade than of Shakespeare because he was a subject of interest to various aristocrats, churchmen, and statesmen whose correspondence has been preserved: for example, he was apprenticed to an ambassadorial mission to Scotland in 1583; he traveled to Paris in 1584 and to Heidelberg in the early spring of 1585; he may have been in Poland in 1586; he is said to be a favorite of the queen in 1587. All three of his twentieth-century biographers—Louise Imogen Guiney writing in 1939, George Wickes in 1954, and Joan Grundy in 1960—provide thoughtful records of these events. The glimpses are, however, just that: unelaborated glimpses.

7. Constable entered St. John's College, Cambridge, in 1578. If he began college at what Joan Grundy designates the usual age of fourteen, his birth year would be the same as Shakespeare's, 1564. Some students entered college as early as twelve, which would make his birth year 1566. Some nineteenth-century scholars assigned Constable the birth year of 1566, perhaps based on the university entrance date: for example, George Ellis, *Specimens of Early English Metrical Romance*, vol. 1 (London: Longman, Hurst, 1803), p. xii; and Oliver Louis Jenkins, *The Students' Handbook of British and American Literature* (Baltimore: John Murphy, 1891), p. 144.

Biographical sketches in the twentieth century follow one another in assigning Constable a birth year of 1562, but most note the absence of documentation. That birth date has no basis other than a herald's visitation in 1575 when the child was designated "thirteen." Did heralds when recording children's ages aspire to precision or approximation? The possible inaccuracy of the report may be surmised by recalling how far off estimates of children's ages are even when made by close family friends or next-door neighbors.

The birth date of 1562 would mean Constable entered Cambridge at the age of sixteen. The biographer Joan Grundy regards this age as surprisingly late, especially for someone intellectually precocious ("Introduction," *The Poems of Henry Constable*, p. 21). The admissions records for Gonville and Caius Colleges, however, suggest that the age of sixteen would be usual. Those records show students entering in 1578 and 1579 who were as young as twelve (especially if they were aristocratic children educated at home) but many more who are fifteen, sixteen, seventeen, eighteen, or older (*Admissions to Gonville and Caius College in the University of Cambridge, March 1558–9 to Jan. 1678–9*, ed. J. Venn and S. C. Venn [London: C. J. Clay and Sons, 1887], p. 43). No similar age records for St. John's during this era are available.

1. Spellbound

1. The modern English of the sonnets is almost always consistent in Stephen Booth's *Shakespeare's Sonnets* (New Haven, CT: Yale University Press, 1977), in Katherine Duncan-Jones's *Shakespeare's Sonnets* (London: Arden Shakespeare, 1997/2007), and in Helen Vendler's *The Art of Shakespeare's Sonnets* (Cambridge, MA: Harvard University Press, 1997). The punctuation, in contrast, varies across editions. I have chosen the punctuation that in any given line seems best.

   In any line where I show Henry Constable's name, the fourteen letters also occur in the spelling of the original 1609 Quarto *Sonnets*, which can be found reprinted in both the Booth and the Vendler editions. I use the original Renaissance English for Henry Constable because no modern English edition exists, and some time may pass before widespread agreement is reached about the modern language for his poems as well as for the rival poet's poems in chapter 5.

2. Joel Fineman in his *Perjured Eye* calls the relation between the two poems "a particularly close parallel" (*Shakespeare's Perjured Eye: The Invention of Poetic Subjectivity in the Sonnets* [Berkeley: University of California Press, 1986], p. 318). Joan Grundy singles out for special notice the pairs of lines I cite, and she observes that since some of the Constable poems that Shakespeare echoes were not published in *Diana*, we can conclude that Shakespeare saw Constable's poems in manuscript (Joan Grundy, ed., "Introduction," *The Poems of Henry Constable* [Liverpool: Liverpool University Press, 1960], pp. 62, 230).

3. Constable, "To his Mistrisse upon occasion of a Petrarch he gave her, shewing her the reason why the Italian Commenters dissent so much in the exposition thereof. Sonet 4," in Grundy, ed., *The Poems of Henry Constable*, p. 133.

4. Henry Constable, "Forgive mee Deere, for thundring on thy name," lines 1–8 and 14, "The sixth Decad. Sonnet. VI," in Grundy, ed., *The Poems of Henry Constable*, p. 206.

5. Constable, "If ever sorrow spoke from soule that loves," "The fifth Decad. Sonnet. III," in Grundy, ed., *The Poems of Henry Constable*, p. 198. Here, as in "Forgive mee Deere, for thundring on thy name," Constable describes the felt experience of being possessed by a person or spirit outside of himself who speaks through him. In this poem it is a feminine presence, "Sorrow," who produces "sigh-swolne words" and "whirlwinds in my brest." In the last six lines he refers to a "she" who is ambiguously Sorrow or the beloved who abstains from providing springs to "help quench my burning hart." Though almost all of the Constable poems cited in *Naming Thy Name* use a male pronoun, or a neutral pronoun, for the beloved, a small number use the feminine. Constable's mixing of male and female genders—for example, his reference to the Judeo-Christian god as a "mistress"—is addressed in chapters 2 and 4.

6. Constable's mother, Christiana Dabridgecourt, came from the town of Astley near Nuneaton, both in Warwickshire. Biographies and biographical sketches usually surmise that Henry Constable grew up in the town of Newark in Yorkshire on a property Christiana inherited when her first husband died. Even if most of his childhood took place in Yorkshire, family visits to Langdon Hall in Warwickshire, and to related family properties in other Warwickshire towns, no doubt took place. In the 1560s, Henry Constable's father, Robert Consta-

ble, was a defendant in a law case in Nuneaton, Warwickshire, and another in Eaton, Warwickshire, both cases involving the leasing of meadowlands (*Fisher v Constable*, 15 June 1562, Chancery Division, Chancery and Supreme Court of Judicature, National Archives, C 78/22/12; and *Forde v Constable*, 14 October 1562, Chancery Division, Chancery and Supreme Court of Judicature, National Archives, C 78/22/16). If Henry Constable's birth or baptism took place in this geography, it is probably not recoverable, since the surviving birth records for Nuneaton begin only in 1577 and those for Astley in 1670 (Parish Records, County Record Office, Warwickshire County Council).

7. William Wordsworth, "There Was a Boy," in *Wordsworth: Poetical Works*, ed. Thomas Hutchinson and Ernest de Selincourt (London: Oxford University Press, 1967), p. 145. The passage is also part of Wordsworth, *The Prelude*, bk. 5, ll. 364–79, p. 525.

8. Constable, "Deere to my soule, then leave me not forsaken," "The fifth Decad. Sonnet. VIII," in Grundy, ed., *The Poems of Henry Constable*, p. 201.

9. My estimate of two accidental occurrences in every hundred lines is based on a hand count of the number of times the fourteen letters of Henry Constable's name turn up in two sixteenth-century sonnet sequences where we can be confident the authors had no intention of inscribing his name: Philip Sidney's *Astrophel and Stella* and Edmund Spenser's *Amoretti*. Sidney's sequence contains 102 pentameter sonnets (it also contains 6 hexameter sonnets, whose lines contain many more letters and hence many more accidental names). In the 102 pentameter sonnets, the name can be found in 34 of the 1,428 lines, which is a rate of 2.3 percent. The rate is only slightly higher—2.5 percent—in Spenser's *Amoretti*, where the name can be found in 31 of the 1,232 lines across the 88 sonnets.

Both Sidney and Spenser sometimes direct our attention to the letters in a poem, as when Sidney in the "Second Song" in *Astrophel and Stella* writes, "Who will read, must first learne spelling," or in the "Seventh Song" cries, "O let them see these heavenly beames, and in faire letters reede," or in the "Eighth Song" writes, "I should blush when thou are naměd." Sonnet 100 includes lines that self-consciously refer to words or vocalized sounds, and these lines twice spell the name "Penelope Rich" (often said by scholars to be the Stella of the poem):

O honied sighs! which from that breast do rise,
Whose pants do make unspilling creame to flow,

. . . .

O plaints! conserv'd in such a sugred phrase,
That Eloquence it selfe envies your praise . . .

The lines are not as self-conscious about their cargo as Shakespeare's lines, and hence the inclusion of the twelve letters in Penelope Rich's name may well be fortuitous.

Spenser wrote *Amoretti* for the woman who became his wife, Elizabeth Boyle. His Sonnet 74—which opens, "Most happy letters!"—says that the three most beneficent women in his life (his mother, his queen, and his beloved) all have the name "Elizabeth." Then the very next poem, Sonnet 75, is about the way time erases the name of the beloved whenever he writes it in the sand, and so he will instead write it in the heaven of verse. The sonnet's eighth line contains the name "Eliza," the ninth line the name "Elizabeth," the tenth line the name "Boyle," and the eleventh line the name "Eliza." No single line manages to spell the full first and last name. This omission reminds us that spelling a name in a pentameter line that simultaneously alerts its reader to the presence of the name is a difficult feat—as Spenser laments in Sonnet 82. There he tells his beloved that her name should be immortalized, but isn't, because heaven, which has endowed her with abundant gifts, has not given equal gifts to her partner. Had heaven done so, the result would be "Some hevenly wit, whose verse could have enchased / Your glorious name in golden moniment."

10. Giles E. Dawson, "A Seventh Signature for Shakespeare," *Shakespeare Quarterly* 43, no. 1 (Spring 1992): 72–79. Ian Wilson observes that Shakespeare's father's name is spelled seventeen different ways in town records, but usually appears as "Shakspere." Wilson, *Shakespeare: The Evidence* (New York: St. Martin's, 1993), p. 135.

11. Only if the line is so awkward that nothing could have motivated its invention other than the attempt to spell the name can one be certain the spelling is intentional. There is in Constable's poems at least one accidental instance of the full name, "William Shakespeare," and a high number of lines if one begins to permit just the first or last name. An accidental occurrence in Shakespeare's sonnets seems, by comparison, easily distinguishable from the intentional instances where the line itself insists that we scrutinize it for the friend's name.

   The rate of accidental occurrences in Shakespeare's sonnets is 38 in 2,155 lines, or 1.76 percent, which is close to the 2 percent rate in the sonnet sequences of Sidney and Spenser (see note 9 above). Shakespeare's second rule (that the line not only contain all fourteen letters but also explicitly instruct the reader to look at the line) creates a bright division between deliberate and inadvertent spellings. In a few cases, however, lines counted as accidental might be considered to fall in a gray zone. For example, Sonnet 11 urges the beloved to "print" multiple "cop[ies]" of himself, and the sonnet has three lines that spell out the beloved's name.

12. Were the word "and" spelled out in this line, the name "Constable" would also be in the line. The ampersand may have been introduced by the printer, or it may have been placed there by Constable himself precisely to avoid including his own name.

13. Constable, "The fifth Decad. Sonnet. IIII," in Grundy, ed., *The Poems of Henry Constable*, p. 199.

14. Henry Constable, "Four Sonnets Written by Henrie Constable to Sir Phillip Sidneys Soule," in *An Apologie for Poetrie, Written by the right noble, virtuous, and learned, Sir Phillip Sidney, Knight* (London: Henry Olney, 1595), pp. 1, 2.

15. Constable, "To Mr. Hilliard upon Occasion of a Picture He Made of My Ladie Rich," in Grundy, ed., *The Poems of Henry Constable*, p. 158. Attention to Constable's poem by Hilliard scholars began with Roy Strong's 1959 article "Queen Elizabeth, the Earl of Essex and Nicholas Hilliard," *Burlington Magazine* 101, no. 673 (April 1959): pp. 145–49. The poem reappears in many other articles about Hilliard.

16. Gretel H. Schueller and Sheila K. Schueller, *Animal Migration* (New York: Chelsea House, 2009), p. 17.

17. Angela Turner, *The Barn Swallow* (London: Bloomsbury, 2010), p. 177.

18. Printings of "England's Sweete Nightingale" in various biographical sketches of Henry Constable all share the same wording except for the word "excite," which is sometimes "encite" or "incite." But they vary in punctuation. Here I follow for the most part the punctuation used both in the *Harleian Miscellany* and again in the "Biographical Notice" of William Carew Hazlitt's 1859 edition of Constable's poems—*Diana: the Sonnets and Other Poems of Henry Constable*. The poem was attached to the Todd manuscript of Constable's poems, as noted by Constable's biographers: Hazlitt, "Biographical Notice," in *Diana* (London: Basil Montagu Pickering, 1859), p. vii; again Joan Grundy, "Introduction," *The Poems of Henry Constable*, p. 34; George Wickes, *Henry Constable: Poet and Courtier, 1562–1613*, in *Biographical Studies 1534–1829*, vol. 2, no. 4 (Bognor Regis, U.K.: Arundel Press, 1954), p. 277; and Louise Imogen Guiney, *Recusant Poets* (New York: Sheed & Ward, 1939), p. 305. Grundy, Wickes, and Guiney each provide fact-laden accounts of Henry Constable (often the same facts), and the three will here be cited many times.

19. Act, scene, and line numbers for Shakespeare's plays here and throughout refer to *The Norton Shakespeare: Based on the Oxford Edition*, eds. Stephen Greenblatt, Walter Cohen, Jean E. Howard, and Katharine Eisaman Maus (New York: W. W. Norton, 1997). Although for any play line numbers vary from one edition to another, a quoted line can usually be found in any edition within approximately ten numbers of the one cited here.

20. The phrase "ten to one" occurs, for example, in the description of the ratio of soldiers on two sides in war, as when in *Henry VI, Part III*, act I, scene ii, York says: "Many a battle have I won in France, / When as the enemy hath been ten to one," and again in scene iv, when Northumberland says, "It is war's prize to take all vantages, / And ten to one is no impeach of valour."

    Sonnets 6 and 37 each use a 10:1 multiplier, though not in the context of a bet. Stephen Booth points out, in his discussion of Sonnet 6, that 10:1 was the highest legally permissible interest rate (*Shakespeare's Sonnets*, p. 142). Shakespeare's attention to multiplication in Sonnet 6 was, of course, biological, not financial, and in Sonnet 37, existential, not financial. The construction—whether as wager, battle odds, genealogical growth, or spiritual elevation—recurs throughout the early writings and does not seem to recur in the later writings. It does appear in the epilogue of the 1613 play *Henry VIII*, where it is used to describe the play itself—"'Tis ten to one this play can never please / All that are here. Some come to take their ease, / And sleep an act or two"—but that is a play for which Shakespeare may have had a coauthor.

21. Goran Stanivukovic, "Shakespeare's Style in the 1590s," in *The Oxford Handbook of Shakespeare's Poetry*, ed. Jonathan F. S. Post (Oxford: Oxford University Press, 2013), pp. 28, 34, 36, 37, 38.

2. The Birthplace of Shakespeare's Sonnets

1. In the nineteenth and early twentieth centuries, scholars also believed Shakespeare's *Venus and Adonis* was indebted to Constable's "The Shepherd's Song

of Venus and Adonis" (published later but believed to have been written earlier). Scholars now believe "The Shepherd's Song" was written by a different poet with the same initials, Henry Chettle. They may well be right, though no thorough study of the poem's authorship appears to have been undertaken.

2. Constable, "The thyrd 7 of severall occasions and accidents happening in the life tyme of his love; Of His Mistrisse upon Occasion of Her Walking in a Garden. Sonet I," in *The Poems of Henry Constable*, ed. Joan Grundy (Liverpool: Liverpool University Press, 1960), p. 130.

3. Grundy, "Commentary on Text," *The Poems of Henry Constable*, p. 228. See also her discussion of Sonnet 99 in the "Introduction" (pp. 61, 62), where she enumerates how many details Shakespeare here borrows from Constable. Though Grundy gives fullest attention to Sonnet 99 (a place where many scholars hear Constable's voice behind Shakespeare's), she also notes an array of other Shakespeare sonnets that she or other scholars believe echo Constable: Sonnets 26, 31, 46, 47, 106, and 128.

   Grundy carefully stipulates that her point is not to argue that Constable influenced Shakespeare, but to show that Constable was "read and appreciated by the greatest of Elizabethan poets" (p. 62). She also identifies echoes of Constable in many other poets of the period: Samuel Daniel, Michael Drayton, Barnabe Barnes, Richard Barnfield, Bartholomew Griffin, and William Alexander (pp. 60–64).

4. Grundy, "Introduction," *The Poems of Henry Constable*, pp. 64, 65; and William Carew Hazlitt, "Biographical Notice," in *Diana: The Sonnets and Other Poems of Henry Constable* (London: Basil Montagu Pickering, 1859), pp. xv, xvi.

5. Katherine Duncan-Jones also sees the "knotted marjoram" as alluding to curls in *Shakespeare's Sonnets* (London: Arden Shakespeare, 2007), p. 322.

6. If the lines of Constable's sonnet are rearranged to follow the sequence in Shakespeare's Sonnet 99, the parallels can be seen at a glance:

The *violet* of *purple* coloure came	The forward *violet* thus did I chide;
Dy'd with the bloud she made my heart to shed	"Sweet **thief**, whence didst thus **steal** thy *sweet that smells*
In briefe all flowers from her theyre virtue take	If not from my love's *breath*? The *purple* pride
From her sweet *breath* theyre *sweet smells* doe proceed,	Which on thy soft cheek for complexion dwells
	In my love's veins thou hast too grossly *dy'd*."
The *lilies* leaves for envy pale became	The *lily* I condemned for thy *hand*.
And her *white hands* in them this envy bred	
	And buds of marjoram had **stol'n** thy hair:
The marygold abroad the leaves did spread	
Because the suns and her power is the same	The *roses* fearfully on thorns did stand
	One *blushing shame*, another white despair;
My Ladies presence makes the *roses red*	A third, nor *red* nor white, had **stol'n** of both,
Because to see her lips they *blush for shame*	And to his **robb'ry** had annex'd thy breath;

The living heate which her eybeames doe make	But for this **theft**, in pride of all his growth
	A vengeful canker eat him up to death
Warmeth the ground and quickneth the seede	
The rayne wherewith she watereth these *flowers*	More *flowers* I noted, yet I none could see,
Falls from myne eyes which she dissolves in shewers	But sweet or *colour* it had **stolen** from thee.

7. Edmund Bolton, *Hypercritica*, cited widely; for example, in Thomas Humphry Ward, *The English Poets: Chaucer to Donne* (London: Macmillan, 1893), p. 381; and Grundy, "Introduction," *The Poems of Henry Constable*, p. 65.

8. Grundy, "Commentary on Text," in *The Poems of Henry Constable*, pp. 219, 221, 244, 245. For additional poets, see note 3 above.

9. Constable, "To his Mistrisse," in Grundy, ed., *The Poems of Henry Constable*, p. 113. Grundy believes this poem may have influenced Shakespeare's Sonnet 31, as does Kenneth Muir in his *Shakespeare's Sonnets* (New York: Routledge, 2013), p. 3.

10. This manuscript—called the Todd manuscript—prefaces many of the poems containing no female pronouns with titles emphatically and defensively specifying a "mistress" or a "lady." On the gender confusion introduced by the incorporation of these titles into modern editions of Constable's poems, see pages 105–107 as well as chapter 6, note 26.

11. Constable, "Carmen 15," lines 19–20, "Adumbratum de Anglico Henrici Conestabilis," in Jani Dousae Filii, *Poemata*, ed. Gulielmo Rabo, J.U.D. (Rotterdam: Adrianum van Dijk, 1704), p. 158. These are the final lines of the poem encountered at the opening of this book.

12. Constable, "To the Queene touching the cruell effects of her perfections. Sonet 2," in Grundy, ed., *The Poems of Henry Constable*, p. 138.

13. For two instances, see letter XXVIII, Elizabeth to James, May 15, 1588, in *Letters of Queen Elizabeth and King James VI of Scotland*, ed. John Bruce (London: Camden Society, 1849), pp. 48, 49.

14. Letter from Henry Constable to Countess of Shrewsbury, cited in Sister Mary Melora Mauritz, "A Study of the Spiritual Sonnets of Henry Constable" (Ph.D. diss., Loyola University, Chicago, 1953), p. 25, drawing on Hazlitt, appendix to *Diana*, p. 79. Hazlitt surmises that the undated letter was written from the Continent in the 1590s.

   Constable's poems to God, the Son, the Holy Spirit, and the Eucharist contain fervent images of male lovemaking, as Sister Mary Mauritz's analysis of these powerful poems registers. In "To God the Holy-Ghost," the Holy Ghost is addressed and defined as "the Love / With which God, and his sonne ech other kysse." In his poem "To God the Father," Father and Son love each other "with passion of lyke kynde, / (as lovers syghes, which meete, become one wynde)." At the close of the sonnet, the speaker asks that God "engrave" his mind with wisdom and that the Son "sence [scent] my hart" ("impregnate with odour; perfume," as Sister Mary writes) with the "syghes of holy Love, / that yt the temple of the Spright may prove." Describing the Eucharist, he writes, "I whyte & liquide see" (Sister Mary Mauritz, pp. 55, 61, 76; and for the poems, see Grundy, ed., *The Poems of Henry Constable*, pp. 183–85).

15. Constable, "To St Mary Magdalen," in Grundy, ed., *The Poems of Henry Constable*, p. 191. The beautiful lines continue:

> . . . but lyke a Magdalen, beere
> for oyntment boxe, a breast with oyle of grace:
> And so the zeale, which then shall burne in mee,
> may make my hart, lyke to a lampe appere
> and in my spouses pallace gyve me place.

16. Constable, "To St Mary Magdalen," in Grundy, ed., *The Poems of Henry Constable*, p. 192.

17. Constable, "To St Margarett," in Grundy, ed., *The Poems of Henry Constable*, pp. 188–89.

18. Constable, "Fayre Grace of Graces, Muse of Muses all," "The seaventh Decad. Sonnet. II," in Grundy, ed., *The Poems of Henry Constable*, pp. 209–10.

19. A more detailed account of this period is given later in the book, in "An Afterword About Afterward."

20. The hourglass figure formed by the parentheses has also been observed by René Graziani, Katherine Duncan-Jones, and the authors of the Oxquarry Books website. John Lennard perceives the parentheses as "little moons," suggestive of waxing and waning, as well as the "empty grave into which the corpse of the *lovely Boy* must sooner or later fall" (cited in Duncan-Jones, *Shakespeare's Sonnets*, p. 366). Helen Vendler sees inside the parentheses the effigy of the youth (*The Art of Shakespeare's Sonnets* [Cambridge, MA: Harvard University Press, 1997], p. 538).

21. Stephen Booth notes that "fickle" and "sickle" would look identical because of the printing of the *s* as a long *f*-like letter (Booth, *Shakespeare's Sonnets* [New Haven, CT: Yale University Press, 1977], p. 427). Helen Vendler observes the "exceptionally dense interphonetic relations" among all the words in the sonnet; almost every word has a phonetic "partner" (Vendler, *The Art of Shakespeare's Sonnets*, p. 535).

22. The definition of "wrack" as "seaweed," which first occurs in 1510, is given by both the *Merriam-Webster* and the *Oxford English* dictionaries.

23. René Graziani (citing Alvan Bregman), "The Numbering of Shakespeare's Sonnets 12, 60, and 126," *Shakespeare Quarterly* 35, no. 1 (1984): p. 81. The single other use Graziani cites is one by the poet Michael Drayton in 1619. The *Oxford English Dictionary* notes that some ancient authors specified various ages as the climacteric year, among them the age of sixty-three; the earliest modern instance cited in the *OED* is 1634, considerably later than Constable's, Shakespeare's, and Drayton's uses. Graziani notes, as I do, the transfer of the sands from the top glass to the augmented youth below in the body of the sonnet (p. 81). In Katherine Duncan-Jones's commentary on Shakespeare's own Sonnet 63, she writes, "It is surely not by chance that this sonnet on the severe

changes brought about by the ageing process is positioned as number 63, the 'grand climacteric,' . . . a figure associated with major life changes" (*Shakespeare's Sonnets*, p. 236).

24. Constable, in Grundy, ed., *The Poems of Henry Constable*, p. 179. Graziani points out that Constable did not include the note in the 1592 or 1594 editions of *Diana*. Grundy specifies that it occurs in the Todd manuscript, the most complete manuscript of Constable's poems and one that Grundy judges had to be collected and arranged by Constable himself. Grundy believes Constable put this manuscript together sometime between late November 1590 and early autumn of 1591 before going into exile (Grundy, "Introduction," p. 84).

25. This image is identical to, but more legible than, the ornaments in the 1592 and 1594 editions of Constable's *Diana* (which have suffered with the passage of time in surviving copies). It is taken from the Bodleian Library at Oxford's copy of Lancelot Andrewes's *The wonderfull combate (for Gods glorie and mans saluation) betweene Christ and Satan Opened in seuen most excellent, learned and zealous sermons, vpon the temptations of Christ, in the wilderness, &c. Seene and allowed* (London: Richard Smith, 1592).

26. A male figure leading a female up out of a cave appears on the title page of both the 1535 and the 1538 editions of the *Goodlye Prymer in Englysshe*. Along the left-hand vertical margin runs the inscription "Tyme reveleth all thinges." No hourglass or sickle resides there. Editions of Petrarch's *The Triumphs* sometimes contained related images; but it would require some luck to happen upon an illustration that contained a sickle and hourglass simultaneously. Among twenty-six sets of fourteenth-, fifteenth-, and sixteenth-century Italian and French illustrations for Petrarch's *The Triumphs*, there seems to be only one illustration—a sixteenth-century French illustration of "The Triumph of Time"—that has all the elements of the Richard Smith seal: a satyr figure, a woman, an hourglass, and a sickle. Among all the other sets, the "Triumph of Time" episode often has an hourglass (but no sickle) and the "Triumph of Death" episode often has a scythe (but no hourglass). These twenty-six sets can be seen at Wikimedia Commons: https://commons.wikimedia.org/wiki/Petrarch%27s_triumphs. For people in eras unassisted by the Internet, the conjunction of elements seemed infrequent enough that Thomas Percy, researching ancient ballads, surmised that it must have been Richard Smith's seal that provided the source for Rubens's *Le Temps découvre la Vérité* (*Reliques of Ancient English Poetry*, ed. J. V. Prichard [London: George Bell and Sons, 1876], p. 345). Since, however, Rubens's winged Truth carries neither hourglass nor scythe, the *Goodlye Prymer* would be as good a source as Smith's seal. See Samuel L. Macey's *Patriarchs of Time: Dualism in Saturn-Cronus, Father Time, the Watchmaker God, and Father Christmas* (Athens: University of Georgia Press, 1987), pp. 48, 53, for images from the *Goodlye Prymer*, a fifteenth-century Italian illustration of the "Triumph of Time," and related images from later centuries.

27. Joan Grundy surmises that since Constable was out of the country, a friend may have helped see the poems through the publication process, though she believes Constable himself must have prepared the manuscript for publication before leaving ("Introduction," *The Poems of Henry Constable*, pp. 93, 94).

It is of course possible that the friend who assisted in publication was Shakespeare.

28. Vendler, *The Art of Shakespeare's Sonnets*, p. 649, noting that "the triviality of expression" makes the two poems seem "odd envoys."

29. Needless to say, to extend this claim to eros causes trouble for the marriage of true minds, or almost any marriage.

30. According to Joan Grundy, an entry for the book appears in the Stationers' Register in 1598, though no surviving book from this year verifies that the printing actually took place ("Introduction," *The Poems of Henry Constable*, p. 98).

31. Sonnets 150 and 151 suggest that the mistress's misdeeds strengthen, rather than diminish, her erotic power. If it seems perverse that the young man has reawakened the poet to the abiding attractiveness of his female beloved, there is nonetheless a logic to it: after long acquaintance, Shakespeare might have forgotten that his female beloved still exercised authority over her own body and the power of consent toward him. The only time in the sonnets that a full sentence of speech by a beloved enters a poem—thus giving the beloved full agency—is when, in Sonnet 145, Shakespeare quotes the mistress-wife, who has said, "I hate not you."

32. Constable, "The sixth Decad. Sonnet. III," in Grundy, ed., *The Poems of Henry Constable*, p. 204.

33. Constable, "The sixth Decad. Sonnet. V," in Grundy, ed., *The Poems of Henry Constable*, p. 205.

34. Perhaps because he had a famous father, Constable was often referred to as "young Constable," not only in 1589, when he was in his twenties, but in 1599, when he was in his mid-thirties and when the adjective is used in a more elaborate description: "a busie yong man al scotishe" (George Wickes, *Henry Constable: Poet and Courtier, 1562–1613*, in *Biographical Studies 1534–1829*, vol. 2, no. 4 [Bognor Regis, U.K.: Arundel Press, 1954], pp. 274, 283; and Grundy, "Introduction," *The Poems of Henry Constable*, p. 15, quoting U.K. National Archives, Public Records Office, S.P. 14 [*State Papers Flanders*], vol. VI, p. 12). By 1599, however, Robert Constable would already have been dead for eight years, so this explanation for the constant use of the adjective is insufficient. It seems more likely that Henry Constable had a youthful or highly animated countenance.

35. Ovid, *Metamorphoses*, book III, ll. 167ff, Loeb Classical ed., trans. Frank Justus Miller, rev. C. P. Goold (Cambridge, MA: Harvard University Press), pp. 136–37. English object names, such as Rain-Drop, can be found in the Perseus Digital Library, Tufts University: www.perseus.tufts.edu/hopper/text?doc=Perseus:text:1999.02.0074:book=3:card=138; as well as the *Theoi Greek Mythology* website at www.theoi.com/Nymphe/NymphaiArtemisiai.html.

36. Malcolm Gladwell, *Outliers: The Story of Success* (New York: Little, Brown, 2008), pp. 35–68.

37. Constable, "The seaventh Decad. Sonnet. VIII," in Grundy, ed., *The Poems of Henry Constable*, p. 214.

38. Grundy, "Introduction," *The Poems of Henry Constable*, p. 26, quoting U.K. National Archives, Public Records Office 31 (*Roman Transcripts*), vol. IX, bundle 3, p. 221. Grundy notes, "The writer is Atilio Amalteo, secretary of the Apostolic Delegate to France, addressing Cardinal Aldobrandino, May, 1597."

3. A Day to Regret

1. In Sonnet 145 the phrase "hate away" (line 13) is widely recognized as "Hathaway." Synonyms for "hath away" also occur in Sonnet 130 ("hath a far" in line 10), Sonnet 133 ("Me from myself thy cruel eye hath taken," line 5), and Sonnet 147 ("Hath left," line 7).

2. Thomas Hobbes, *On the Citizen*, trans. and ed. Richard Tuck and Michael Silverthorne (Cambridge: Cambridge University Press, 1998), p. 86; and Hobbes, *Leviathan*, ed. C. B. Macpherson (London: Penguin, 1968), pp. 382–83.

3. Joan Grundy writes, "The dating of the manuscript as 1588 makes it the earliest source of Constable's sonnets that we have" ("Introduction," *The Poems of Henry Constable* [Liverpool: Liverpool University Press, 1960], p. 86).

4. Constable, "The last 7 of the end and death of his love. Sonet 5," in Grundy, ed., *The Poems of Henry Constable*, p. 175.

5. Earlier version of Constable, "Myne eye with all ye deadly sins is fraught," cited in Grundy, ed., *The Poems of Henry Constable*, pp. 175–76n14.

6. This failure to serve as watchman over himself is also registered in another sonnet, which opens: "My reason absent did myne eyes require / To watch and ward and such foes to descrie / As neare my heart they should approaching spy / But traytoure eyes my hearts death did conspire" (Constable, "The last 7 of the end and death of his love. Sonet 3," in Grundy, ed., *The Poems of Henry Constable*, p. 173).

7. An example of the instability in descriptions of hair color is provided by the multiple paintings of Henry Wriothesley, Earl of Southampton: one depicts him with long light blond hair and very light blue eyes (the Hilliard miniature of 1594, painted when he was twenty-one, now in the Fitzwilliam Museum), another with long black-brown hair and dark eyes (the painting by John de Critz when Southampton was about seventeen; a second painting done in 1603 by this same painter again has dark brownish-red hair that is slightly lighter than the earlier portrait); another has brown hair that contains black, red, and gold highlights (a full-length portrait completed in 1600 when he was twenty-seven). Portraits of Penelope Rich from the period similarly show painters' varying perceptions of hair color: Hilliard's miniature gives her luminous blond hair; another miniature by Hilliard shows her hair light brown; a portrait at Lambeth Palace shows it as light red; and a portrait believed to depict Penelope Rich and her sister shows her hair as brown.

8. Constable, "Of the thoughtes he nourished by night when he was retired to bed. Sonet 7," in Grundy, ed., *The Poems of Henry Constable*, p. 136.

9. Almost equally beautiful are Shakespeare's Sonnets 28 and 43, though these are written during periods when the two friends are separated both by night and by day (as would take place, for example, when Henry Constable was out of the country). Sonnet 61 is also an extraordinary account of nightly torment: "Is it thy will thy image should keep open / My heavy eyelids to the weary night?" The final line—"From me far off, with others all too near"—expresses not only the pain of separation but the fear that another person at the moment may be with the beloved; alternatively, it may be the person Shakespeare himself at that moment lies next to who seems "too near."

10. Constable, "The seaventh Decad. Sonnet. IIII," in Grundy, ed., *The Poems of Henry Constable*, p. 211.

11. Constable, "The last 7 of the end and death of his love. Sonet 1," in Grundy, ed., *The Poems of Henry Constable*, p. 171.

12. In *The Two Gentlemen of Verona*, Valentine suddenly offers all his share in Sylvia to Proteus in act V, scene iv, lines 86–87. The play just as quickly drops the event as though it had not taken place. For a fascinating account of this "astonishing line" and the volatile critical response to it, see Marjorie Garber, *Shakespeare After All* (New York: Anchor Books, 2004), pp. 50–53.

13. G. Wilson Knight, *The Crown of Life: Essays in Interpretation of Shakespeare's Final Plays* [1947] (London and New York: Routledge, 2002), p. 17.

14. Philip Fisher has made me aware of these puzzling (because wholly unwarranted) denunciations in Shakespeare.

15. Constable, "The fifth Decad. Sonnet. II," in Grundy, ed., *The Poems of Henry Constable*, p. 198.

16. Constable, "The first 7 of severall complaynts of misfortune in love onlye. Sonet 6," in Grundy, ed., *The Poems of Henry Constable*, p. 164. Punctuation throughout and italics in second quatrain added.

17. Oxquarry Books' website calls attention to the importance of the word "impediments" in the Marriage Service of the Book of Common Prayer, and of Shakespeare's three uses of the term in conversations about marriage in *Much Ado About Nothing*. In his eloquent meditation on the sonnets in his recent book, *Ideas of Order: A Close Reading of Shakespeare's Sonnets*, Neil L. Rudenstine also describes the relation between Shakespeare and the beloved as a marriage or "a metaphorical 'marriage'" ([New York: Farrar, Straus and Giroux, 2014], p. 27).

18. Or worse: Katherine Duncan-Jones reports that literary scholars often see the couplet as "bombast" and she herself reluctantly concedes it has the needless "swagger" of Pistol—needless because Shakespeare has already written 115 sonnets (*Shakespeare's Sonnets* [London: Arden Shakespeare, 2007], p. 343). But as I argue here, the "evidence" of writing can serve as evidence only if the writing is available to view—that is, if the sonnets have been published. The act of publishing them—bringing them and their account of male marriage into the public space—is a valiant act, full of potential consequence, and hence meriting the portentous announcement of the couplet.

19. The poem translated into Latin is the love sonnet "Blame not my hearte for flying up so high." The two poems appearing in Dutch are Constable's "Thyne eye the glasse where I behold my hearte" and "Promethius, for stealing living fire" (Constable in Jani Dousae Filii, *Poemata*, ed. Gulielmo Rabo, J.U.D. [Rotterdam: Adrianum van Dijk, 1704], pp. 156, 163, 164). The recognition of the second Dutch poem was made by J. A. van Dorsten. Dorsten points out that the 1591 Latin poem appeared in its English version only in 1592, when the first edition of Constable's *Diana* was published. Janus Dousa the Younger must therefore have had the poem in manuscript, though not necessarily (as Dorsten notes) from Constable himself (*Poets, Patrons, and Professors: Sir Philip Sidney, Daniel Rogers, and the Leiden Humanists* [Leiden: Leiden University Press, 1962], pp. 83, 88, 89).

20. "Adumbrate" and "foreshadow" came into the world together: according to *The Merriam-Webster's Collegiate Dictionary*, eleventh edition (online), the first known use of "foreshadow" was 1577 and "adumbrate," 1581. Dousa would have been sensitive to the root word in "adumbration," since he uses the word *"umbra"* constantly throughout his poems and entitled one poem "Proso-popoeia Umbrae."

21. This imprint of the Cupid image is identical to, but more legible than, the one that appears on the title page of *Shakespeare's Sonnets*. It is taken from the British Museum copy of Jean François Le Petit's *The Low-Country common wealth contayninge an exact description of the eight united Provinces*, trans. from the French by Ed. Grimeston (London: George Eld, 1609). See note 23 below.

22. The mythological figures in Sonnets 53, 55, 98, and 102—Adonis, Helen, Mars, Saturn, and Philomela—all contribute to the fabric of the sonnets; but unlike Sonnets 153 and 154, the poems are not centrally "about" them.

23. George Eld's many different ornaments across twenty years of printing include five different genres of Cupid ornaments, two of which occur much more frequently than the one we find in Shakespeare: in one, two Cupids turn away from one another and aim arrows at serpents; in the other, a single Cupid presides over the design. Prior to 1609, the ornament that provides the gateway into Shakespeare's sonnets seems seldom to have been used. It does appear in the 1604 printing of William Alexander's *The Monarchicke Tragedies*; in this same book we also find the ornament that occurs on the first page (as opposed to the title page) of Shakespeare's sonnets. In 1609, the image appears not only in Shakespeare's sonnets but also in a book about the Netherlands; in 1610 it graced the dedication page of St. Augustine's *City of God*.

 Shakespeare's elegant integration of the ornament into the sonnet sequence seems unusual. As the occurrence of the ornament in Augustine's *City of God* suggests, printers' ornaments were not necessarily intended to reflect the specific substance or tone of the book to which they served as gateway. The third volume of Raphael Holinshed's *Chronicles*, for example, shows two horned and hoofed satyrs sitting meditatively back to back on either side of a ram's head whose headdress—whether horn or vine—swirls out to the edges in an Ovidean riot of prancing horses, delighted snails, curious rabbits, and flower blossoms that spin upside down and right side up.

 If such ornaments have any consistent meaning, it is that graphemes—letters and scrolls—can at any moment break into three-dimensional creatures. In the Holinshed ornament, for example, the scrolls—or vines or extended rams' horns—are roomy enough in their interior for horses to break out of them into the open. The materialization of speech is the key theme here in Holinshed: the central ram's head has some substance emanating from its mouth that continues in, and is hence the source for, the overall design. In the more sober ornament on the page to the reader, tongues of twin snakes, tongues of twin greyhounds, and the tongue of the towering bear-like figure at the center seem a special concern.

 Likewise, in the facing Cupids gracing the entryway to Shakespeare's sonnets, the two dolphin-dogs whose manes the Cupids grasp for steerage have some event proceeding out of their mouths; and the three open-mouthed fishes at the bottom center may be the source from which the design as a whole emanates. "Who can say?" the ornament seems to say; "Who can say what will happen?" Reader, anything might happen, for you are about to enter a book.

4. Brief Names, Beloved Names: Hal, Hyella, Hen

1. The phrase "phonetic jewel" is Seamus Heaney's.
2. For example, the opening line of Sonnet 18; the opening and closing lines of Sonnet 63; the opening line of Sonnet 2.
3. The word "shalt" occurs once in a dark lady sonnet (Sonnet 142), but sonically "shalt" is closer to the word "shout" than to the word "Hal." "Shalt" also occurs in Sonnet 146, the poem addressed to Shakespeare's soul rather than to the beloved man or to his mistress-wife.
4. Constable, "Carmen xix," "Adumbratum de Anglico Henrici Conestabilis," in Janii Dousae Filii, *Poemata*, ed. Gulielmo Rabo, J.U.D. (Rotterdam: Adrianum van Dijk, 1704), p. 160. The Latin reads:

   Cum te lux video, videor mihi cuncta videre,
   Etsi aliud nostri nil videant oculi;
   At tua si quando facies mihi, Hyella, negatur,
   Aspiciam quamvis omnia, cerno nihil.

   Richard Thomas provides the literal translation: "When, my Light, I see you, I seem to myself to see everything, even if our eyes see nothing else. But whenever your face is denied to me, Hyella, although I look on everything, I discern nothing."
5. Here the Latin, *"demeritura,"* is—in order to agree with the feminine ending in "Hyella"—a future feminine participle (indicating Hyella is destined to be deserving). If therefore one were to use a pronoun instead of "the fair one" in the previous line, one might have to say "she." In other Hyella poems, the pronoun or adjective is given in the masculine. The gender complications introduced by the Hyella poems are addressed at the end of the Hyella section.
6. Constable, "Carmen xiii," "Adumbratum de Anglico Henrici Conestabilis," in Dousa, *Poemata*, p. 157. My thanks once again to Richard Thomas.
7. It may be more accurate to say Constable devotes four lines to the forest image: the woodland springs up in line 5, grows luxuriant branches in line 6, and then comes to be filled with wildflowers and streams in lines 7 and 8.
8. Constable, "Carmen xviii," "Adumbratum de Anglico Henrici Conestabilis," in Dousa, *Poemata*, p. 160.
9. See the article on "Hermes" at "Myth Index: Greek," www.mythindex.com /greek-mythology/H/Hermes.html.
10. Francesco Flamini, *A History of Italian Literature, 1265–1907*, trans. Evangeline M. O'Connor, introd. William Michael Rossetti (New York: National Alumni, 1907), p. 154.
11. Andrea Navagero, "Lusus XXI: On Cupid and Hyella," trans. I. D. McFarlane, in *Renaissance Latin Poetry* (Manchester, U.K.: Manchester University Press, 1980), p. 28.

12. Navagero, "Lusus XXII: Prayer to Night That His Love Remain Hidden," trans. McFarlane, in *Renaissance Latin Poetry*, p. 51.
13. J. A. van Dorsten, *Poets, Patrons, and Professors: Sir Philip Sidney, Daniel Rogers, and the Leiden Humanists* (Leiden: Leiden University Press, 1962), pp. 77–82. Dorsten believes the French diplomat Jean Hotman may have been the intermediary between Dousa and Constable.
14. Katherine Duncan-Jones, *Shakespeare: An Ungentle Life* (London: Methuen Drama, 2010), pp. 36–38.
15. Joan Grundy, "Introduction," *The Poems of Henry Constable* (Liverpool: Liverpool University Press, 1960), p. 24.
16. Here the Latin is *"artificemque pedem."* The play between human feet and metrical feet occurs often in Ovid, and *"pedem"* is here used in both capacities. Like Ovid, the poet wants to rotate through body parts (from eyes to cheeks to feet) and simultaneously move from the physical (body parts) to the abstract (talents). As Richard Thomas notes, the adjective *"artificem"* here almost excludes the physical reading of human feet and requires the translation of "poetry" or "verses."
17. The Latin for this opening section of the poem reads as follows:

TRIUMPHUS XXI

Vicimus hei tandem, & saevos restinximus ignes;
Vicimus, e rigido pectore cessit Amor.
Ite leves lusus, joca blanditiaeque valete:
Tuque vale mentis carnificina meae:
Non ego, Hyella, tuos posthac mirabor ocellos,
Purpureasque genas, artificemque pedem:
Non ego perpetiar fastus & jurgia mille,
Florea non rigidis serta dabo foribus.

18. Again, the Latin:

Nec te spumigena referam cum Matre Cupido,
Pejus habet Stygii quo nihil aula Jovis.
Ex te odia & furor & caedes & bella cruenta,
Ex te hominum generi plurima nata mala;
Mortali gestas tu tela madentia caede,
Tu jacis in tenerum spicula dira jecur;
Credula tu blandis corrumpis corda venenis,
Ut solet AEaeo saga ministerio;
Tunc curae subeunt, lachrymaeque, at cura salubris
Nulla subit Bacchi, nulla subit Cereris.

19. And again, the Latin:

Cingite victrices ergo mea tempora lauri,
. . . .
Cingite victrices iterum mea tempora lauri . . .

20. Richard Thomas points out the use of the word "savage" for Hyella and Cupid in lines 1 (*saevos*) and 38 (*saeve*) of the Latin.

21. Here is the Latin for these closing lines of "Triumphus xxi":

> *Sic ego sim, sic & liceat consumere, Parca*
> *Dum sinit, aetatis tempora verna meae,*
> *Ut mulier nostres non sentiat ulla furores,*
> *Nec vinctum, collo sub sua jura trahat.*
> *Ergo tua, o Bona Mens, tua me in sacraria condo;*
> *Tu mala de corde haec omnia pelle meo,*
> *Quae mihi nec noctes, nec sunt mihi passa quietos*
> *Ire dies, dum me torfit acerbus Amor.*

22. See chapter 2, pp. 40–41.

23. The editor of the 1640 edition was John Benson and that of the 1711 edition Bernard Lintott. Margreta de Grazia writes that these changes (which are sometimes overstated in scholarship) are indicative of a many-centuries-long reluctance to see Shakespeare's beloved as a male, or to see their love as something other than an instance of "Platonism . . . or the Renaissance ideal of friendship" ("The Scandal of Shakespeare's Sonnets," *Shakespeare Survey* 46 [1994]: pp. 35–49).

24. Grundy, "Introduction," *The Poems of Henry Constable*, p. 51.

25. Grundy, "Introduction," *The Poems of Henry Constable*, p. 52.

26. The 1592 *Diana* has only two poems with titles (the other poems are simply prefaced by a sonnet number). One is the opening poem, "To his absent Diana." The other is a poem on the birth of Lady Rich's daughter, "A calculation upon the birth of an honourable Ladies daughter, borne in the year, 1588. & on a Friday." The 1594 *Diana* has, other than the indication of sonnet number, only the title accompanying the poem about the birth of the infant. The poem to the absent Diana is not in this edition.

27. Margreta de Grazia points out that Shakespeare has "an astonishing number of sonnets that do not make the gender of the addressee explicit" and says that "Shakespeare is exceptional among the English sonneteers (Sidney, Spenser, and Daniel, for example) in leaving the gender of the beloved unspecified in so many of the sonnets: about five sixths of them in the first 126 and just less than that in the collection entire" ("Scandal of Shakespeare's Sonnets," p. 41).

28. In Grundy, ed., *The Poems of Henry Constable*, p. 135.

29. In Grundy, ed., *The Poems of Henry Constable*, p. 121.

30. In Grundy, ed., *The Poems of Henry Constable*, p. 128.

31. Grundy, "Introduction," *The Poems of Henry Constable*, p. 84.

32. Grundy, "Introduction," *The Poems of Henry Constable*, p. 36.

33. William Carew Hazlitt, *Diana: The Sonnets and Other Poems of Henry Constable* (London: Basil Montagu Pickering, 1859), p. 1. The footnote is by Thomas Parks, who worked with Hazlitt to provide notes and illustrations to the edition. Whether intentionally or unintentionally, the word "prefix" (rather than "title") is well chosen, since the title works to fix or repair a potential problem in the body of the poem, and to do so preemptively. ("Fix" did not

have this meaning in the 1590s but it did by the time of the nineteenth-century Hazlitt edition.)

34. Henry Constable, letter to Anthony Bacon, October 6, 1596, in Hazlitt, "Biographical Notice," in *Diana*, p. xxi.

35. Henry Constable, letter to Anthony Bacon, January 8, 1596, from Rouen, France, and Constable, letter to the Earl of Shrewsbury, May 11, 1604, from the Tower of London, in Hazlitt, "Biographical Notice," in *Diana*, pp. xi–xiv. In addition to Constable's own signature, the abbreviation was used by other people referring to Constable. The biographer George Wickes describes a copy of Constable's treatise on religious tolerance now in the British Museum: onto the title page someone has noted, in seventeenth-century handwriting, "It was written by Mr. Hen: Constable a lay papist" (George Wickes, *Henry Constable: Poet and Courtier, 1562–1613*, in *Biographical Studies 1534–1829*, vol. 2, no. 4 [Bognor Regis, U.K.: Arundel Press, 1954], pp. 295–96n21).

36. The act of abbreviating one's first name and following it with a colon was a wide practice in signatures of sixteenth-century England.

37. The manuscript for *Naming Thy Name* was submitted to Farrar, Straus and Giroux in July 2014 with the passages about the *Fritillaria meleagris* in *Venus and Adonis*, and the accounts of the flower in Gerard and Duodens, already completed. The identity of the flower at the end of *Venus and Adonis* has since that time also been affirmed by the botanist Mark Griffiths in his May 2015 article in *Country Life*. Many Shakespearean scholars have long identified the flower (incorrectly) as an anemone (which is indeed the flower Ovid specifies but which bears no resemblance to the description Shakespeare gives). Griffiths's important observation about *Venus and Adonis* was largely ignored because he made a second, more dramatic, and probably also incorrect claim that the frontispiece to Gerard's *Herball* portrays Shakespeare holding a *Fritillaria* (see Mark Brown, "Shakespeare: Writer Claims Discovery of Only Portrait Made During His Lifetime," *The Guardian*, May 19, 2015). As numerous correspondents to the controversy have pointed out, the figure holding the *Fritillaria* on the frontispiece is almost certainly the botanist Dioscorides. It is not impossible, however, that Shakespeare posed for the Dioscorides portrait (or as Griffiths argues, the Apollo portrait), just as even kings and queens sometimes dressed as ancient or mythological figures (an analogy proposed to me by Matthew Spellberg in conversation). Leaving aside the identity of the figure, Griffiths's attention to the delightful magnification of the *Fritillaria* on the frontispiece is a benefit to us, as is his confirmation of the identity of the flower in *Venus and Adonis*.

38. John Gerard, *The Herball or Generall Historie of Plantes. Gathered by John Gerarde of London Master in Chirurgerie* (London: John Norton, 1597), p. 122.

39. Gerard, *The Herball*, p. 123. Rembert Dodoens's *A New Herball, or Historie of Plants*—translated from German into French and then into English by Henrie Lyte in 1578 and printed in a second edition in 1586—also ends by acknowledging the small flower's mystery and beauty: though the "nature and vertues of these floures are yet unknown," they are "beautiful to looke on" (Dodoens, *A New Herball, or Historie of Plants wherein is contained the whole discourse*

and perfect description of all sorts of Herbes and Plants: their divers and sundrie kindes: their Names, Natures, Operations, & Vertues: and that not onely of those which are heere growing in this our Countrie of England, but of all others also of forraine Realms commonly used in Physicke, trans. Henrie Lyte, [London: Ninian Newton, 1586], part 1, p. 241).

40. Writers across the centuries (including authors today) usually note that "*fritillus*" is the Latin word for dice box rather than chessboard, and that those originally naming the flower (who intended the Latin for chess) were confused on this point. Gerard notes this same slip in language: after giving his chess description, he continues, "some thinking that it was named *Frittillus*, whereof there is no certainty; for *Martialis* seemeth to call *Frittillus, Abacus,* or the tables whereat men plaie with dice, in his fifth booke of his Epigrams" (*The Herball,* p. 123). Kew Gardens is one of the few plant houses that assumes that dice box was the intended designation; they say that dice boxes were originally checkered. (Even if the dice boxes were ornamented on six sides with the dots on the six sides of the dice they would have an almost checkered appearance.) The conception of the blossom as a tiny box is not unwarranted, for though it is like an inverted cup or bell, it has four raised pleats at the top of the blossom which give it a squared-off or box-like appearance.

41. Gerard, *The Herball,* p. 122.

42. Dodoens, *A New Herball,* part 1, p. 241.

43. Although Gerard does not place the ginnie hen flower with tulips, he does immediately follow his chapter on tulips with his chapter on the ginnie hen flower. He also notes that it is sometimes called a "checkerd Daffodill" (pp. 122, 123).

44. Constable, "Carmen xiv," "Adumbratum de Anglico Henrici Conestabilis," in Dousa, *Poemata,* pp. 157, 158. Here again, as with all the Latin poems, I am grateful to Richard Thomas for his generous help.

45. Shakespeare brings together "checkered" with wicker in *Romeo and Juliet* when Friar Laurence describes the morning sky while filling with flowers a wicker basket made of willow wands: "The grey-eyed morn smiles on the frowning night, / Chequ'ring the eastern clouds with streaks of light / . . . I must up-fill this osier cage of ours / With baleful weeds and precious-juicèd flowers" (II.iii. 1–2, 7–8).

5. The Rival Poet

1. James VI, "A complaint against the contrary wyndes that hindered the Queene to com to Scotland from Denmarke," in James Craigie, ed., *The Poems of James VI of Scotland* (Edinburgh: William Blackwood, 1958), vol. 2, p. 68.

2. Joan Grundy, ed., *The Poems of Henry Constable* (Liverpool: Liverpool University Press, 1960), p. 142.

3. Allan F. Westcott, "Alexander Montgomerie," *Modern Language Review* 6, no. 1 (January 1911): pp. 1–8 (observing that Montgomerie changes the rhyme scheme and the phrasing in the sestet). See also Ronald D. S. Jack, "Imitation in the Scottish Sonnet," *Comparative Literature* 20, no. 4 (Autumn 1968). Constable's poem about the eyes as windows was, as noted earlier, also translated into Dutch by Janus Dousa—the poem begins, "*U oog is een glas, daar*

mijn hart is ingegreven" (Jani Dousae Filii, *Poemata*, ed. Gulielmo Rabo, J.U.D. [Rotterdam: Adrianum van Dijk, 1704], p. 163). But unlike Montgomerie, Dousa credited the poem to Constable, since it appears in 1591 with the poems under the title "Adumbratum de Anglico Henrici Conestabilis."

4. Constable, "Of the conspiracie of his Ladies eyes and his owne to ingender love," in *The Poems of Henry Constable*, ed. Grundy, p. 117. For Montgomerie's poem, see *The Poems of Alexander Montgomery*, ed. David Irving (Edinburgh: Ballantyne, 1821), p. 83.

5. Adam Nicolson, *God's Secretaries: The Making of the King James Bible* (New York: HarperCollins, 2003), p. 7.

6. Nicolson, *God's Secretaries*, p. 7.

7. "The Danish Account of the Marriage of James VI and Anne of Denmark," trans. Peter Graves, in David Stevenson, *Scotland's Last Royal Wedding: The Marriage of James VI and Anne of Denmark* (Edinburgh: John Donald, 1997), p. 99, and see 50–51.

8. Allan Ferguson Westcott, ed., *New Poems by James I of England from a Hitherto Unpublished Manuscript (Add. 24195) in the British Museum* (New York: Columbia University Press, 1911), p. xxii. The diarist James Melville speaks of the child's "strange and extraordinar gifts of ingyne, judgement, memorie and language," and reports, "I heard him discours, walking upe and doun in the auld Lady Marr's hand, of knawlage and ignorance, to my greit mervell and estonishment" (Melville, *Diary* [Edinburgh: Bann. Club, 1574], p. 38, cited in Westcott, ed., *New Poems by James I of England*, p. xx).

9. Nicolson, *God's Secretaries*, p. 151.

10. Westcott, ed., *New Poems by James I of England*, p. lxviii.

11. Stephen Booth, ed., *Shakespeare's Sonnets* (New Haven, CT: Yale University Press, 1977), p. 271.

12. Constable's poem "To the King of Scotland" is printed in the king's book with many variant spellings and additional commas. The first word is "Where" rather than "When." In line 6, "taught" rather than "schoold" occurs. The title and attribution here are as printed in the king's book, but the text is that which occurs in "To the K. of Scots touching the subject of his poems dedicated wholie to heavenly matters," in Grundy, ed., *The Poems of Henry Constable*, p. 141.

13. James VI, *His Majesties Poeticall Exercises at Vacant Hours* (Edinburgh: Robert Walde-grave, 1591), reprinted in *The Poems of James VI of Scotland*, vol. 1, ed. James Craigie (Edinburgh: William Blackwood, 1955), p. 102. Constable was one of many who credited James VI's poetic abilities.

14. The National Gallery of Scotland houses two portraits of James VI at the age of eight with a sparrow hawk, one by Arnold Bronckorst, the other by an unknown hand.

15. See http://collections.glasgowmuseums.com/starobject.html?oid=37492.

16. "Hawks Yesterday and Today," National Archives of Scotland: A National Records of Scotland Website, October 2006, www.nas.gov.uk/about/060704 .asp.

17. Constable, "To the K. of Scots whome as yet he had not seene. Sonet 4," in Grundy, ed., *The Poems of Henry Constable*, p. 140. Whether this means

Constable had never before seen King James or, instead, has not yet arrived on this particular visit (the poem is part of the 1589 sequence) is unclear.

18. Craigie, "Appendix A," in *The Poems of James VI of Scotland*, vol. 1, p. 274. Craigie here includes many other poetic tributes to James VI.

19. M. Oppenheim, "The Royal Navy Under James I," *English Historical Review* 7, no. 27 (July 1892): pp. 487–88.

20. Oppenheim, "The Royal Navy Under James I," p. 472.

21. "The Danish Account of the Marriage," in Stevenson, *Scotland's Last Royal Wedding*, pp. 80, 89.

22. Stevenson, *Scotland's Last Royal Wedding*, p. 28. When James first realized that he could no longer wait for the Danish fleet and would have to set sail himself, he instructed the country's admiral to prepare a fleet, but he was quickly informed that existing ships would need to be equipped; James was unable to provide the money. Thirlestane then came to the rescue.

23. Nicolo Molin (Venetian ambassador in England), despatch, July 6, 1604, in *Calendar of State Papers Relating to English Affairs in the Archives of Venice, Volume 10: 1603–1607* (1900), pp. 165–71, available at British History Online.

24. "A True Reportarie of the Most Triumphant, and Royal Accomplishment of the Baptisme of the Most Excellent, Right High, and Mightie Prince, Frederik Henry; By the Grace of God, Prince of Scotland, Solemnized the 30. Day of August. 1594" (Edinburgh: Robert Walde-grave, Printer to the King), pp. 21–23. The description I give, even when not in quotation marks, is a close paraphrase of the exact language, but the spelling has been modernized (for example, "A True Reportarie" tells us "All her Sayles were double of white Taffata") or modern names used (the word "oboe" is used rather than its precursor "howboy"). Though the extravagant ship is a piece of pageantry rather than an actual ship, the festivities entailed actual ships whose extravagance is noted. At the end of the ceremonies, for example, James and Anne were invited by the ambassadors of Denmark to banquet on a ship too large to have entered the harbor.

25. Anne's attempt to sail for Scotland began at Copenhagen on September 5; the ships encountered bad winds and were stranded at Kronborg for two days and at Flekkerøy for six days; they then sailed for three days, but were forced to turn back to Rekefjord; the ships lost one another, were eventually reunited (one was lost) and sailed in adverse conditions for nine days, after which they arrived back at Flekkerøy (where Anne slept in a farmhouse; James, when he eventually reached Norway, insisted on sleeping in the same farmhouse). The Danish nobility decided Anne should abandon the attempt to reach Scotland and should continue on to Oslo, Norway. This part of her trip was almost equally difficult with many delays in various harbors so that she only arrived in Oslo on October 25, where, according to the Danish account, she was reverentially received: "the whole clergy was gathered on the quay, the citizenry lined the street fully armed, and the governor and the chief men of the country humbly wished her grace good fortune and happiness." James's ocean voyage to Oslo (where he arrived on November 19) and Anne and James's five-week (December 22–January 29) overland trip by sledge from Norway through Sweden to Denmark (where they stayed until spring) were equally arduous. They

arrived in Scotland on May 1, 1590 ("The Danish Account of the Marriage," in Stevenson, *Scotland's Last Royal Wedding*, pp. 86–88, 91, 100).

26. James VI, "A Complaint of His Mistressis Absence from Court," in Craigie, ed., *The Poems of James VI of Scotland*, vol. 2, p. 80. This poem is part of a manuscript entitled "All the kings short poesis that ar not printed" (MS. Add. 24195 in the British Museum). According to Craigie, the probable time of composition for the poems in this manuscript is the period of James's early years with Anne (late 1589 and early 1590s), even though the manuscript itself was probably prepared for publication between 1616 and 1618 when James was readying his prose essays for publication (Craigie, "Introduction," *The Poems of James VI of Scotland*, vol. 2, pp. xxii–xxiii). According to Allan Ferguson Westcott, Constable was a key person in James's poetic life ("Introduction," *New Poems by James I of England*, pp. xxxvi–xxxviii). It is therefore reasonable to suppose that Constable would be one of the intimate circle to whom James would show or send the unpublished poems.

27. Westcott, ed., *New Poems by James I of England*, pp. 78, 79, cited in Craigie, ed., *The Poems of James VI of Scotland*, vol. 2, p. 228n8. Craigie observes that the verse form of "A Complaint of His Mistressis Absence from Court" is what James identifies in his *Reulis and Cautelis* as "*Troilus verse*," appropriate for "tragicall materis, complaintis, or testamentis."

28. James VI, "A Dreame on His Mistris My Ladie Glammis," in Craigie, ed., *The Poems of James VI of Scotland*, vol. 2, pp. 82–89, quoting lines 181–98. The poem is included in James's manuscript "All the kings short poesis that ar not printed."

29. This photograph of Adrian Vanson's painting of James VI is a Private Collection Photo © Philip Mould Ltd, London/Bridgeman Images.

30. James VI, *Daemonologie*, in *King James VI and I: Selected Writings*, ed. Neil Rhodes, Jennifer Richards, and Joseph Marshall (Aldershot, U.K.: Ashgate, 2003), p. 150.

31. Glossary in Craigie, ed., *The Poems of James VI of Scotland*, vol. 2, pp. 290ff.

32. James VI, *Daemonologie*, in Rhodes, Richards, and Marshall, eds., *King James VI and I*, chap. 6, pp. 163, 164, 165, 399. We also learn that the "contract" between the magician and the familiar may be written in the "*Magicians* owne bloud" or else, "being agreed upon," can be sealed by an act of bodily touch that leaves no mark.

33. David Stevenson shows that James probably derived his fear of witches from his bride's country: even before James and Anne left Copenhagen, the possibility that witches had attempted to kill Anne by "rais[ing] storms" and "scattering . . . the fleet" was under discussion in the Danish court, and trials of witches in Denmark began several months before similar trials were initiated in Scotland. Stevenson observes that "nautical *maleficum*" was a Norwegian and Danish "speciality," with prosecutions for the crime of raising a storm at sea in order to imperil a monarch occurring as early as 1540 (*Scotland's Last Royal Wedding*, pp. 72–73).

34. James VI, "The Azured Vault," in Craigie, ed., *The Poems of James VI of Scotland*, vol. 2, p. 99 (italics added). The poem, like two others already looked at, was part of the manuscript "All the kings short poesis that ar not printed."

35. According to the glossary, "roares" means noise, especially the noise of waters; "sadd" means steadfast; "rearding" means roaring or resounding.

36. James VI, "The Reulis and Cavtelis to be Observit and Eschewit in Scottis Poesie," in Craigie, ed., *The Poems of King James VI of Scotland*, vol. 1, p. 81. The following are some of the words from the Halloween poem that may not be self-evident: "Benwod": beanstalk. "Sadland": saddling. "Sho": she. "Grathed": arrayed. "Hotcheand": fidgeting. "Hovand": rising. "Heicht": height. "Elrage": supernatural. "Rydand": riding. "Bratshard": little brat. "Bus": bush. "Fand": found (glossary in Craigie, vol. 2). The excerpt is from a section of Alexander Montgomerie's poem "Flyting betwixt Montgomery and Polwaet" that describes the health care offered by "the Weird Sisters" (*The Poems of Alexander Montgomerie*, ed. James Cranstoun and George Stevenson [Edinburgh: Blackwood, 1887], p. 31).

   In providing translations for the Scots vocabulary in the poems that follow, I rely primarily on Craigie's glossary but have also consulted the online *Dictionary of Scots Language/Dictionar o the Scots Leid* (www.dsl.ac.uk), which in turn draws on both the twelve-volume *Dictionary of the Older Scottish Tongue* and the ten-volume *Scottish National Dictionary*.

37. James VI, "Sonnet of the Authour," in Craigie, ed., *The Poems of James VI of Scotland*, vol. 1, p. 94.

38. James VI, "Ane Quadrain of Alexandrin Verse," in Craigie, ed., *The Poems of James VI of Scotland*, vol. 1, p. 8.

39. James VI, "The Translators Invocation," in Craigie, ed., *The Poems of James VI of Scotland*, vol. 1, p. 112 (italics added).

40. James VI, "Sonnets 1–12," in *The Essayes of a Prentise, in the Divine Art of Poesie*, in Craigie, ed., *The Poems of James VI of Scotland*, vol. 1, pp. 9–14.

41. James was sometimes an insightful describer of poetic style, as in his account of the harsh, hammering, tumbling style of the metaphysical poets. According to Allan Westcott, a person close to James's court is the first to apply the word "metaphysical" to the style of John Donne and company (Westcott, "Introduction," *New Poems by James I of England*, p. xc).

42. James VI, "Song I," in Craigie, ed., *The Poems of James VI of Scotland*, vol. 2, p. 94. Another candidate is his sonnet on "the Cheviott hills," the hills that separate Scotland from England, and James from someone for whom he burns (Craigie, vol. 2, p. 70).

   Where "Song I" begins and ends changes from one printing of James's poems to another. In a biography by D. H. Willson (*King James VI and I* [London: Jonathan Cape, 1962], p. 89), the poem stops one stanza earlier than in the version I have given. In both Craigie's and Westcott's editions, the poem continues for another four stanzas, and in the fifth stanza explicitly speaks of a "she." Craigie assumes that the entire poem is written to Anne of Denmark at the time the 1589 storm delayed their marriage: "This poem would seem to be addressed to Anne of Denmark, and from ll. 5–6 ['The seas are now the barr / Which makes us distant farr'] to have been written between 15th September and 22nd October 1589" (*Poems of James VI of Scotland*, vol. 2, p. 230). Westcott assumes the same (*New Poems by James I of England*, p. 83). But it is hard to see how the first four stanzas permit this reading. The poem explicitly says that the pain of separation is caused by the sheer joy and sense of "oneness" they experienced when (after long wishing to meet) they did meet; at the time that James and Anne were stranded from one another by the storm, they had never met; their engagement and marriage negotiations had been carried out by intermediaries. Further, though the poem describes the two people as separated by the sea, the sea is not here designated the cause of their separation: instead the cause is an obligation to another loved person. The two are like star-crossed lovers in other literature (the poem's third stanza tells us) but separated by an unusual cause that does not appear in that literature. It therefore seems reasonable to think that James may have written the poem while in Denmark, united with Anne but separated by the sea from a newly discovered companion back in England or Scotland.

As the end point of "Song I" varies across editions, so the starting place varies. In the 1901 edition by R. S. Rait (*Lusus Regius, being Poems and Other Pieces by King James Ye First. Now first set forth and Edited by R. S. Rait* [Westminster: Constable, 1901]), the sixth and seventh stanzas in the Craigie and Westcott editions are the first and second stanzas. Here James "rejoices" that the two are companions ("marrowes"), is comforted by the knowledge that they share the pain of separation, and hopes that they will soon meet again.

43. Constable, "To the K: of Scots upon occasion of his longe stay in Denmarke by reason of the coldnesse of the winter and freezing of the sea. Sonet 7," in Grundy, ed., *The Poems of Henry Constable*, p. 143.

44. Anonymous, "To H.C upon occasion of his two former Sonets to the K. of Scots," in *Harleian Miscellany: A Collection of Scarce, Curious, and Entertaining Pamphlets and Tracts, as well in Manuscript as in Print*, vol. ix, ed. Thomas Park (London: White & Cochrane, 1812), pp. 517, 518.

45. See, for example, Stevenson, *Scotland's Last Royal Wedding*, p. 66.

46. Grundy, "Introduction," *The Poems of Henry Constable*, p. 18; and George Wickes, *Henry Constable: Poet and Courtier, 1562–1613*, in *Biographical Studies 1534–1829*, vol. 2, no. 4 (Bognor Regis, U.K.: Arundel Press, 1954), p. 276.

47. Grundy, "Introduction," *The Poems of Henry Constable*, p. 27. Grundy's description suggests that Constable was one of several in this position and not necessarily the major intermediary. David Stevenson in *Scotland's Last Royal Wedding* points out that the choice between Anne and Catherine (neither of whom James had ever met) turned in part on the size of the dowry and in part on age: Anne was fourteen, Catherine thirty-one.

48. Henry Constable, "To the divine protection of the Ladie Arbella, the author commendeth both his Graces honoure, and his Muses aeternitye," in *Harleian Miscellany*, p. 517. Joan Grundy does not mention Arabella's eligibility for marriage with James, but does mention that she and Constable were good friends once Arabella (at the age of twelve) first appeared in court in 1587. Grundy also mentions that Arabella was perceived as James's main competitor for the English throne, should Elizabeth die ("Introduction," *The Poems of Henry Constable*, pp. 26, 29). See also Wickes, *Henry Constable: Poet and Courtier*, p. 274; and Louise Imogen Guiney, *Recusant Poets* (New York: Sheed & Ward, 1939), p. 304.

49. In *Contested Will: Who Wrote Shakespeare?*, James Shapiro shows not only how starkly unfounded are the attributions of the plays to authors other than

Shakespeare, but how massive is the evidence that the plays were indeed written by Shakespeare ([New York: Simon & Schuster, 2010], pp. 221–60).

50. Sir Edward Duning, *Bacon Is Shake-speare* (1910), reprinted in George McMichael and Edgar M. Glenn, *Shakespeare and His Rivals: A Casebook on the Authorship Controversy* (New York: Odyssey Press, 1962), p. 75.

51. Joan Grundy details Constable's movements in each of these countries, and says he also had plans to go to Switzerland that may or may not have been fulfilled (see "Introduction," *The Poems of Henry Constable*, pp. 21, 23, 24, 26, 34, 35). George Wickes and Louise Imogen Guiney in their earlier biographical studies (*Henry Constable: Poet and Courtier* and *Recusant Poets*) also describe Constable's travels.

52. James VI, "The CIIII. Psalme, Translated out of Tremellius," in Craigie, ed., *The Poems of James VI of Scotland*, vol. 1, pp. 86–88.

53. Craigie, "Introduction," *The Poems of James VI of Scotland*, vol. 2, pp. xv, xvi. The watermark on the paper of the manuscript is consistent with James's other 1580s manuscripts (though also with later manuscripts); eight of the psalms are followed by initials indicating James is King of Scotland (and therefore not yet King of England); they all, like Psalm 104, appear to be translated primarily out of Tremellius's sixteenth-century Latin version (though James possessed and drew on ten Bibles—one in Greek, one in Italian, three in Latin, three English, two French—as well as multiple versions of the psalms); and he mentions his manuscript in his 1591 published book of poems.

54. Craigie, "Introduction," *The Poems of James VI of Scotland*, vol. 2, pp. xx, xxi.

55. Craigie cites (*The Poems of James VI of Scotland*, vol. 2, p. xxxn8) an account of the 1601 General Assembly of the Kirk given in Spottiswoode's *History of the Church of Scotland* (1655, p. 465). The assembly, discussing problems with existing translations of the Bible, witnessed how knowledgeable James was about the Scriptures in general and the psalms in particular: "and when he came to speak of the Psalmes, [he] did recite whole verses of the same, shewing both the faults of the meeter and the discrepance from the text. It was the joy of all that were present to hear it, and bred not little admiration in the whole Assembly, who approving the motion did recommend the translation to such of the brethren as were most skill'd in the languages, and revising of the Psalmes particularly to Mr Robert Pont; but nothing was done in the one or the other." Though this 1601 story is late, James's intricate knowledge about and ability to recite many of the psalms were surely noticed and transmitted orally in much earlier years.

56. Katherine Duncan-Jones, ed., *Shakespeare's Sonnets* (London: Arden Shakespeare, 2007), p. 284.

57. Stevenson, *Scotland's Last Royal Wedding*, p. 38.

58. It also invites us to rethink the tone of the closing couplet in "England's Sweete Nightingale." Earlier we described the tone of these lines—"Come, feare thou not the cage, but loyall be, / And ten to one thy Soveraigne pardons thee"—as cavalier, high-handed. But the author of this sonnet, as we can now appreciate, had good reason to surmise that Constable stood so high in the view of sovereigns that he had a strong chance of being exonerated.

59. James Shapiro, *The Year of Lear: Shakespeare in 1606* (New York: Simon & Schuster, 2015), pp. 21, 22.

60. I have long assumed that in James and Henry Constable's many conversations about poetry, Constable would surely have voiced his admiration for Shakespeare's poetic genius. It had not occurred to me, however, that Constable's reverential endorsement might have actually contributed to James's choice of Shakespeare's company for the King's Men. The suggestion was made to me by Matthew Spellberg (conversation, December 17, 2008).

61. Grundy, "Introduction," *The Poems of Henry Constable*, p. 40.

6. Last Names

1. Stephen Booth, ed., *Shakespeare's Sonnets* (New Haven, CT: Yale University Press, 1977), p. 337.

2. Katherine Duncan-Jones, ed., *Shakespeare's Sonnets* (London: Arden Shakespeare, 2007), p. 300.

3. Richard R. Heiser, "Castles, Constables, and Politics in Late Twelfth-Century English Governance," *Albion: A Quarterly Journal Concerned with British Studies* 32, no. 1 (Spring 2000): pp. 21, 23.

4. Shelagh Bond, "The Medieval Constables of Windsor Castle," *English Historical Review* 82, no. 323 (1967): pp. 227, 230, 232, 236.

5. Joan Grundy, ed., "Introduction," *The Poems of Henry Constable* (Liverpool: Liverpool University Press, 1960), p. 16. The position—constable of Chester—was held by the brother of the Robert Constable line that eventually led to Henry Constable.

6. Despatch from Nicolo Molin, Venetian Ambassador in England, to the Doge and Senate, September 1, 1604, in "Venice: September 1604," *Calendar of State Papers Relating to English Affairs in the Archives of Venice, Volume 10: 1603–1607* (1900), pp. 178–84. British History Online.

7. *Calendar of State Papers Domestic: James I, 1603–1610*, vol. 9, August–October 1604, entry for September 6. British History Online.

8. Despatch from Nicolo Molin, *Archives of Venice*.

9. Joan Kent, "The English Village Constable, 1580–1642: The Nature and Dilemmas of the Office," *Journal of British Studies* 20, no. 2 (Spring 1981): p. 31.

10. M. S. Giuseppi, ed., introduction to *Calendar of the Cecil Papers in Hatfield House*, vol. 17, 1605 (London: His Majesty's Stationery Office, 1938), p. 492.

11. Lines 10 and 11 alternatively read: "That you yourself may privilege your time / Do what you will . . ." The change from "To" to "Do," as Stephen Booth explains, was made by Edmond Malone in the eighteenth century, and is a change many editions now follow; but the meaning of the two versions is the same, so the change (according to Booth) is needless (*Shakespeare's Sonnets*, p. 235).

12. Constable, "But beeing care, thou flyest mee as ill fortune," "The fifth Decad. Sonnet. VII," in Grundy, ed., *The Poems of Henry Constable*, pp. 200–201.

13. Constable, "I Am no modell figure, or signe of care," "The fifth Decad. Sonnet. VI," in Grundy, ed., *The Poems of Henry Constable*, p. 200.

14. Constable, "Deere to my soule, then leave me not forsaken," "The fifth Decad. Sonnet. VIII," in Grundy, ed., *The Poems of Henry Constable*, p. 201.

15. Constable, "Whilst Eccho cryes, what shall become of mee," "The fifth Decad. Sonnet. IX," in Grundy, ed., *The Poems of Henry Constable*, p. 202.

16. This etymology and explanation are given in the *Encyclopaedia Britannica* article on "diapason."

17. Since Pan's pipe was Syrinx, who transformed herself into a reed, there is perhaps here the implication that Henry Constable is not a string instrument but himself the reed or weed that the poet has fashioned into a flute, an object with notes.

18. Here is one way of understanding the line while retaining the "my"—"That every word doth almost tell my name." If someone were to ask, "Who are you?" I could answer, "I am William Shakespeare" or "I am the person who can't stop writing about my beloved" because my writing about him is almost who I am as much as my name is who I am.

19. Katherine Duncan-Jones points out the "fel"/"tell" misprint (*Shakespeare's Sonnets*, p. 262).

20. Henry Constable, "Carmen xv," "Adumbratum de Anglico Henrici Conestabilis," in Jani Dousae Filii, *Poemata*, ed. Gulielmo Rabo, J.U.D. (Rotterdam: Adrianum van Dijk, 1704), p. 158. My thanks to Richard Thomas for his help in this translation; all errors are my own.

21. The Latin uses the word "*Dominae*," which I have here translated as "from on high." "*Domina*" is ordinarily the word for lady or mistress. The uppercase, as Jeff Dolven observes, seems to license the translation "from on high." Numerous goddesses had the name "Domina" added to their names: Venus Domina, Diana Domina, Isis Domina, Cybele Domina, Proserpina Domina, Juno Domina. The list, given by B. L. Hijmans, is provided in the *Thesaurus Linguae Latin*.

22. Constable, "Carmen xvii," "Adumbratum de Anglico Henrici Conestabilis," in Dousa, *Poemata*, p. 160. My thanks to Richard Thomas and to Jeff Dolven. Here is the Latin:

> *Quid mirum, valido quum sese obsessus ab igne*
> *Colligat, & vires sumat ab hoste rigor;*
> *Fulminibus Dominae & flammati cordis ab aestu*
> *Pressa stupent rigido si mea membra gelu?*

23. "Thunder much / that made the lande to shake / And lightning great fro heaue on hye / which causd them all to quake" occurs in the 1551 *The abridgemente of goddes statutes in myter, set oute by Wylliam Samuel*; and shaking lightning periodically reappears in sermons, histories, polemics, plays, and meditations up through George Abbot's bone-shaking lightning in his 1600 Oxford lecture *An exposition vpon the prophet Ionah Contained in certaine sermons*, and continuing on to John Donne's earth-shaking lightning in his 1610 *Pseudo-Martyr* and Cyril Tourneur's bulwark-shaking lightning in *The Atheist's Tragedy*.

24. The illustration for *The Tempest*—drawn by François Boitard and engraved in copper by Elisha Kirkall—appears in Nicholas Rowe's 1709 *The Works of Mr. William Shakespeare*. For this and other illustrations in the Rowe edition,

see the British Library, www.bl.uk/collection-items/the-first-illustrated-works
-of-shakespeare-edited-by-nicholas-rowe-1709.

25. Constable, "Carmen xviii," "Adumbratum de Anglico Henrici Conestabilis," in Dousa, *Poemata*, p. 160. My thanks yet again to Richard Thomas for his patient help in this translation; all errors are my own.

26. For example, Constable has a beautiful sonnet about being touched by a gloved hand that contains the phrase "Thy arrowes quiver," wording which might be understood as parallel to "thy spear's shaking." As mentioned earlier, I have abstained throughout this study from drawing on Constable's many gender-neutral poems (that may be about a male beloved) in cases where the Joan Grundy edition gives them lengthy titles about women (titles that occur only in the Todd manuscript). This sonnet about the glove is in some volumes of poetry entitled "Love's Franciscan" and is potentially lovely in relation to Shakespeare, since his father was a glove-maker, since the final line possibly alludes to his name, and since the poem is about the afterimage of the act of touch. So radically different is the felt experience of reading the poem when prefaced by the title "To his Ladies hand upon occasion of her glove which in her absence he kissed" (Grundy, ed., *The Poems of Henry Constable*, p. 131) that the editors of poetry collections printing the poem under the title "Love's Franciscan" do not recognize it as the same poem and believe it is missing from the Grundy edition and that its source is unknown. (See Sister Mary Melora Mauritz, "A Study of the Spiritual Sonnets of Henry Constable" [Ph.D. diss., Loyola University, Chicago, 1953], p. 41, for multiple collections that print "Love's Franciscan.")

27. Grundy, "Introduction," *The Poems of Henry Constable*, pp. 51, 52.

28. Grundy prints the word "than" here, which is hard to understand (*The Poems of Henry Constable*, p. 210). Either "them" (a near rhyme, and highly coherent in meaning) or "then" (an exact rhyme, and not incoherent in meaning) seems a likely alternative.

29. Constable, "What view'd I deere when I thine eyes beheld?" "The seaventh Decad. Sonnet. III," in Grundy, ed., *The Poems of Henry Constable*, p. 210.

An Afterword About Afterward

1. See the account of Sonnets 126, 153, and 154 in chapter 2 and the account of Sonnet 107 later in this chapter.

2. Jane Kingsley-Smith, *Shakespeare's Drama of Exile* (Houndmills, U.K.: Palgrave Macmillan, 2003), p. 1.

3. Jane Kingsley-Smith opens her book by quoting Joyce's Stephen Daedalus on Shakespeare's obsession with exile (*Shakespeare's Drama of Exile*, p. 1).

4. James Shapiro, *A Year in the Life of William Shakespeare: 1599* (New York: HarperCollins, 2005), p. 275.

5. Francis Meres, *Palladis Tamia: Wit's Treasury* (1598), cited in Ian Wilson, *Shakespeare: The Evidence* (New York: St. Martin's, 1993), p. 244. Cited also in James Shapiro, *A Year in the Life: 1599*, p. 16. Shapiro notes that some of the sonnets did indeed appear in print in 1599 in *The Passionate Pilgrim* but, despite Shakespeare's name on the title page, he had nothing to do with the

book's publication (p. 188). One nineteenth-century scholar, C. Elliot Browne, identified what he believes to be a 1595 reference to the sonnets in a piece of marginalia which couples the phrase "Sweet Shakspeare" with the phrase "Watson's heyre." Thomas Watson (who had died in 1592) was called "the English Petrarch" because of his sonnets ("The Earliest Mention of Shakespeare," *Notes and Queries* 4–11 [May 10, 1873]: p. 378).

6. Shapiro, *A Year in the Life: 1599*, pp. 189, 198.

7. George Wickes, quoting the Talbot manuscript M, pp. 489–90, in *Henry Constable: Poet and Courtier, 1562–1613*, in *Biographical Studies 1534–1829*, vol. 2, no. 4 (Bognor Regis, U.K.: Arundel Press, 1954), p. 292.

8. Seamus Heaney, "On Sonnets: A Reading in the Parlour" (lecture, Harvard University Department of English, Cambridge, MA, October 18, 2004).

9. The successive appearances of the ornament in *Poeticall Exercises at Vacant Hours* can be seen on Early English Books Online, image numbers 2, 9, 32, and 52.

10. Again, the ornament can be seen at Early English Books Online, in *Essays of a Prentise* on pages with the following image numbers: 7, 29, 17, 29, 39, 42, and 54. See also the title page (image number 1) in *A True Reportarie of the Most Triumphant, and Royal Accomplishment of the Baptisme of the Most Excellent, Right High, and Mightie Prince, Frederik Henry*. Printings of Shakespeare's plays in the 1600 period occasionally include the identical (or close variant of the) *HC* ornament: for example, the 1603 (but not the 1604, 1605, 1611, or 1625) printing of *Hamlet*; the 1600 printing of *Henry IV, Part II*; the 1600 and 1602 printings of *Henry V*; the 1594 and 1600 printings of *Henry VI, Part II* (under the "York/Lancaster" title). An ornament similar to the *HC* ornament appears in the first chapter of Philip Sidney's 1590 *Shepherd's Calendar*.

11. Henry IV converted to Catholicism in 1594 and successfully entered his residence in Paris (impossible before his conversion); the actual writing of the Edict began in 1597.

12. Noel B. Gerson, *The Edict of Nantes*, illus. Bob Pepper (New York: Grosset & Dunlap, 1969), pp. 11, 93, 106, 107, 110, 112. For a summary of the French edicts preceding the Edict of Nantes, see N. M. Sutherland, *The Huguenot Struggle for Recognition* (New Haven, CT: Yale University Press, 1980), pp. 333–72.

13. Francis M. Higman, *Lire et découvrir: la circulation des idées au temps de la Réforme* [Read and Discover: The Circulation of Ideas in the Reformation] (Geneva: Droz, 1998), p. 583.

14. Higman, *Lire et découvrir*, p. 596.

15. Constable may have been younger than twenty-seven. Higman bases the age on the birthdate of 1562, the date often attached to Constable's name. As noted earlier, however, the only documentation of this date is the mention by a herald in 1575 who visits the Constable home and reports the presence of a thirteen-year-old child. In any event, Constable does not seem too young to have written the treatise.

16. Joan Grundy and George Wickes, for example, who are highly aware of Constable and Du Perron's close working relation and the various manuscript entanglements, accept Constable's authorship of *Examen pacifique de la doctrine des Huguenots* (Grundy, ed., "Introduction," *The Poems of Henry Constable*

[Liverpool: Liverpool University Press, 1960], p. 31; and Wickes, *Henry Constable: Poet and Courtier*, p. 281). Constable's authorship is accepted by many other past and present historians and literary historians, such as W. B. Patterson in *King James VI and I and the Reunion of Christendom*, J. A. Van Dorsten in *Poets, Patrons, and Professors*, Katy Gibbons in *English Catholic Exiles in Late Sixteenth-Century Paris*, and Brian Lockey in *Early Modern Catholics, Royalists, and Cosmopolitans*.

Henry Constable's friendship with Jacques Davy Du Perron was crucial for its own sake and for the proximity to the king it ensured. Like Constable, Du Perron was steeped in—and wrote—secular and spiritual poetry. His influence on the king extended across the final decade of the sixteenth century. In 1592 (in the midst of the country's military campaigns), Du Perron participated in two theological debates that pressed the king in the direction of tolerance and the decoupling of church and state (Janine Garrisson, *L'Édit de Nantes* [Paris: Fayard, 1998], pp. 48–49). In 1593, Du Perron was the king's spiritual advisor during his conversion to Catholicism. In 1598–99, Du Perron was a frequent guest in the king's household, and the one Catholic whose voice the king's sister (constantly "harassed" by her brother and other court officials to convert) listened to and whose words she read with delight (Martha Walker Freer, *History of the Reign of Henry IV, King of France and Navarre: Henry IV and Marie de Medici* [London: Hurst and Blackett, 1861], pp. 298–99).

17. Gerson, *Edict of Nantes*, p. 102. Gerson's lively account ends by attributing to Catherine de Bourbon a charismatic capacity to negotiate not only with the Protestants but with the Catholics (pp. 119–25); I have not found the second confirmed in other modern or sixteenth-century sources.

18. These dates are given by Constable's biographers: for example, on Constable's arrival in Leith, see Louise Imogen Guiney, *Recusant Poets* (New York: Sheed & Ward, 1939), p. 309; and Wickes, *Henry Constable: Poet and Courtier*, p. 283. On his aspiration to return to Scotland in 1600, as communicated to Pope Clement VIII, in Rome, see Grundy, "Introduction," *The Poems of Henry Constable*, p. 45.

19. Public Records Office, Scottish Papers, Flanders, vol. VI, p. 12, cited in Wickes, *Henry Constable: Poet and Courtier*, p. 283. Also cited in Grundy, "Introduction," *The Poems of Henry Constable*, p. 40.

20. Louise Imogen Guiney thinks this poem may be by James, but acknowledges that its quality is too high. She resists Constable's authorship in part because she resists the idea that the poet supported divine-right monarchy; but we know from Constable's *A Discovery of a Counterfeit Conference* (a treatise discussed later) that he did support James's hereditary right.

21. Henry Constable (possible author), "The Argument: Sonnet" ("God gives not Kings the stile of *Gods* in vaine"), in King James VI, *Basilicon Doron*, in *King James VI and I: Selected Writing*, ed. Neil Rhodes, Jennifer Richards, and Joseph Marshall (Farnham, U.K.: Ashgate, 2003), p. 200. This edition does not question James's authorship of the poem. The 1599 edition of *Basilicon Doron* included, in addition to the sonnet summarizing the argument of the treatise, the king's dedicatory poem to the prince. Its quality is much less high, and James omitted it from the 1603 and 1616 editions (p. 199).

22. Portrait of James VI by Paul van Somer (1618?), oil on canvas, described by paintings curator, Palace of Holyroodhouse, October 12, 2014. The painting can be seen in the Throne Room, Palace of Holyroodhouse, or online at www .royalcollection.org.uk/collection/401224/james-vi-i-1566-1625. Another portrait, by Adam de Colone, again pictures James dressed in black with his hand on the medal of the Order of the Garter; on display at the National Galleries of Scotland, or online at www.nationalgalleries.org/collection/artists-a-z/c/artist /adam-de-colone/object/james-vi-and-i-1566-1625-king-of-scotland-1567 -1625-king-of-england-and-ireland-1603-1625-pg-2172.

23. Henry IV had been elected to the Order of the Garter in 1590. The 1596 investiture ceremony was titled "Oath of Henry IV, King of France, to keep and observe the statutes of the Order of the Garter. Rouen, 20 October, 38 Eliz. Illuminated" (Diplomatic Documents in the Deputy Keeper of the Public Records). A day earlier, Henry IV had taken an oath at Rouen to observe and uphold the treaties with England concluded the previous May; in these treaties, Elizabeth agreed to send troops to support Henry IV in his wars with French citizens opposing his ascension to the throne. *Parliamentary Papers, House of Commons and Command*, vol. 44 (H.M. Stationery Office, 1887), p. 567.

24. Gilbert Talbot, the seventh Earl of Shrewsbury, was the son of Gertrude Manners. Henry Constable was the grandson of Catherine Manners.

25. Grundy, "Introduction," *The Poems of Henry Constable*, pp. 18, 20.

26. Henry Constable, "H.C. To the Gentleman Reader," in Edmund Bolton, *The Elements of Armories* (London: George Eld, 1610), Early English Books Online, image no. 6. Also in Grundy, ed., *The Poems of Henry Constable*, p. 182.

27. Katherine Duncan-Jones provides this wonderful insight about "shaking" in falcony in *Shakespeare: An Ungentle Life* (London: Methuen Drama, 2010), p. 110.

28. The March 1599 through September 1599 visit to Scotland is certain. Biographers Wickes, Guiney, and Grundy cite correspondence about Constable's preoccupation with James's potential conversion that suggests he may also have traveled to Scotland in the fall of 1598 and in the spring of 1600.

29. Grundy, "Introduction," *The Poems of Henry Constable*, p. 39.

30. John Petit, cited in Wickes, *Henry Constable: Poet and Courtier*, p. 281. Guiney in *Recusant Poets* (p. 309) gives a slightly different phrasing.

31. Queen Anne's biographers—Ethel Carleton Williams in *Anne of Denmark: Wife of James VI of Scotland, James I of England* (London: Longman, 1970), p. 110; Leeds Barroll in *Anna of Denmark, Queen of England: A Cultural Biography* (Philadelphia: University of Pennsylvania Press, 2001), p. 163; and David Stevenson in *Scotland's Last Royal Wedding: The Marriage of James VI and Anne of Denmark* (Edinburgh: John Donald, 1997), p. 67—all date the conversion to 1600, since this is the year in which she underwent formal training by Father Robert Abercromby. J. D. Mackie, for many years Scotland's historiographer royal, also identifies 1600 as the formal conversion year in *A History of Scotland* (London: Penguin, 1964), p. 178. The Lutheran pastor who had come with Anne from Denmark eventually converted to Presbyterian-Calvinism; her spiritual isolation is believed by Williams (p. 110) and by Stevenson (p. 67) to have contributed to her vulnerability to Catholicism.

32. Joan Grundy describes Constable's aspiration to convert Anne and James, then notes that Anne converted: "Anne did become a Catholic, but we do not know by what means." The sequencing of this information contains at least the suggestion that Constable may have contributed to the conversion ("Introduction," *The Poems of Henry Constable*, p. 39). George Wickes notes that when Constable first arrived in Scotland, there was a delay in his seeing James but that he was quickly received by Anne, "who thinck him but simple." Her words may be pejorative, or they may instead suggest that she trusted him—that she regarded him as guileless and modest, a description given by many. It is also possible that the source for Anne's opinion is Constable himself, since the quotation occurs in a report by Roger Aston that is based in part on his conversations with Constable (Wickes, *Henry Constable: Poet and Courtier*, p. 283, citing "Report from Roger Aston to Lord Cecil," Public Records Office, *State Papers, Scotland*, vol. 64, p. 37). In this same report, James attributes his own delay in meeting with Constable to the fact that Constable has not only announced his plan to convert James, but announced that conversion is possible, perhaps easy, because "he had conferred with me long senes and fond me nott so grounded in religion butt I mought be persuaded to becom a catholig."

33. By September 1600 Queen Elizabeth accuses James of a plan "to sell his son to the Pope," which James vigorously denies; he does not, however, assure her that Henry will not become Catholic, only that his education will not be put in the hands of any pope or king or queen of another country. James to Elizabeth, no. LXX, September 1600, *Letters of Queen Elizabeth and King James VI*, ed. John Bruce (London: Camden Society, 1849), pp. 132–33.

34. Grundy, "Introduction," *The Poems of Henry Constable*, p. 42.

35. Constable's frequent contact with the Pope and the French or Belgian nuncio is documented, for example, by Grundy, ed., *The Poems of Henry Constable*, pp. 39, 41, 46, 47, 48; by Wickes, *Henry Constable: Poet and Courtier*, pp. 285, 286, 287, 289, 291; and by Guiney, *Recusant Poets*, p. 314.

36. On the Spanish attempt during these negotiations to bring about in England greater tolerance for Catholics, see Albert J. Loomie, S.J., "Toleration and Diplomacy: the Religious Issue in Anglo-Spanish Relations, 1603–1605," *Transactions of the American Philosophical Society* 53, no. 6 (September 1963): pp. 1–60.

37. W. B. Patterson, *King James VI and I and the Reunion of Christendom*, Cambridge Studies in Early Modern British History (Cambridge: Cambridge University Press, 1997), p. ix.

38. Patterson, *King James VI and I and the Reunion of Christendom*, p. 148.

39. Patterson, *King James VI and I and the Reunion of Christendom*, pp. 57, 58, 63.

40. Patterson, *King James VI and I and the Reunion of Christendom*, pp. 148, 150.

41. George Wickes says that even before its translation into English, *Examen* had circulated to many people in England by the time Henry's father, Sir Robert Constable, died in November 1591 (*Henry Constable: Poet and Courtier*, p. 276). Wickes notes that the book was admired by his kinsman the Earl of Shrewsbury (p. 276).

42. *Calendar of State Papers, The Scottish Series*, Elizabeth, 1589–1603 (London: Eyre and Spottiswoode, Public Records Office, 1858), pp. 702, 784. Guiney in *Recusant Poets* mentions the second event on p. 311; Wickes in *Henry Constable: Poet and Courtier*, p. 286, believes the book is *A Discoverye of a Counterfecte Conference.*

43. Henry Constable, "Author's Epistle to the Reader" prefacing *Examen pacifique*, "To All the Kings Faithful subjects, and principally to those Catholikes, that are Desirous of the quiet of the Church and State," trans. from Constable, *The Catholike moderator: or A moderate examination of the doctrine of the Protestants Proving against the too rigid Catholikes of these times, and against the arguments especially, of that booke called, The Answer to the Catholike apologie, that we, who are members of the Catholike, apostolike, & Roman Church, ought not to condeme the Protestants for heretikes, until further proofe be made* (London: Eliot's Court Press, 1623), Early English Books Online page image 6 (italics added).

44. Since (as mentioned in an earlier note) no copy of the 1598 edition has been found, Joan Grundy concludes that, though entered into the Stationers' Register, it probably was never printed. Conversely, the Stationers' Register contains no record for the 1594 edition, which of course *was* printed. ("Introduction," *The Poems of Henry Constable*, pp. 97, 98.)

45. "The Passionate Shepherd to His Love" was actually authored by Christopher Marlowe, even though it had Shakespeare's name affixed to it. "The Shepherd's Song of Venus and Adonis," signed "H.C.," is now thought to be by Henry Chettle rather than Henry Constable, though, as observed earlier, its authorship is still uncertain. (Guiney, *Recusant Poets*, p. 307, mentions the retraction of Constable's authorship of the "Venus and Adonis" poem, as does Joan Grundy, "Introduction," *The Poems of Henry Constable*, p. 69.)

46. William Dunn Macray, ed., *The Pilgrimage to Parnassus with the Two Parts of the Return from Parnassus: Three Comedies Performed in St. Johns College, Cambridge, MDXCVII–MDCI* (Oxford: Clarendon Press, 1886; repr. London: Forgotten Books, 2012), pp. 85, 87. Shakespeare's mention by name occurs in *Part Two*, p. 138.

47. Macray, ed., *Return from Parnassus, Part II*, pp. 148, 150, 152. Philomusus is explicitly asked to play "Richard the 3" (p. 141), a play Constable had been in when at St. John's College (see below, note 66). Imagining their shepherd's life together in the countryside, Studioso twice speaks lines about having one's lament echoing from sympathetic woods and rocks (pp. 150, 152) that seem close to Constable's poem on this subject quoted in chapter 1. An "oaten reede" (that Shakespeare alludes to in his "noted weed" of Sonnet 76; see pp. 166–67) also makes an appearance here (p. 152).

48. Grundy believes that the work may no longer survive. ("Introduction," *The Poems of Henry Constable*, p. 42.) In a letter, Constable describes this work as a theological treatise in the form of a dialogue between two French ministers. Wickes in *Henry Constable: Poet and Courtier* (p. 281) thinks this could be the English translation of *Examen pacifique*, but that work does not take the form of a dialogue between two French ministers. Guiney (*Recusant Poets*, p. 308) points out that Henry Constable sent the manuscript to Anthony Bacon from Rouen.

The description—a theological debate between two French pastors—comes close to matching the treatise Constable wrote defending Du Perron against criticisms made by the Protestant minister Daniel Tilenus. The work takes the form of a dialogue between two speakers: paragraphs excerpted from Tilenus's previously published attack on Du Perron alternate with paragraphs by a speaker designated H. Connestable. On the basis of the preface Du Perron added when it was published in 1601, Louise Imogen Guiney believes Du Perron rather than Constable is the author (p. 308), even though Constable is named as author on the title page and as speaker throughout. But the occasion of Du Perron's preface makes clear why he might present it as his own even if it was his friend's. He there says that he is giving it to the Duke of Sully (the king's financial minister and himself a Huguenot) in order that he might read it and give it to "Madame" (Catherine, the king's Huguenot sister) at the very time Catherine has agreed to read Du Perron's writings if others in the court agree to cease pressuring her about the need to convert to Catholicism (see note 16, above). Du Perron may say he wrote it because he did, in fact, write it; but even if he was not the author, the appropriation would be understandable: it is Du Perron's own ideas that are being summarized and defended in the treatise, and the purpose is not to acquire authorial credit but to persuade Catherine of the wisdom of the Catholic position (and by her hoped-for conversion, soothe the never-ending alarm of French Catholics). H. Connestable, *Refutation de l'Escrit de D. Tilenus Contre un Discours Recueilly despropos de Monsieur L'Evesque D'Evereux, touchant les Traditions Apostoliques*, in *Les Diverses Oevvres de L'Illustrissime Cardinal Du Perron* (Paris: Antoine Estiene, 1622), pp. 359–465.

49. William C. Carroll, *Macbeth: Texts and Contexts* (Boston: Bedford/St. Martin's, 1999), pp. 201–202. Constable's book was written against a book by his former friend Robert Persons that argued against the legitimacy of James's succession.

50. Grundy, "Introduction," *The Poems of Henry Constable*, p. 34; and Wickes, *Henry Constable: Poet and Courtier*, p. 276, both citing a statement from Anthony Tyrrell enclosed in a letter from Justice Young to Sir Robert Cecil and Sir John Wolley, October 20, 1593. In *Calendar of the Cecil Papers in Hatfield House*, vol. 4, 1590–1594, ed. R. A. Roberts (London, 1892), pp. 381–406, www.british-history.ac.uk/cal-cecil-papers/vol4/pp381-406. The gathering took place in the quarters of the Welshman Sir Roger Williams, who had supported Henry of Navarre. The papers do not indicate where Williams's quarters were at this moment; he had earlier military victories near the coast at Dieppe and Rouen and in the Netherlands, so his residence may have been in this coastal region or instead in Paris. If the coastal region, it is possible Constable fled in the morning in order to go to England.

51. Wickes, *Henry Constable: Poet and Courtier*, p. 277, quoting Public Records Office, Scotland, vol. XLIV, p. 37.

52. George Wickes, in *Henry Constable: Poet and Courtier*, believes Constable may have been in Rome from 1593 to August 1595 (p. 278, drawing on *Historical Manuscript Commission, Calendar of the Manuscripts of the Marquis of Salisbury [Robert Cecil], Hartfield House, Hertfordshire, Part V* [London: Her Majesty's Stationery Office, 1895], p. 313). Guiney, in *Recusant*

Poets (p. 307), also notes that Constable left Italy for France in the summer of 1595, and cites the same report to Cecil from Rome on August 11: "Henry Constable is departed from Rome and gone into France: they do not trust him . . ."

53. Shakespeare's Sonnets 97 and 98, describing many months of absence, are distinctly different from those in which he refers only to the friends' separation at night. Other sonnets also imply long separation: in Sonnets 44 and 45, Shakespeare regrets that while his thoughts and desires can leap the distance across oceans and countries, he himself cannot do so; in Sonnet 61, the friend is "So far from home." Sonnet 56 expresses the hope that even when they are separated only by the hours of the night, they should renew their longing as though they were new lovers standing on two facing shores of an ocean, or separated by the length of winter. Shakespeare's sonnets record his effort to carry out the feat of sustaining love during long absences, and keeping love fresh when the friends are every day together.

54. Even as early as 1583 Constable, according to his three biographers, participated in an ambassadorial mission to Scotland; he carried out such missions intermittently throughout the 1580s. Shakespeare's Sonnet 45 uses embassy language ("In tender embassy of love to thee," "By those swift messengers return'd from thee") to describe his aspiration to leap over the huge geographical distance which separates them.

55. Wordsworth's contemporaries reported that he walked between ten and twenty miles a day and that over his lifetime he walked 180,000 miles (Stanley Plumly, *The Immortal Evening: A Legendary Dinner with Keats, Wordsworth, and Lamb* [New York: W. W. Norton, 2014], p. 14). Constable's record—though carried out on horse and ship, as well as foot—must have been, even if not comparable, remarkable.

56. Jean Vanes, *Documents Illustrating the Overseas Trade of Bristol in the Sixteenth Century* (Bristol, U.K.: Bristol Record Society, 1979), appendix 6, pp. 169, 170. The two-year period in this case is 1598–99.

57. Vanes, *Documents Illustrating the Overseas Trade*, p. 74. Here the two-year period is 1589–90 (thus, a year before Constable left England; but the traffic is being offered by Vanes as a sample of other years).

58. Entry from June 13, 1592, in *Calendar of State Papers, Domestic Series, of Elizabeth 1591–1594*, vol. ccxli (London: Longman, 1872), p. 234 (italics in original).

59. Account from 1601 in *Calendar of State Papers, Domestic Series, of the Reigns of Elizabeth and James, Addenda 1590–1625*, vol. xxxiv (London: Longman, 1872), p. 415.

60. Letter, "Sir Henry Neville to Mr. Secretary Cecyll," Paris, 27 June 1599, in *Memorials of Affairs of State in the Reigns of Q. Elizabeth and K. James I, Collected (chiefly) from the Original Papers of the Right Honourable Sir Ralph Winwood, Kt. Sometimes one of the Principal Secretaries of State. Comprehending likewise the Negotiations of Sir Henry Neville, Sir Charles Cornwallis, Sir Dudley Carleton, Sir Thomas Edmondes, Mr. Trumbull, Mr. Cottington and others, at the Courts of France and Spain, and in Holland, Venice, &c. wherein the Principal Transactions of those Times are faithfully*

related, and the Policies and Intrigues of those Courts at large discover'd. The whole digested in an exact Series of Time, vol. 1 (London: T. Ward, 1715), p. 52.

61. Letter, "Sir Henry Neville to Mr. Secretary Cecyll," Orleans, 18 July 1599, in *Memorials of Affairs of State in the Reigns of Q. Elizabeth and K. James,* vol. 1, p. 73.

62. Wickes, *Henry Constable: Poet and Courtier,* p. 281; and Guiney, *Recusant Poets,* p. 309.

63. Wickes, *Henry Constable: Poet and Courtier,* p. 282.

64. Guiney, *Recusant Poets,* p. 312n61, citing *Calendar of State Papers, Spanish, 1587–1603,* no. 704.

65. For example, Elizabeth's State Papers record on September 22, 1599, "Mr. Constable going to France," *Calendar of State Papers, The Scottish Series, Elizabeth, 1589–1603,* p. 776.

66. Thomas Legge's *Richardus Tertius* was performed at St. John's, Cambridge, in 1579. A transcript of the play residing at Emanuel College, Cambridge, gives the cast list that specifies the roles played by Henry Constable: "Mr. Constable, Gent. Filius Stanlei Dominus / Strange. / Centurio / Braa Servus comitissae Richmond." Cast list for act III, printed in Barron Field, ed., *The True Tragedy of Richard the Third; to which is Appended the Latin Play of Richardus Tertius by Dr. Thomas Legge. Both Anterior to Shakespeare's Drama* (London: Shakespeare Society, 1844), p. 128.

   In his introduction (pp. 73–74), Barron Field enumerates the Elizabethan and Jacobean works that mention the *Richardus Tertius* production: John Harrington's 1591 *Apologie of Poetry,* Thomas Nash's 1596 *Have with You to Saffron Walden,* and Thomas Heywood's 1612 *Apology for Actors.*

   In addition, the production is in the background of the *Parnassus* plays, which are in part about the interaction between university-trained and non-university-trained actors, as when in *Return from Parnassus Part II,* act IV, scene iii (pp. 138ff.), William Kempe and Richard Burbage interact with Philomusus and Studioso. As noticed earlier, both Shakespeare and Constable are mentioned by name in the play, and both have been among the historical persons believed to have been represented in the play by various characters, such as the Ovid-loving Amoretto.

67. Henry Foley, S.J., *Records of the English Province of the Society of Jesus,* vol. vi, *The Diary of the English College, Rome, from 1579 to 1773, with Biographical and Historical Notes; the Pilgrim-Book of the Ancient English Hospice Attached to the College from 1580 to 1656, with Historical Notes; Addenda to Previous Volumes* (London: Burns and Oates, 1880), alphabetical index, passim.

68. Foley, *Records of the English Province of the Society of Jesus,* vol. vi, p. 107.

69. For the suggestion that Constable was sometimes in conflict with the Jesuits, see Grundy, "Introduction," *The Poems of Henry Constable,* pp. 38, 44. See also Wickes, *Henry Constable: Poet and Courtier,* pp. 282, 283. For the Benedictine use of aliases, see, for example, Terence Benedict Snow's *Obit Book of the English Benedictines, 1600–1912* (Edinburgh: Mercat Press, 1913), which contains 213 instances of "alias."

70. *Calendar of State Papers, Domestic Series, of the Reigns of Elizabeth and James, Addenda 1590–1625*, vol. xxxiv, 1601 (Elizabeth), p. 415. The volume for Elizabeth's papers for the ten years immediately prior to this one contains eighty-four instances: *Calendar of State Papers, Domestic Series, of the Reign of Elizabeth, 1581–1590*, ed. Robert Lemon (London: Longman, 1865), for example, pp. 31, 55, 60, 93, 121, 141, 142, etc. Unlike the Jesuit records, the aliases in the *State Papers* sometimes just register alternative spellings of the surname or a maiden name; but some refer to Catholics: "Examination of George Breton . . . as to lending his white gelding to Cotton, *alias* Martin, the priest. Has been acquainted with Cotton for six years" (p. 149).

71. Letter, "Sir Henry Neville to Mr. Secretary Cecyll," Paris, 25 January 1599, in *Memorials of Affairs of State in the Reigns of Q. Elizabeth and K. James*, vol. 1, p. 147.

72. See, for example, Patterson, *King James VI and I and the Reunion of Christendom*, pp. 51, 52.

73. Wickes, *Henry Constable: Poet and Courtier*, p. 284, citing Edmund Sawyer in *Memorials of Affairs of State*, vol. 1, p. 37.

74. Wickes, *Henry Constable: Poet and Courtier*, pp. 284, 297n55, citing and translating Alexandre Teulet, *Relations Politiques*, vol. IV, pp. 222–23. "I learn here that the King of that country [Scotland] is much pressed by His Holiness, through the mediation of Constable, an Englishman, and Bomton [i.e., Bonnington], a Scotsman, both of whom recently arrived from France, to grant to Catholics liberty of conscience and to declare war on the Queen of England; and that for this purpose His Holiness has offered the King money and the assistance of all the Catholic princes of Christendom and of a large number of Catholics in this kingdom."

75. Elizabeth's state papers record that in April 1600, "advertisement [was] given to the King [of Scotland] by Henry Constable, from Arragon; confederation of a great number of nobles, being all papists." As Constable is reporting on the mental disposition of people in foreign countries, so his own actions appear to have been constantly monitored in England. On August 21, 1599, to cite another example, the British court recorded the fact that "Mr. Constable and the Laird of Bonitan [are] with the Scottish King on behalf of the Pope." *Calendar of State Papers, The Scottish Series, Elizabeth 1589–1603*, vol. lxv, pp. 773, 781.

76. Constable's 1597 letter to Essex cited in Wickes, *Henry Constable: Poet and Courtier*, pp. 279, 280.

77. Letter from Edward Wylton in Paris to Essex, in cipher, September 22, 1595, cited in Guiney, *Recusant Poets*, p. 307.

78. The words in quotation marks are Guiney's summary of Constable's letter, *Recusant Poets*, p. 308.

79. Wickes, *Henry Constable: Poet and Courtier*, p. 284. This report from John Colville to Secretary of State Cecil is cited by Wickes as overlapping in many details with the report by the French ambassador in London (see note 74 above), both of which mention Constable by name.

80. Grundy, "Introduction," *The Poems of Henry Constable*, p. 45.

81. A narrative about Borromeo (written by a monk but approved by Borromeo) records the 1600 visit of "the illustrious Henry Constable" and designates him

"an intimate friend of the illustrious Frederick, Cardinal Borromeo." Frank Salmon draws on this document and many others to show that their friendship originated during Constable's residence at the College of Rome in the fall of 1593, a period during which Borromeo sponsored a new painting school, arranged for several northern European painters such as Jan Brueghel to reside there, and began an art collection which included Titian's painting of Mary Magdalene. Salmon proposes that Titian's painting may have influenced Constable's four ecstatic and erotic sonnets to Mary Magdalene in the "Spiritual Sonnets." "Praedatrix Praeda Fit Ipsa Suae: Mary Magdalen, Federico Borromeo and Henry Constable's Spirituall Sonnettes," *Recusant History* 18, no. 3 (1987): pp. 228, 229, 232.

82. Letter, "Mr. Winwood to Mr. Secretary Cecyll," Paris, 21 July 1602, in *Memorials of Affairs of State in the Reigns of Q. Elizabeth and K. James,* vol. 1, p. 427, italics in original. Ralph Winwood was a diplomat, and later England's secretary of state.

83. Charles Nicholl, *The Lodger Shakespeare: His Life on Silver Street* (New York: Viking Penguin, 2008), pp. 59, 62, 69.

84. Nicholl, *The Lodger Shakespeare*, p. 17.

85. Nicholl, *The Lodger Shakespeare*, pp. 104, 143, 144, 164, 165.

86. Nicholl, *The Lodger Shakespeare*, pp. 94ff, 133, 176.

87. Joan Grundy ("Introduction," *The Poems of Henry Constable*, p. 48) gives the imprisonment date as April 14; Louise Guiney specifies "about April 15" (*Recusant Poets*, p. 34). The biographies all give July as the month of release, but see note 89 below for a possible August date.

88. Drawing on Public Records Office, *Roman Transcripts*, vol. IX, bundle 88, p. 119, George Wickes writes, "In Paris the Nuncio received news that Constable was once again in the King's grace, indeed more than ever." Wickes surmises Constable may have been exaggerating (*Henry Constable: Poet and Courtier*, p. 291).

89. For example, on August 3, 1604, the Privy Council forwarded an instruction to the lieutenant of the Tower "to restrain the too free access of visitors" (*Calendar of State Papers, Domestic: James I, 1603–1610* [1857], pp. 140–63, entry for August 2). This date is later than the July date usually given as the day of Constable's release from prison. However, the Venetian papers seem to report that he and Anthony Standen were released together on August 18, 1604 (*Calendar of State Papers Relating to English Affairs in the Archives of Venice, Volume 10: 1603–1607* [1900], pp. 171–77). For an example of James's sudden flamboyant visits, opening of the prison doors, and release of those within (other than those accused of treason, who had been moved to another prison), see *Report to the Master of the Rolls on Documents in the Archives of Venice* (1866).

90. Original despatch, Venetian Archives, Nicolo Molin, Venetian ambassador in England, to the Dodge and Senate, April 28, 1604, *Calendar of State Papers Relating to English Affairs in the Archives of Venice, Volume 10: 1603–1607.* Originally published by Her Majesty's Stationery Office, London, 1900, available at British History Online, www.british-history.ac.uk/cal-state-papers /venice/vol10/pp140–148. Guiney (*Recusant Poets*, p. 314), Wickes (*Henry Constable: Poet and Courtier*, p. 290), and Grundy (*The Poems of Henry*

Constable, p.48) each quote the ambassador's description of Constable's fatal letter; Wickes and Grundy cite his request that the letter be interpreted generously; Guiney includes his plea for visitors.

91. Letter from the Tower, 11 May 1604, in *Calendar of Cecil Papers in Hatfield House*, vol. 16, May 1–15, 1604, ed. M. S. Giuseppi. Here the official state record summarizes Constable's letter as "beseech[ing] [Secretary of State] Cecil in matters of double construction in them to take that sense which is most conformable to the loyal mind he has always been known to bear his majesty."

92. Mary Anne Everett Green, ed., *Calendar of State Papers, Domestic: Elizabeth, 1598–1601* (London: Longmans, Green and Co., 1867), vol. 273, p. 356. The passage is cited in Guiney, *Recusant Poets*, p. 311.

93. It may well be that James used this poem on multiple occasions, assuring more than one petitioner he had treated coldly that warm friendship lay ahead. Though the date on which the poem surfaces is early 1604, G.P.V. Akrigg in his *Letters of King James VI & I* attaches this poem (without explanation) to a 1586 letter from James to Elizabeth in which James says he is including a poem, but from which in other editions of the letters the poem is missing ([Berkeley: University of California Press, 1984], pp. 71, 72, letter 19). There may exist excellent reasons for believing this is the poem that was sent to Elizabeth (before it then disappeared for twenty years), but those reasons are not currently legible; and there are strong reasons to doubt James would have sent it to Elizabeth.

Peter C. Herman, drawing on the Akrigg edition, accepts the yoking of the poem and letter, but gives three reasons why sending the poem to Elizabeth was a spectacular "blunder": first, the poem is inappropriately erotic (and wholly out of register with the correspondence between the two monarchs); second, since James and Elizabeth are blood relations, it is incestuous; third and perhaps most egregious, the speaker in the poem presents himself as superior to the person addressed (James would be addressing Elizabeth as though he were an archer and she his bow, as though he were a smith and she one of his tools, as though he were the husband and she his wife). (*Royal Poetrie: Monarchic Verse and the Political Imaginary of Early Modern England* [Ithaca, NY: Cornell University Press, 2010], pp. 157–65.)

Throughout James's letters he tends to be extremely deferential to Elizabeth; and it seems almost inconceivable that during a time when he is requesting that she formally name him her successor, he would speak to her in this way. Other scholars have nominated other poems as the one missing from the letter to Elizabeth (see, for example, Edith Rickert, "Political Propaganda and Satire in *A Midsummer Night's Dream*," *Modern Philology* 21, no. 2 [1923]: p. 153). The John Bruce edition of the correspondence between James and Elizabeth states that the missing poem's identity is unknown and that the letter itself is undated. Bruce surmises that the letter was sent "very late in the reign of Elizabeth," presumably in the mid-to-late 1590s (*Letters of Queen Elizabeth and King James VI of Scotland*, pp. 170–71).

Even if it can be convincingly shown that James did send this poem to one or more persons in an earlier decade, there must be a reason why the sonnet surfaces in early 1604. The king's meetings with Constable may provide that reason.

94. As noted earlier, when Constable first arrived in Scotland in 1599, Anne welcomed him but James held off for several weeks, after which his pleasure in Constable's presence was visible enough to third parties that it was remarked on in correspondence. Again in 1603, James took some time to grant Constable's request to enter England; once Constable arrived, James waited several weeks to receive him, after which their friendship resumed.

95. *Holograph. Endorsed* (terms indicate the poem is in the King's handwriting and that he has signed his initials.): "1604. Sonnet of his Majesty" (133. 49.), Cecil Papers—Miscellaneous 1604, in Giuseppi, ed., *Calendar of the Cecil Papers in Hatfield House*, vol. 16. The papers do not give a month or date, but as it is the first entry in the 1604 volume, it would be in the winter or early spring. For this same year, see also "1604 Sonnet of his Majesty" in James Craigie, ed., *The Poems of James VI of Scotland*, vol. 2 (Edinburgh: William Blackwood, 1955), p. 171.

96. Emily Vasiliauskas points out how singular Shakespeare's assertion of his own immortality is in Sonnet 107 and how "underappreciated" that feature of the sonnet has been: "Nowhere else in the sequence does Shakespeare include a similar gesture, in which the speaker asserts that a poem will perpetuate his own life." ("The Outmodedness of Shakespeare's Sonnets," *ELH: English Literary History* 82, no. 3 [2015]: p. 768.)

97. Letters, James to Elizabeth, no. LXX, September 1600, and Elizabeth to James, no. LXXI, April 1601, in Bruce, ed., *Letters of Queen Elizabeth and King James VI of Scotland*, pp. 132, 133, 134, 136.

98. George Walter Prothero, ed., *Select Statutes and Other Constitutional Documents: Illustrative of the Reigns of Elizabeth and James I* (Oxford: Clarendon Press, 1906), p. 78.

99. Shapiro, *A Year in the Life: 1599*, pp. 175–77, 282. Shapiro describes the fear of a second Spanish Armada as well as Elizabeth's fear of James VI's takeover of England while she was still alive.

100. James Shapiro observes that the presence in *Hamlet* of an internal coup (Laertes) and an external threat (Fortinbras) would resonate with the Elizabethan audience (*A Year in the Life: 1599*, p. 183).

101. See the intricate plot of the twelfth-century Danish legend of Amleth summarized by James Shapiro, *A Year in the Life: 1599*, p. 285.

102. This line expresses Hamlet's puzzlement about Fortinbras, in his "How all occasions do inform against me" soliloquy where Hamlet both regrets his own inability to act and derides Fortinbras's readiness to act (*Hamlet* IV.iv.47). Joan Grundy observes that pro-war sentiments are occasionally attributed to Constable, but seem "uncharacteristic" given his "pacifist statements." ("Introduction," *The Poems of Henry Constable*, p. 41.)

103. Henry Constable, quoted in Wickes, *Henry Constable: Poet and Courtier*, p. 290. As the letter continues, Constable states that so long as the king does not think him "unduetifull," the Earl of Shrewsbury and other friends are not "discontented" with him, and no other man "have damage by me, I shall repute my selfe happy in all other miserys."

104. Adam Nicolson, *God's Secretaries: The Making of the King James Bible* (New York: HarperCollins, 2003), pp. 2, 20, 21. The feeling of abundance also came

from James's willingness to distribute honors which Elizabeth in her last years had refused to do (p. 2). James conferred large numbers of baronies, viscountcies, earldoms, and dukedoms which he "scattered like sequins across the country" (p. 19).

105. Nicolson, *God's Secretaries*, p. 41.
106. Robert Lemon, ed., *Calendar of State Papers: Domestic Series, of the Reign of Elizabeth 1581–1590, Preserved in the State Paper Department of Her Majesty's Public Record Office* (London: Longman, Green, Roberts, 1865), vol. 209, pp. 467, 468 (italics added), 469 (italics added), 470, 471. All items occur under the specified date, except for the information about March 10, which occurs on "January ?" [*sic*].
107. John Roche Dasent, ed., *Acts of the Privy Council*, vol. 16, 1588 (London: Her Majesty's Stationery Office, 1897), p. 198.
108. Entry 38, May 12, 1588, in Lemon, ed., *Calendar of State Papers Domestic: Elizabeth, 1581–1590* (1865), vol. 212, July 1–21, 1588, pp. 497–508.
109. Entry 52, July 16, 1588, in Lemon, ed., *Calendar of State Papers Domestic.*
110. Entry 52, entry 29, August 4, 1588, in Lemon, ed., *Calendar of State Papers Domestic.*
111. Jean Vanes, *Bristol at the Time of the Spanish Armada* (Bristol, U.K.: Bristol Historical Association, 1988), p. 23.
112. Vanes, *Bristol at the Time of the Spanish Armada*, p. 21.
113. Thomas Hobbes, *The Life of Mr. Thomas Hobbes of Malmesbury, Written by Himself in a Latine Poem, and Now Translated into English* (London: Andrew Cooke, 1680; repr. Exeter: The Rota, 1979), pp. 1, ll. 1–8.
114. The March 3 (new calendar, March 13), 1588, eclipse is documented on the NASA website, http://eclipse.gsfc.nasa.gov/5MCLEmap/1501-1600/LE1588 -03-13T.gif and http://eclipse.gsfc.nasa.gov/LEcat5/LE1501-1600.html. It is reproduced with additional maps here: http://moonblink.info/Eclipse/eclipse /1588_03_13. To my knowledge, no account of Sonnet 107 mentions the 1588 lunar eclipse (the eclipses in 1595 and 1605, in contrast, are often cited in connection with the poem).
115. Tycho Brahe's description of this dark eclipse is cited by Wendelinus in his 1644 *Eclipses Lunnares*, which is in turn cited by S. J. Johnson, "Lunar Eclipses of 1588 and 1623," *The Observatory* 11 (April 1888).
116. John Harvey, writing about the March 1588 total eclipse (which he dates as March 2), quotes passages about the dire consequences of both solar and lunar eclipses: "it cannot choose, but there must needs follow some great accident in the world." J. H. Physition, *A Discoursive Probleme Concerning Prophesies, How Farre They are to be Valued, or Credited according to the Surest Rules, and directions in divinitie, philosophie, astrologie, and other learning: Devised especially in abatement of the terrible threatenings, and menaces, peremptorily denounced against the kingdoms, and states of the world, this present famous yeere, 1588, supposed the Greatwoonderfull, and Fatall yeere of our Age* (London: John Jackson, 1588), p. 117 (document image 59 on Early English Books Online).

Quite apart from the eclipse, the year 1588 had, according to Holinshed's *Chronicles*, for several centuries been named as the year in which catastrophes (up to and including the end of the world) would occur; and these predictions put "the great yeare of 1588 in everie mans mouth" (Raphaell Holinshed,

Chronicles of England, Scotland, and Ireland, vol. III [London, 1587], pp. 1,356–57, cited in Sarah Dodson, "Holinshed's Sources for the Prognostications About the Years 1583 and 1588," *History of Science Society* 38, no. 1/2 (November 1947): p. 61. When the year passed without catastrophe, the predictions were treated with derision.

117. All of these Thanksgivings except Bristol's are described in Robert Hutchinson, *The Spanish Armada* (New York: Macmillan, 2014), pp. 218–20. Bristol's is given in Vanes, *Bristol at the Time of the Spanish Armada*, p. 25.

118. Stephen Booth notes that it is line 8, the proclamation of peace, that—more than any other line—initiates the sense that the poem is topical, that it refers to actual historical events (*Shakespeare's Sonnets* [New Haven, CT: Yale University Press, 1977], p. 342).

119. The grounding of Sonnet 107 in the year 1588 is compatible not only with the practice of prophecy in that cultural era but also, more specifically, with one of Henry Constable's poems dated "1588" in its title: "A calculation upon the birth of an honourable Ladies daughter borne in the yeare, 1588, on a Friday" (*Diana*, penultimate page, 1592; and Grundy, ed., *The Poems of Henry Constable*, p. 157). The poem celebrates a baby girl born to Lady Penelope Rich by predicting a great future for the child; to confirm his high confidence in the prediction, Constable refers to 1588 as "the wondrous yeare" and also invokes a celestial event, the position of a particular planet. The infant soon died, however, and Constable had to write a second poem addressing the incorrect prediction. Prophecy and the failure of prophecy were, then, on Constable's mind, as they were on Shakespeare's mind (Shakespeare's second quatrain begins with a bleak prospect that gives way to euphoria, while Constable's two poems begin with euphoria, then give way to sorrow).

120. Helen Vendler, *The Art of Shakespeare's Sonnets* (Cambridge, MA: Harvard University Press, 1997), p. 455.

121. Booth, ed., *Shakespeare's Sonnets*, p. 346. Booth writes, "The syntax of quatrain 1 . . . contributes to an impression of mystical and majestic superhuman pronouncement" (p. 346).

122. Queen Anne's biographers—Leeds Barroll and Ethel Carleton Williams—both mention the production (*Anna of Denmark*, p. 56; and *Anne of Denmark*, p. 99). We know Constable was in London that month, since he wrote a letter from the Kingston district of London on January 9, 1694/5 (Guiney, *Recusant Poets*, p. 315).

123. British Museum, Additional Manuscript 11,402, folio 159 verso, 31 July 1610, printed by F. P. Wilson, "Marston, Lodge, and Constable," *Modern Language Review* ix (1914), pp. 99–100, cited in Grundy, "Introduction," *The Poems of Henry Constable*, p. 49. I follow Wilson's spelling.

124. Wickes, *Henry Constable: Poet and Courtier*, p. 293.

125. Letter from John Chamberlain to Dudley Carleton, *Public Records Office, State Papers, James I*, vol. 67, p. 67, cited in Wickes, *Henry Constable: Poet and Courtier*, p. 293.

126. This event is reported in Guiney, *Recusant Poets*, p. 315; by Grundy, "Introduction," *The Poems of Henry Constable*, p. 49; and by Wickes, *Henry Constable: Poet and Courtier*, p. 293.

127. John Lechmere, "To the Reader," *The Relection of a Conference Touching the Reall Presence* (Doway: Laurence Kellam, 1635), p. 5.

128. Samuel Schoenbaum, *Shakespeare: A Compact Documentary Life* (New York: Oxford University Press, 1987), pp. 234–36. Shortly after purchasing New Place, Shakespeare carried out extensive renovations.

129. Katherine Duncan-Jones in *Shakespeare: An Ungentle Life* surmises that Shakespeare, though residing in Stratford, planned to visit London regularly, as does Stephen Greenblatt in *Will in the World: How Shakespeare Became Shakespeare* (New York: W. W. Norton, 2004), p. 379. Duncan-Jones notes that even with John Robinson living there, the house had enough room for a second person to occupy several rooms (pp. 283, 284). The property was directly across the river from the Globe Theatre, and several hundred yards from Blackfriars Theatre, used during the winter by Shakespeare's company (p. 283). An atmosphere congenial to the theater was also provided by the many "clothing-related craftsmen" such as "feather sellers, silk workers" in the Blackfriars environs (Sarah Dustagheer, "Acoustic and Visual Practices Indoors," in *Moving Shakespeare Indoors*, ed. Andrew Gurr and Farah Karim-Cooper [Cambridge: Cambridge University Press, 2014], p. 145). Duncan-Jones notes that most other biographers reject the idea that Shakespeare himself intended to reside in the Blackfriars property, even for visits.

130. Identifying a property by its current resident does sometimes occur in bills of sale from the period, so perhaps its occurrence in a will is less pregnant with meaning than the scholarship (including the present study) assumes.

131. The 1623 mass is mentioned in many works about Shakespeare. In addition, Joseph Pearce in *The Quest for Shakespeare* (San Francisco: Ignatius Press, 2008) three times mentions that Catholic services were held at Blackfriars from the mid 1580s onward; but he seems to provide no documentation, so his basis for that assertion is at present unclear.

132. See "Is it lawful for Catholics to buy monastic property, to sell it, or to keep it?" in P. J. Holmes, *Elizabethan Casuistry* (Norfolk, U.K.: Catholic Record Society, 1981), pp. 43–44. The Catholic Church was still making this same recommendation in the early and middle seventeenth century. See case 109, "Is it lawful for Catholics in England to buy and sell the possessions of monasteries or other ecclesiastical benefices," in Peter Holmes, *Caroline Casuistry: The Cases of Conscience of Fr Thomas Southwell SJ* (Suffolk, U.K.: Catholic Record Society and Boydell Press, 2012), pp. 89–90.

133. Biographers of Shakespeare have researched John Robinson's identity and found that there was a John Robinson living in Stratford and there was a John Robinson living in London, but both of them appear to have died by the time Shakespeare was writing his will.

   Here is a more detailed summary of the scholarship. Some scholars have proposed that the John Robinson who signed the will lived in Stratford and was a different man from the John Robinson who lived in Shakespeare's London property (Schoenbaum, *Shakespeare: A Compact Documentary Life*, pp. 304, 306; Alan and Veronica Palmer, *Who's Who in Shakespeare's England* [London: Palgrave Macmillan, 1999], pp. 204, 205). But the weight of opinion falls on the side of the will signer and the Blackfriars resident being a single man. The John Robinson who lived in Stratford was a laborer (Schoenbaum) while the signature on the will seems to be that of a well-educated individual (Ian Wilson, *Shakespeare, the Evidence* [New York: St. Martin's Press, 1993], p. 396; and Reg Mitchell, *Tho Quiney—Gent* [Warwick, U.K.: Stratford Play Scripts, 2007], p. 62). Furthermore, the Stratford John Robinson died on December 5, 1614—hence was not alive to sign the will in the spring of 1616 (Mitchell). It is possible there lived more than one Stratford John Robinson, an idea invited by the multiple town documents cited by Alan Palmer, though none is later than 1613; Reg Mitchell notes there is only a single baptism record.

In London, a man named John Robinson was steward to Sir John Fortescue, who worked in the Royal Wardrobe in the Blackfriars district; he performed lively tasks such as buying the flowers for a revelry at Whitehall in 1608 (Glynn Wickham, *The London Shakespeare*, vol. 2 [New York: Simon & Schuster, 1957], p. 79). But this John Robinson was dead by 1613 (three years prior to Shakespeare's will), according to the testimony of his son Edward at the College of Rome in that year (*Records of the English Province of the Society of Jesus* 6, no. 451, p. 264). In that same testimony, twenty-one-year-old Edward reports that he has a brother; several scholars surmise that this brother's name may have been John and that he may be the person living in the premises Shakespeare purchased (Wilson; also Peter Ackroyd, *Shakespeare: A Biography* [New York: Random-Anchor, 2005], p. 497; also Pearce, *Quest for Shakespeare*). Even if the brother's name turns out to be John, it seems unlikely that fifty-two-year-old Shakespeare arranged for the living quarters of someone in his late teens or early twenties, and that so young a person was present in Stratford in the final weeks of the poet's life and asked to witness the will.

134. Benjamin Carier, *A Treatise, Written by M. doctor Carier, wherein hee layeth downe sundry learned and pithy considerations by which he was moved, to forsake the Protestant congregation, and to betake himselfe to the Catholke Apostolike Roman Church. Agreeing verbatim with the written copye, addressed by the sayd doctor to the King his most excellent Maiestie* (England: English Secret Press, 1614), p. 12. Bodleian Library, University of Oxford. Early English Books Online.

135. *Public Records Office, Roman Transcripts*, vol. ix, bundle 88, pp. 5–6, cited in Wickes, *Henry Constable: Poet and Courtier*, p. 288. Since Constable differentiates the two chaplains—one Protestant, the other Puritan—and Carier was Protestant, it seems almost certain that he is the person about whom Constable is here writing.

136. Carier's overall argument—as George Hakewill correctly summarizes it in his attempted refutation—is identical with the aims to which Constable's life was dedicated: "The maine end which it drives at, is either totall reconcilement to the Church of Rome; or if that cannot be, a partiall toleration of the Romish Religion" (George Hakewill, *An Answere to a Treatise written by Dr. Carier, by way of a Letter to his Maiestie wherein he Layeth Downe Sundry Politike Considerations; by which hee pretendeth himselfe was moved, and endevoureth to move others to be reconciled to the Church of Rome, and imbrace that Religion, which he calleth Catholike. By George Hakewil, Doctour*

of Divinity, and chapleine to the Prince his Highnesse (London: John Bill, 1616), p. 2.

137. Hakewill, *An Answere to a Treatise*, p. 5. Hakewill introduces Constable's death immediately after he has given a climactic denunciation of the treatise: "I have not met within the narrow compasse of so short a treatise, so formally pend, and carrying so fair an outside; so many weake arguments, so many grosse mistakes, so many notorious falsehoods, so many irreconciliable contradictions, so many sandie and disjoynted consequences: howsoever were his proofes never so strong, so sure, so true, so consonant, so coherent; yet was hee a man most unfit to intermeddle in a business of union, and pacification" (pp. 4, 5). In pages that King James probably would not have appreciated, Hakewill proves the necessity of his own treatise by quoting many admiring responses to Carier in Latin and French publications (p. 10).

138. Joan Grundy does not mention either the oddity or the potential untruth of the death date: she describes the Carier visit without noting the two-year delay in the reporting of the death; her footnote identifies (without commenting upon) Hakewill's treatise as the source of the information. Wickes observes the discrepancy between Constable's renown and his "obscure death"; but his sentences describing the Carier–Hakewill connection are themselves somewhat opaque and require several rereadings in order to recognize that the death is not mentioned in the first, only in the second. Wickes says the date of death is in a herald's report from a Nottingham visitation, but it does not appear to be in the 1614 visitation, and the next visitation does not occur until 1664. Guiney openly states that the death date is "assigned without citation or authority." She also calls attention to the errors in the Westminster Cathedral eulogy (as well as the incorrect location of the printed eulogy in the volume dedicated to events occurring in 1586–94). She states that the particular day of death is specified as October 9 in Joseph Foster's *Yorkshire Pedigrees*, but she does not alert us to the date of that book, which is 1874. (See Grundy, "Introduction," *The Poems of Henry Constable*, pp. 49, 50; Wickes, *Henry Constable: Poet and Courtier*, pp. 293, 294, 299n102; and Guiney, *Recusant Poets*, pp. 315, 316, 318nn18, 79.)

139. The names and aliases in this paragraph and the one following are from the alphabetical index in Foley, *Records of the English Province of the Society of Jesus*, vol. vi, passim; for clarification of family ties among people with the last name "Scarisbrick," see page 690.

140. Like our Henry, this one is from Yorkshire; in 1611 he came to the Continent to be educated; afterward he studied in Italy and was ordained a priest, before being sent by Rome back into England in 1619. (The Yorkshire record indicates he died in 1619.) His brother William attended St. Omer's College, leaving it in 1616 to go to Rome. Foley, *Records of the English Province of the Society of Jesus*, vol. vi, pp. 260, 268, 275. (Henry and William had, among many other siblings, a brother named Robert, but he does not seem to be the same Robert who appears here in the Jesuit records. See note 142, below.)

141. Alphabetical index, Foley, *Records of the English Province of the Society of Jesus*, vol. vi, p. 757. For the account of Henry, William, and Robert Constable, see Foley, *Records of the English Province of the Society of Jesus*, Fifth Series, vol. iii, pp. 205ff.

142. The siblings indicate that their parents were Philip and Margaret and enumerate the names of their other brothers and sisters (Foley, *Records of the English Province of the Society of Jesus*, vol. iii, p. 205). The elaborate pedigree chart of the Constable family in Yorkshire shows Philip (eldest son of Marmaduke) and Margaret as the parents of Henry and William, as well as of the other children explicitly named by the brothers in the Jesuits' account, Marmaduke, Robert, Michael, Roger, Francis, Frances, and Jane (Joseph Foster, *Pedigrees of the County Families of Yorkshire*, vol. iii, "North and East Riding" [London: W. Wilfred Head, 1874], p. 96n). This same Yorkshire chart confirms that the grandfather of these children is the uncle of our Henry Constable.

The youth with the Salvin alias (Robert Constable) almost certainly belongs to a different branch of the extended Yorkshire Constable family. The Jesuit volume that first introduces Henry, William, and Robert (Foley, vol. iii, p. 205) specifies Yorkshire as the home ground of all three, but does not identify Robert as a sibling of Henry or William, nor does it describe Robert as the offspring of Philip and Margaret. A later volume does identify Robert—probably incorrectly—as the brother of Henry and the son of Philip (Foley, vol. vi, p. 275). The Yorkshire genealogy chart gives Henry and William a brother Robert, but specifies he was married.

Another young relative, Ralph Greene, invokes our Henry Constable as a reference in presenting himself to the Jesuits (Foley, *Records of the English Province of the Society of Jesus*, vol. iii, p. 179; and see vol. vi, p. 246, describing the youth as "a remarkable example of virtue to all"); George Wickes notes Ralph Greene's invocation of Henry Constable in *Henry Constable: Poet and Courtier*, p. 292.

143. Godfrey Anstruther, *The Seminary Priests: A Dictionary of the Secular Clergy of England and Wales 1558–1850*, vol. 2, *Early Stuarts 1603–1659* (Great Wakering, U.K.: Mayhew-McCrimmon, 1975), pp. 69, 390.

144. Foley, *Records of the English Province of the Society of Jesus*, vol. vi, p. 264. The Edward Robinson described here is the son of the Blackfriars John Robinson who was dead by 1613 (see note 133 above) and thus not the John Robinson we are looking for.

145. Report, Captain Duffield to Robert Cecil, November 9, 1593, *Calendar of the Manuscripts of the Most Hon. Marquess of Salisbury Preserved at Hatfield House, Herfordshire*, p. 496; also cited in Wickes, *Henry Constable: Poet and Courtier*, p. 277.

146. Robin is Ariel's precursor in *A Midsummer Night's Dream*. Asked by a fairy to confirm that he is Robin (II.i.33), he is called by name only by Shakespeare (in registering who is speaking or giving a stage direction such as "*Enter Robin*") and by Oberon, the precursor of Prospero, who is widely recognized as a figure representing Shakespeare (III.ii.*passim*). The one exception is when Robin refers to himself by name in the epilogue. Since Henry Constable was in London by December 1603, it is fascinating that the 1604 New Year's Day production of *A Midsummer Night's Dream* at Hampton House was performed under the title *Robin Goodfellow*, or at least that is the only title we have for the production which is mentioned in a contemporary letter (Leeds Barroll, cited by John H. Ashington, "The Globe, the Court, and Measure for

Measure," in Stanley Wells, *Shakespeare Survey*, vol. 52 [Cambridge: Cambridge University Press, 2004], p. 135). Constable had not yet been received at court, so it is almost inconceivable that he would have trespassed into the production, even well disguised.

147. Remarkably, we have both Henry Constable's and John Robinson's signatures, though it is not clear whether in exploring whether the two are the same person, we ought to expect similarities or differences in the handwriting: a person enacting an alias might aspire to produce a different hand, just as Hamlet disguised his hand in the document arranging for the death of Rosencrantz and Guildenstern. For instances in which characters in Shakespeare's plays identify handwriting as a way to recognize a person, see George Koppelman and Daniel Wechsler, *Shakespeare's Beehive: A Compleat Recording of the Annotations* (New York: Axletree Books, 2014).

    Henry Constable's signature appears to be in the Italian style and John Robinson's in the mixed English secretary style. Italian script—with its evenly slanted letters and many letters attached—is the style from which both the practice and the name "italics" is derived: this hand was beginning to be learned throughout England during this period and was regularly used for international correspondence and letters of state. The English secretary hand (learned before other hands and thus an accomplishment which any Englishman using the Italian would also have) consisted of "an angular script with Gothic features" and was "the hand most widely used by Elizabethan and Jacobean Englishmen" (Heather Wolfe, "Women's Handwriting," in Laura Lunger Knoppers, *Cambridge Companion to Early Modern Women's Writing* [Cambridge: Cambridge University Press, 2009], pp. 21, 24).

148. Tiffany Stern, " 'A ruinous monastary': The Second Blackfriars Playhouse as a Place of Nostalgia," in *Moving Shakespeare Indoors*, ed. Gurr and Karim-Cooper, p. 99.

149. Duncan-Jones, *Shakespeare: An Ungentle Life*, p. 284.

150. See above, text accompanying notes 131 and 132.

151. Excerpts from both *The Doleful Even-Song* and contemporary letters are reprinted in Henry Foley, *Records of the English Province of the Society of Jesus: Historic Facts Illustrative of the Labours and Sufferings of Its Members in the Sixteenth and Seventeenth Centuries*, vol. 1 (London: Burns and Oates, 1877), pp. 78–85.

152. See, for example, the entry for "Edmondes, Sir Thomas, of Blackfriars," who was agent to France throughout most of the 1590s, and envoy to the Spanish Netherlands in 1599–1600, in *The History of Parliament: British Political, Social, and Local History*, www.historyofparliamentonline.org.

153. Grundy, "Introduction," *The Poems of Henry Constable*, pp. 21, 22; Wickes, *Henry Constable: Poet and Courtier*, p. 273; and Guiney, *Recusant Poets*, p. 304, all citing state papers. The three biographers also note that the English ambassador, in turn, soon wrote to Walsingham proposing that Queen Elizabeth send Constable to "comfort" Henry of Navarre "in his religion."

154. Park Honan, cited in Duncan-Jones, *Shakespeare: An Ungentle Life*, p. 283; and Mark Eccles, cited in Schoenbaum, *Shakespeare: A Compact Documentary Life*, p. 306.

155. Germaine Greer, *Shakespeare's Wife* (New York: HarperCollins, 2007), p. 347.

156. Edmund Spenser, stanza lxxv, *Amoretti*, ed. Teresa Page (Kent, U.K.: Crescent Moon Publishing, 2007), p. 75. (I have used modern spelling in these closing moments of this book—for example, "again" rather than "agayne," as available from the Bartleby website: www.bartleby.com/40/81.html.)

157. Constable, "Sonet 1," in Grundy, ed., *The Poems of Henry Constable*, p. 115. I have used, for this final poem, spelling close to the modern; the spelling of "Sonetto primo" in the 1592 and 1594 editions of *Diana* is closer to the modern spellings than is the Todd manuscript spelling Grundy follows in her edition (and which, with the exception of this poem, I have followed throughout). I have also followed the wording in the 1592 *Diana*: "favors" rather than, as in Grundy, "favoure" in line 12; "your ear" rather than "thine eare" in line 14; "my voice" rather than "the voice" in line 14.